Fences and Neighbors

≣IGCC

*A project of the University of California
Institute on Global Conflict and Cooperation*

Fences and Neighbors

The Political Geography of Immigration Control

JEANNETTE MONEY

Cornell University Press

ITHACA AND LONDON

#40043699

First published 1999 by Cornell University Press

Printed in the United States of America

Library of Congress Cataloging-in-Publication Data
Money, Jeannette.
    Fences and neighbors: the political geography of immigration control / Jeannette Money.
        p.   cm.
    Includes bibliographical references and index.
    ISBN 0-8014-3570-6 (cloth: alk. paper)
        1. Emigration and immigration—Government policy.   2. Great Britain—Emigration and immigration—Government policy.   3. France—Emigration and immigration—Government policy.   4. Australia—Emigration and immigration—Government policy.   I. Title.
    JV6271. M66   1999
    325′. 1—dc21   98-46766

Cornell University Press strives to use environmentally responsible suppliers and materials to the fullest extent possible in the publishing of its books. Such materials include vegetable-based, low-VOC inks and acid-free papers that are recycled, totally chlorine free, or partly composed of nonwood fibers.

Cloth printing   10 9 8 7 6 5 4 3 2 1

For George

Contents

Preface

Robert Frost's neighbor, he tells us in "Mending Wall," believes that "good fences make good neighbors." This is a book about fences, literal or figurative, that nations erect at their borders. I was interested originally in the fences or barriers to trade that nations periodically erect and subsequently dismantle. It was only later that I turned my attention to the various mechanisms that states employ to encourage or discourage immigration. I wanted to know whether the same forces that affect trade policy are at work in the immigration arena or whether, as the literature suggests, people who move across international borders are somehow distinct from the flow of goods or, for that matter, from flows of capital, technology, and information.

First I systematically tested the received wisdom. Is immigration policy driven by economic interests, or is it affected by cultural values, notions of identity, and citizenship? After having spent a substantial amount of time trying to determine the relative weights of economic, social, and political determinants of immigration control, I realized that, by focusing on the nation-state, policy analysts have overlooked an important aspect of immigrant behavior: the concentration of immigrant communities in host states. So began my exploration of the determinants of immigration policy at a disaggregated level, the local communities in which immigrants settle.

It is well established that immigrants are not evenly distributed within the host population. Some cities, counties, states, and regions have many immigrants, others have few or none. Although policy analysts acknowledge this social phenomenon, they tend to overlook its political consequences. To explain why states raise or lower their barriers to immigration, I argue that the uneven geographic distribution of immigrants creates an uneven geographic distribution of the costs as well as the benefits of immigration, thereby providing a spatial context for immigration politics. As a result, politically organized opponents and proponents of immigration tend to be organized on the basis of local communities. Organized support for immigration is attributed to employers who confront tight and inflexible labor markets but are unable to move their production facilities to places where labor is cheaper. Organized opposition to immigration is attributed to individuals who bear the brunt of the short-term costs associated with immigration—those who compete with immigrants for jobs, social services, or cultural dominance. Competition is not constant but varies with the level of economic growth, the rate of immigration, and the level of immigrant incorporation within the local community.

Because immigrants are geographically concentrated, local political pressures rarely amount to the national political majority required to pass national legislation. So national politicians tend to ignore those local pressures unless they are important to maintaining a national electoral majority. Only when pro- or anti-immigrant constituencies can swing national electoral outcomes do electoral incentives cause politicians to add immigration issues to the national legislative agenda. I substantiate this argument through an analysis of the politics of immigration control in three advanced market economy countries: Britain, France, and Australia.

One of the pitfalls of research on immigration is the political charge the topic generates. Researchers who point out the potential or real costs of immigration are sometimes branded anti-immigrant or racist, whereas those who emphasize the benefits of immigration are accused of being beholden to special interests, employers, and the immigrants themselves. I therefore reveal the normative base of my research on immigration: the issue of equity. Robert Frost disputes his neighbor's belief that "good fences make good neighbors." I question it, too. In the contemporary international system, the distribution of power and wealth is highly inequitable. One means of diminishing that inequality is through migration from poorer countries to countries where power and wealth are concentrated. To reduce this disparity, I favor continued openness to immigration. Moreover, I believe that to ensure immigrants are treated equitably in host states, they should have access to full membership in those societies, even if periods of apprenticeship are required. But, as this book suggests, continuing openness to international migration has resulted in an inequitable distribution of costs and benefits among members of the host society. To ensure continued openness, we need policies that do not aggravate inequality within the host state. This research elucidates the distribution of costs and benefits, in the hope of providing policy recommendations that redistribute them more equitably. Discrimination against individuals based on their group membership, often labeled "racism," should never be tolerated, but policies that promote equity among members of the host society should relieve some of the tensions created by immigration and diminish an often ugly backlash.

Since Dick Rosecrance, at the UCLA Center for International Relations, first encouraged me to pursue this research, many individuals have helped me. I have presented parts of my work to various groups who generously provided feedback that helped me to clarify my thinking and my presentation. They include Paul Papayoanou and the members of the Seminar in International Relations at the University of California, San Diego; Bill Hagen and the seminar participants at the Center for Comparative Research in History, Society, and Culture at the University of California, Davis; Georges van den Abbeele and the conference participants at the Davis Humanities Institute; Phil Martin and the members of the Comparative Immigration and Integration Policy working group at the Center for German and European Studies at the University of California, Berkeley; John Ravenhill and the international relations faculty at the Australian National University; and Peter Lindert and the members of the Agricultural History Center at the University of California, Davis.

Parts of Chapters 3 and 4 were first published, in slightly different forms, as "No Vacancy: The Political Geography of Immigration Control in Advanced Industrial Countries," *International Organization* 41 (Autumn 1997): 685–720, © 1997 The IO Foundation and Massachusetts Institute of Technology. The editor, John Odell, and two anonymous reviewers provided feedback that helped me clarify my argument and improved my knowledge of British immigration control. James Jupp read the Australian chapter twice and kindly pointed out necessary modifications. Gary Freeman, Phil Martin, and Marty Schain commented on the manuscript as a whole; they contributed both to my understanding of the politics of immigration and to the improvement of the manuscript.

My field research remains a source of great pleasure, both for the environment it provided for testing my understanding of politics and for the many human contacts that make the research pleasurable. James Jupp, director of the Centre for Immigration and Multicultural Studies at the Australian National University (ANU), welcomed me to Canberra, as did John Ravenhill, also of ANU. Andrew Kopras, of the Australian Parliamentary Library, shared both data and expertise in the analysis of the Australian censuses. The hospitality I received there has motivated future research projects involving Australia. In France, my "French parents," Leo and Dorothy Packer, offered free lodging and sympathetic ears as I made my daily journeys to various archives and libraries. Catherine Wihtol de Wenden and Patrick Weil provided welcome support and feedback. In Britain, Zig Layton-Henry made the valuable resources of the Centre for Research in Ethnic Relations available to me. Chris Husbands, at the London School of Economics and Political Science, greeted my project with enthusiasm and useful input. The Social Science Research Centre at the University of Essex provided data necessary for the analysis of British immigration policy. To these and the many staff members I encountered at various centers, archives, and libraries I extend my thanks.

Financial support has been provided by the Institute on Global Conflict and Cooperation at the University of California, San Diego, for which I thank David Lake in particular; by the Center for German and European Studies at the University of California, Berkeley; and by the Faculty Senate of the University of California, Davis.

On a more practical level, research was facilitated by the participation of several graduate students, including Jan Breemer, Stacy Burnett-Gordon, Tressa Tabares, and Kimberly Cole. The first three helped gather and analyze the quantitative data, and Kim provided the first draft of Chapter 6, for which she has earned the position of co-author. A whole bevy of undergraduate students, many supported by Institute of Governmental Affairs undergraduate research fellowships, also assisted my research by providing bibliographic essays. Jean Stratford, Shelagh Mackay, and Alan Olmstead, of the Institute of Governmental Affairs at UC Davis, aided in the location and purchase of data. And the technicians at the Social Science Data Service helped convert the raw data to a statistically manageable form. Without such support my task would have been much more difficult and time-consuming.

My colleagues at UCLA and UC Davis have also contributed to this project, either indirectly or directly. At UCLA I had the good fortune to work with Ron Rogowski, Michael Wallerstein, Jeffry Frieden, and David Lake, who provided both excellent training and infectious enthusiasm for research. I remain amazed that I stumbled upon such a talented group of scholars and only hope to live up to the standards they set. At UC Davis, I have been joined by a congenial group of junior faculty (some no longer junior) with whom to share ideas. I have also benefited from the encouragement of senior faculty members, including Don Rothchild, Randy Siverson, and especially Robert Jackman, who read and commented on every word in the manuscript. I could not have wished for more helpful and supportive colleagues.

I am lucky enough to have two Georges in my life. George Tsebelis is a colleague, a friend, and a mentor, who helped me learn the craft of political science. George Waters is my partner in life, a friend and companion who provides an environment outside the profession in which I can relax. I thank them both.

JEANNETTE MONEY

Sacramento, California

Fences and Neighbors

I   *The Politics of Immigration Control*

At the close of the twentieth century, immigration remains a salient political issue in advanced market economy countries. Efforts by politicians to
"solve" immigration issues often provide only a brief respite, or generate an
organized opposition, or create new controversies. In the United States, 1986
marked the passage of the Immigration Reform and Control Act, aimed
at reducing undocumented immigration while providing amnesty to large
numbers of resident aliens. Eight years later, in 1994, California voters
approved Proposition 187, barring the provision of social services, including
education, to the growing numbers of undocumented immigrants, an indication that the 1986 reform had not eliminated illegal immigration. And in
1996, while the California initiative was being tested in the court system, the
U.S. government approved legislation to withdraw certain state services and
benefits from both legal and undocumented immigrants. This law generated
a counteraction of its own; state governors petitioned the national government to relax some of the more onerous restrictions.

Legal immigration in the United States has also been controversial. The
1990 Immigration Act expanded opportunities for legal migration to the
United States and contained provisions to encourage immigration of skilled
workers. A mere four years later, the Presidential Commission on Immigration Reform released a report recommending reduction of these quotas
(United States 1994). Even refugees have become targets of political controversy. The Haitian flotilla of 1992 prompted U.S. intervention in Haiti as
a means to avoid accepting thousands of new residents.

Immigration to Europe has been equally controversial and in many countries has given rise to extreme right parties with anti-immigrant platforms.
Jean-Marie Le Pen's anti-immigrant National Front continues to obtain substantial electoral support in France, garnering 10 to 15 percent of the vote
in national polls and winning elections in some communities. Yet when the

Gaullist government introduced legislation to control undocumented immigration more strictly by requiring citizens to report the departure of foreign visitors, more than 100,000 protesters demonstrated in the streets (*Economist*, March 1, 1997). Politicians are walking a thin line between the Scylla of anti-immigrant pressures and the Charybdis of their societies' egalitarian ethos.

These contemporary controversies have generated substantial public interest, media attention, and academic research. In this book I examine one dimension of immigration policy, immigration control. Immigration control can be distinguished from the broader concept of immigration policy by its emphasis on state policies that define the permissible level of resident alien admissions.[1] I ask why some advanced market economy countries welcome large numbers of resident aliens while others are less hospitable and why the policies within countries change over time.[2]

Variations in Immigration Control Policy

The tolerance for resident aliens—individuals who enter a host country with permission to reside for at least one year—varies substantially among advanced market economy countries.[3] A variety of indicators substantiates such differences.[4] One indicator is the average annual gross flow of legal resident aliens per capita.[5] As depicted in Table 1.1, the intake range is broad. At the low end, Japan permitted only 3 aliens per 10,000 resident population per year, on average, between 1962 and 1991. Australia and New Zealand are at the high end of the spectrum, allowing the entrance of 81 and 136 resident aliens per 10,000 resident population respectively. Belgium and Canada are closest to the unweighted annual average of the data set, 58 per 10,000, or about one-half of 1 percent of the resident population. These data are

1. Hammar makes a similar distinction between "the actual regulation and control of immigration and policy formulations which influence the condition of immigrants"; see Hammar 1985:x. My definition of control, however, is narrower than his; control is limited to the number of entries, whereas policies that affect the length of stay, such as the requirement of a residence permit—which Hammar classifies as immigration control—really govern the condition of the immigrants.

2. Although immigration control includes temporary visitors who enter the country for a short time, such as tourists and business visitors, I focus only on those who enter on a nontemporary basis. I also exclude from the analysis policies controlling refugees and asylum seekers. See Chapter 2 for a more detailed discussion of the various types of migrant flows.

3. Readers who object to the pooling of "guest workers" with "settlers" in the common terminology of "immigrants" and "resident aliens" may find a defense of this usage in Chapter 2.

4. See Chapter 2 for additional details on the data, including problems of comparability across countries.

5. Countries employ different labels for different categories of individuals who cross national borders. I employ the terms "resident alien" and "immigrant" interchangeably to encompass individuals who enter a host country with permission to reside for at least one year.

Table 1.1. Average annual inflows of legal resident aliens in selected OECD countries, 1962–1991 (per 10,000 resident population)

Country	Mean intake	Standard deviation	Number of years
Japan	3	1	23
France	23	14	29
United States	24	13	29
Finland	26	6	11
United Kingdom	38	7	28
Netherlands	40	10	14
Norway	47	9	29
Sweden	51	15	30
Belgium	53	13	28
Canada	62	21	28
Denmark	66	9	30
Australia	81	30	29
Germany (West)	122	48	29
New Zealand	136	26	28
Colonial countries[a] (with Japan)	32	20	122
Colonial countries[a] (without Japan)	38	16	99
Settler countries[b]	75	47	114
Average	58	41	365

[a] Japan, France, United Kingdom, Netherlands, Belgium.
[b] United States, Canada, Australia, New Zealand.
Source: See Chapter 2 for a detailed discussion of data and appendix for an enumeration of the sources.

similar to those reflecting arrivals for a single year, 1990, indicating that the patterns of immigration during the past thirty years are still present (Smith and Edmonston 1997: Table 2.11).

Some surprising facts emerge from these data. For example, the United States is widely perceived as a country of immigrants with a tradition of openness to immigration. Yet, although the United States admits large absolute numbers of immigrants, on a per capita basis it is located toward the low end of the scale, with 24 aliens per year per 10,000 residents, on average. Another anomaly is Germany. Even though it proclaims that it is not a country of immigration, (West) Germany admits relatively large flows of aliens on a per capita basis, even when excluding the ethnic Germans migrating from central Europe and the Soviet successor states, as these figures do.

Paired comparisons of particular countries also reveal wide contrasts in the acceptance of alien residents. (West) Germany and Japan, for example, have similar postwar economic and political histories. Both were defeated in

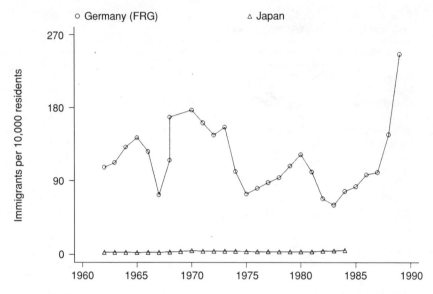

Figure 1.1. Immigration in Germany and Japan, 1962–1989. (*Source:* Statistische Bundesamt, *Statistische Jahrbuch für die Bundesrepublik Deutschland*, various years; Statistics Bureau, Management and Coordination Agency, *Japan Statistical Yearbook*, various years.)

war, adopted postwar constitutions influenced by the liberal democratic traditions of the victors, and went on to achieve economic "miracles." But in response to tight labor markets in both countries, Germany opted to import large numbers of "guest workers" to fill its factories whereas Japan chose to retain a homogeneous labor force. The dramatic differences in these countries' immigration policies are illustrated in Figure 1.1.

A second comparison can be drawn between Australia and the United States, both "settler" states, sparsely populated countries whose resources attracted millions of European migrants. Both adopted policies of racial exclusion by the turn of the twentieth century that were ultimately rejected in the 1960s.[6] Both accept immigrants as permanent settlers, facilitate naturalization of immigrants, and grant citizenship to those born in their territories. Yet Australia has opted for levels of immigration at more than three times the U.S. average, as illustrated in Figure 1.2.

The picture becomes even more variegated when these data are disaggregated over time. The United States shows an upward trajectory even after

6. Australia began to admit non-Europeans informally in 1966 and modified its laws governing alien admissions de jure in 1973. The United States passed legislation in 1965 revising its ethnic quota system.

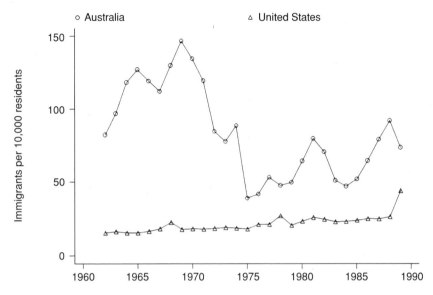

Figure 1.2. Immigration in Australia and the United States, 1962–1989. (*Source:* Australian Bureau of Statistics, *Yearbook Australia*, various years; U.S. Department of Labor, Bureau of the Census, *Statistical Abstract of the United States*, various years.)

accounting for the amnesty program instituted as part of the 1986 Immigration Reform and Control Act (IRCA). Many European countries, such as Sweden and Belgium, are experiencing a downward trend, initiated as early as the 1960s. Other countries, such as the United Kingdom, appear to maintain a relatively constant level of immigration over time.

The national stock of foreigners is another measure that demonstrates substantial differences in the countries' desire to accommodate newcomers. The stock of foreigners in a nation represents the cumulated net flows from previous years: gross intake of migrants, the rate at which migrants acquire citizenship (including children born in the host country who may remain "foreign"), and the rate of return migration to the country of origin. As Table 1.2 illustrates, the proportion of the foreign population varies from less than 1 percent to more than 20 percent.[7]

These data, although imperfect indicators of national openness to a resident alien population, do indicate significant variation among advanced industrial countries and therefore represent an important empirical puzzle. What, then, accounts for these patterns?

7. Migration patterns reflect both "push" factors in countries of emigration and "pull" factors in countries of immigration. Given the infinite supply of immigrants in the period under review, however, flows and stocks of foreign population are determined predominantly by the host country's policies.

Table 1.2. Number and percent of foreign population in selected OECD countries, 1991

Country	Number (thousands)	Percent of total population
Australia	3,940.5	22.8%[a]
Austria	512.2	6.6
Belgium	922.5	9.2
Canada	4,342.9	16.0[a]
Denmark	169.5	3.3
Finland	35.8	0.7
France[b]	3,596.6	6.3
Germany (West)	5,882.3	7.3
Italy	896.8	1.5
Japan	1,218.0	1.0[a]
Luxembourg[b]	109.1	28.4
Netherlands	732.9	4.8
Norway	146.8	3.5
Sweden	493.8	5.7
Switzerland	1,163.2	17.1
United Kingdom	1,750.0	3.1
United States[b]	19,767.3	7.9[a]

Note: As the data are collected in accordance with different criteria in the various countries, they are not strictly comparable.
[a] Calculated by author.
[b] 1990.
Source: SOPEMI 1993.

Contending Explanations of Immigration Control

A variety of explanations have been advanced to account for variation in immigration control policies among advanced industrial countries.[8] Most point either to aspects of national identity, to economic factors, or to a combination of the two variables.

One group of analysts focuses on conceptions of ethnicity, citizenship, or national identity to predict immigration policy.[9] Doris Meissner (1992:70), for example, argues that "for Europeans, membership in their societies is tied to shared ethnicity and nationality." She then juxtaposes the European perspective with attitudes in such "traditional settler nations" as Australia, Canada, and the United States, "where nation building through immigration led to ideas of membership based on civic participation and a generally shared commitment to democratic values." From this perspective, "settler" states are those where national identity and citizenship are based on civic

8. A more detailed and comprehensive survey of the literature is developed in Chapter 2; here I provide only a brief overview of the major contending explanations.
9. See, for example, Foot 1965 on Britain, Higham 1963 on the United States, and Meissner 1992 for a comparative analysis. Brubaker 1989 applies this concept to citizenship policies.

values of participation; immigrants are viewed as potential citizens and the state is relatively open to immigration. In contrast, "nonimmigrant" nations are those where citizenship and national identity are based on ethnicity; where these cultural values hold, immigrants are viewed as aliens or foreigners, and low levels of immigration are anticipated.[10]

This "primordial" perspective defines immigration control in terms of national identity. Moreover, national identity is fixed; societies have a predetermined tolerance for aliens. To account for the variation over time, the analyses introduce additional exogenous variables.[11] Elites, institutional structures, and extremist groups, for example, can damp down or kindle pressures to control entry of aliens.[12]

Economic interests of domestic political actors are a second major explanatory scheme. One group of analysts privileges employers' interests in explaining levels of openness. According to Marxian analyses, employers' interests are dominant because of their privileged access to the capitalist state (Castells 1975, Castles and Kosack 1973, Petras 1981); for public choice analysts, employers influence policy because they face fewer collective action problems than do employees or the public at large (Freeman 1995); those who focus on labor market segmentation believe that employers' interests are consistent with other societal interests because migrant labor is concentrated in the secondary labor market and therefore complements and enhances the returns to the native labor force deployed in the primary labor market (Piore 1979). Variation in immigration control is attributed to employers' demand for labor and hence for immigrants.

Alternatively, groups whose economic interests are affected by immigration are believed to compete in the political arena. According to Helga Leitner (1995:262), "Different social classes within the national territory will have conflicting interests which can result in opposing positions on immigration." She cites employers as one important class of political actors who favor immigration but adds unions to the political equation as actors who "might be opposed on the ground that this will harm workers' wages and working conditions." Variation in openness to immigration is explained in terms of power balances among societal actors, some who support immigration, others who oppose it.

Finally, many analysts point to the tension between economic benefits that accrue from immigration and the cultural costs that openness entails. One

10. The influx of migrants to the "nonimmigrant" nations of Europe during the 1950s, 1960s, and 1970s is often explained as a mistake; the policymakers responsible for encouraging or tolerating the inflows, it is said, failed to understand the permanence of a portion of those flows.

11. Alternatively, "this view assumes that ethnic and racial strife is inevitable and invariant" (Olzak 1992). In this case, the framework is unable to account for variation over time.

12. Philip Roeder 1994, for example, argues that institutional change in the former Soviet Union accounts for the outbreak of ethnic strife.

method of modeling the relationship between economic and cultural variables and political outcomes attributes tension to competition for scarce resources.[13] National or ethnic identity is seen as a contested social boundary rather than as fixed. National identity becomes politically significant when competition for scarce resources arises between the native and the immigrant populations. Susan Olzak (1992:27), for example, contends that "competition potentially occurs . . . when two or more groups come to exploit the same realized niche." "Niche overlap" triggers ethnic competition and, with it, opposition to immigration. From the "competition" perspective, anti-immigrant pressures are not constant but change as circumstances change: the size of the immigrant community, its rate of growth, as well as other socioeconomic factors.

How well do these hypotheses fare when compared with the empirical evidence? Analysts can always point to cases that substantiate a particular hypothesis and critics can usually find one or more exceptions to the rule. But systematic efforts to evaluate the explanatory power of these hypotheses are absent. My research was initiated in an attempt to evaluate the various contending hypotheses. As I show in Chapter 2, none of the hypotheses is fully substantiated. The only variable that consistently accounts for some of the variance in immigration control policy, unemployment, is consistent with several hypotheses and therefore does not permit us to distinguish among them.

Rather than discard the hypotheses, however, I suggest that, because immigrants are geographically concentrated within the host state, national-level variables may be insufficiently sensitive to the economic or cultural impact of immigrants. If the unit of analysis is shifted from the national level to the local community, each of these perspectives may fare better and may provide some insight into the dynamics of immigration policy. Those who emphasize national identity suggest that analyses must also be sensitive to factors that mediate between public opinion and policy outputs, that is, the political institutions of the nation. Those who emphasize economic variables suggest that important political actors are not limited to those who are concerned with national identity. Societies have political actors who actively promote immigration as well as those who oppose it. Those who focus on the interaction of cultural and economic variables suggest that the intensity and hence the political significance of national and ethnic identity may vary and that explanations should incorporate variables that affect the intensity of public opinion. The explanation I offer builds on these insights while emphasizing a fourth element, the geographic concentration of the immigrant community.

13. Also see Hollifield 1992, Freeman 1995, Zolberg 1983, and Leitner 1995 for alternative ways of modeling the relationship between the economic and cultural variables.

Costs and Benefits of Immigration

If migration is generated by "push" factors in the home countries of immigrants and by "pull" factors in the host country, the process is facilitated and sustained by migrant networks. These social organizations link new migrants to resources available in the established immigrant community. Earlier migrants provide information about opportunities in the host country, economic support until the new migrant is self-sustaining, and social support to endure and adjust to the new environment. Migrant networks are powerful social agents that draw newcomers to areas of old migrant settlement. Ultimately, migrant networks work to concentrate the immigrant population in a small number of communities within the host nation.

The spatial concentration of immigrants creates both benefits and costs for the host community. Employers are the primary recipients of the benefits of immigration.[14] They enjoy a more flexible and lower-cost labor market than in the absence of immigration. These benefits are especially appreciated by employers such as primary producers of agricultural goods and raw materials and in-person service providers who cannot move their production facilities and rely more on local labor markets than do other employers. Concentrated benefits create incentives for local employers to organize politically and petition in support of immigration.

The costs of immigration are borne by members of local host communities, but only under conditions of competition. Where immigrants replace a departing host population, they create little competition and can even revive declining neighborhoods. Where they compete with the host population, for public services, for employment, and for cultural dominance, they create costs for the local community. Economic recession aggravates competition and generates the rise of political pressures against immigration.

The concentration of costs and benefits facilitates the political organization of proponents and opponents of immigration (Olson 1965). Yet, because immigration is concentrated, local representatives have difficulty in generating majority support for a policy change at the national level, where immigration policy is determined. The result is inertia in immigration policy. If these local constituencies are critical to maintaining or retaining a national electoral majority, however, national politicians have an incentive to adopt local preferences and translate them into policy. Hence local demands for expanded or reduced immigration are catapulted to the national political

---

14. Consumers also enjoy lower-priced goods as a result of immigrants' participation in the host country's labor force (Smith and Edmonston 1997). But because these benefits are diffuse—that is, small benefits accruing to a large number of individuals—it rarely, if ever, pays consumers to organize in support of immigration. None of the literature cites consumers as important actors in immigration policy making.

agenda only when these local political actors are capable of swinging the national electoral outcome. Local conditions drive local preferences, but national politicians are driven by national electoral incentives to play or not to play the "immigrant card."

This is the basic argument put forward in this book. It is developed in more detail in Chapter 3, where I specify the conditions that affect employers' demands for immigrant labor and the types and degree of competition generated by an immigrant community. I also define more precisely the criteria for creating a national electoral majority and the conditions under which incentives exist to play the immigrant card. Although standard explanations of immigration policy privilege domestic political factors, my approach is distinctive in three ways. It focuses on the local community as the primary unit of political analysis; it provides a theory to explain changing local preference structures of both support for and opposition to immigration; and it systematically includes institutional aspects of the political system through which societal demands are funneled.

The framework presented here reflects an interdisciplinary perspective that is crucial to understanding the dynamics of immigration control. From demographers and sociologists comes the insight that immigrant communities are geographically concentrated and that concentration is generated by migrant networks and chain migration. From economists comes the framework for evaluating the distribution of the costs and benefits of immigration—a method of determining societal preferences—associated with both labor markets and government services. Although economists rarely include noneconomic costs of immigration, these can be incorporated into the cost-benefit framework as well. And from political scientists come insights regarding the problems of collective action and the role of political institutions in channeling societal preferences. Each of these dimensions is crucial to building an accurate model of immigration policy making.

The Changing Context of International Migration

That states can decide how many individuals cross their borders is a function of a particular, and modern, context. In the contemporary era, advanced market economy countries confront a virtually unlimited supply of immigrants and can decide the number and characteristics of those to admit. In the past, immigrants' destinations were different and boundaries more porous. To understand the contemporary context of global migration, it is useful to describe how that context has changed over time.

Migration—the movement of individuals from one geographic location to another—is a constant in human behavior, yet it tends to be the exception rather than the rule (Zolberg 1983). Less than 2 percent of the world's population now reside in nations other than those of their birth (Smith and Edmonston 1997). Migration is motivated by a variety of factors. Some individuals flee individually targeted political or religious persecution or move to avoid the volley of gunfire in civil or international wars. Others migrate to escape the effects of natural catastrophes such as floods and droughts. Another important impetus for migration comes from the desire to improve one's economic position, giving rise to a distinction in the migration literature between "involuntary" refugees and "voluntary" migrants.[15] But if the determinants of migratory pressures remain constant, the economic and political context within which migration takes place has changed dramatically.

The changing distribution of economic resources has modified both the sources and destinations of migrants. With the rise of the modern world system, beginning in the sixteenth century, Europe became a supplier of migrants to the rest of the globe. The processes of capital accumulation, industrialization, and economic development generated a steady stream of migrants, some who moved locally, others who looked beyond their national horizons (Massey 1989). Sparsely populated regions of the world with vast, untapped natural resources attracted these migrants, along with those who desired greater political and religious freedom. Lacking a sufficient voluntary migratory base, Europeans also organized various forms of involuntary migration, including the slave trade, systems of indentured servitude, and the transportation of convicts. These extra-European flows were massive in scope and reached a peak about the turn of the twentieth century. Approximately 11 percent of the European population in 1900 migrated to non-European destinations between 1846 and 1924 (Massey 1989:6).

In the contemporary era, these migratory patterns have changed.[16] One element in the broader global migratory context is the movement from peripheral areas of the global economy to the core, commonly referred to as the migratory movement from "the South" to "the North," in defiance of the geographic reality.[17] Wealth is concentrated in a set of advanced market economy countries—Western Europe, North America, and Australia, New Zealand, and Japan on the Pacific Rim—providing large economic incentives to migrate, the "pull" factors of international migration. In the periphery, high population growth and insufficient economic development, aggravated in

15. This book concentrates on the latter group of migrants, those whose dominant motive for migration is to improve their lot in life.
16. See Castles and Miller 1993 for an overview of the broader, global context of migration.
17. This global pattern of periphery-to-core flows was replicated in the core in the early postwar period, when individuals from less developed semiperipheral states moved to wealthier and more dynamic states in the core. Now these nations as well as some peripheral developing nations are attracting immigrants of their own. See *Migration News* for details of the latter flows.

some instances by political instability and natural disasters, have provided the "push" for individuals to leave their homes. These disparities in wealth—combined with the beginnings of economic development in the South that generate a flow of migrants—have created a reverse flow of migrants, from previously colonized countries to the earlier colonizers. The settler states of Canada, the United States, Australia, and New Zealand, early destinations of European emigrants, continue to attract immigrant flows as well. This south-to-north flow has been compounded in the 1990s by an east-to-west movement, as barriers to exit from former Soviet bloc countries have disappeared (Heisler 1992).

Even in this periphery-to-core migration, patterns vary. Russell King (1993b) contrasts the "industrial migration" of the 1950s, 1960s, and 1970s with the "postindustrial" migration of the 1980s and 1990s. The former consists of unskilled and semiskilled workers attracted to the industrial plants of the North, along with their families. The latter is more complex, made up of high-skill workers, asylum seekers, and undocumented migrants. High-skill workers often have professional credentials and find employment in transnational firms producing for global markets.[18] Asylum seekers claim persecution in their home countries but also have strong economic motives as the sole or additional reason for migrating. Undocumented migrants are those who, in the absence of opportunities for lawful entry, enter or stay in host countries unlawfully.

The political context of global migration has changed dramatically as well. In the past, "foreigners" were defined as newcomers to the local community. In ninteenth-century France, for example, new arrivals to the village or town were required to register with the local government, regardless of whether they were French citizens or citizens of foreign states (Lequin 1992). As the consolidation of nation-states and national markets proceeded during the nineteenth century, a distinction arose between "internal" and "international" migration. The former refers to movement within a single national political jurisdiction while the latter indicates movement between national political jurisdictions. At the same time, the political jurisdiction over migration was contested. Communities or, in the United States, states that had previously decided who would be admitted within their borders lost that control to the national government.

Contemporary international migration takes place within a network of nation-states whose governing principle is sovereignty, including the legal authority to permit or deny entrance to their territory. Thus migrants are not free to move as they please as they often did in an earlier era. Rather, they confront a particular set of states that are strong and capable of controlling

---

18. A significant portion of this flow appears to be between states within the core.

their borders, despite growing interdependence. These wealthy countries of destination cannot completely prevent illegal or undocumented migration; where incentives are large, if population movement is controlled, an illegal movement will develop. But this does not mean that states have lost control of their borders.[19] In fact, the increasing costs of illegal migration suggest that states are developing their capacity to control population flows in response to new situations.

Thus contemporary patterns of migration are distinctive from those of the past. Both pull and push factors in the post–World War II era have generated a flow of migrants from poorer, developing nations to the wealthy, powerful, advanced market economy countries. Because these states have both the de jure and de facto ability to control that flow, they must decide which immigrants and how many to admit.

This book provides a framework for analyzing the political determinants of this decision in advanced market economy countries, within this particular global context. The wealthy countries on which the book focuses share three characteristics: their wealth attracts immigrants; their state capacity allows them to control their borders more or less effectively; and their democratic political institutions provide mechanisms for citizens to express their policy preferences. The theoretical framework developed here is applicable to other countries that share all three characteristics but not to countries with fewer shared attributes.

Evidence on the Politics of Immigration Control

I begin in Chapter 2 by evaluating the alternative explanations of immigration control via a cross-national quantitative data set for twelve advanced market economy countries. This is the basic starting point for general readers as well as policy analysts. If there is a straightforward way to distinguish why some countries are more open to immigration than others, there is no need to proceed. But, although anecdotal evidence abounds, there have been no systematic analyses to evaluate some of the most commonsensical and straightforward hypotheses. Do concepts of citizenship and national identity matter? Are homogeneous European states, where citizenship is based on ethnicity, less open than heterogeneous North American states where citizenship is based on political participation? Does national history make a difference? Do long-standing ties and commitments of colonial countries provide privileged access to members of previously colonized states? Do

---

19. There is a dispute among migration specialists over whether states have lost control of their borders. Mark Miller 1994 is one who supports the position put forward here.

unemployment rates make a difference? Do states institute controls in periods of high unemployment only to relax controls in periods of low unemployment?

To answer these questions, I begin by describing the cross-national, time-series data set. It consists of twelve wealthy democratic nations with competitive party systems, where politicians must respond in some fashion to societal interests. I define the dependent variable, the annual gross flow of legal resident aliens per capita, defend this choice against alternative formulations, and describe the limits of the analysis. The brief summary of the literature on immigration control policy provided above is expanded and various hypotheses are delineated and operationalized. Finally, I evaluate the results of the analysis. The quantitative analysis demonstrates that most of the commonsense approaches offered in the literature cannot explain patterns of immigration control. These results suggest that national-level variables may be insufficiently sensitive to capture either the impact of immigration on the national population or the political processes by which societal preferences are translated into policy.

In Chapter 3, I lay out the theoretical foundations of the argument and discuss the research strategies employed to test the various hypotheses. In essence, the argument has two levels. The initial level defines societal preferences toward immigration. The second layer takes into account the specific national political institutions through which societal demands are funneled.

In Chapters 4 through 6, I substantiate my argument by analyzing the transition in Britain, France, and Australia from a period of relative openness to one of greater closure. In the quantitative analysis, immigration control policy is operationalized as the annual gross flow of legal resident aliens per capita. In the country analyses, I employ a broader variety of indicators. Most significantly, I trace government policy through the issuance of various administrative decrees, the passage of legislation, and, in the case of Australia, where target intake levels are set annually, I examine both the projected target and the actual intake level. These indicators—executive orders, legislation, targeted and actual immigration levels—provide a reasonably full and accurate picture of a country's immigration control policy.

The three nations were selected for analysis on the basis of a "most different case" research strategy (Przeworski and Teune 1970).[20] Each country has a distinctive immigration history and different political institutions. Yet each had a similar policy outcome in immigration control, a restriction of immigration after a period of relative openness. Because the differences

20. Although the vocabulary is different, this research design is similar to John Stuart Mill's 1970 "method of agreement."

cannot account for the similar policy outcomes, the researcher can attribute the cause to the single common feature, in this case the rise of opposition to immigration in constituencies that are important to maintaining or gaining a national electoral majority.

The three cases provide variance on the independent variables hypothesized to influence immigration control policy. Britain and France are European states, with long histories of state-building and a sense of national identity based on a shared history. Yet France, confronting an early demographic transition and slow population growth, actively encouraged immigration during the nineteenth and twentieth centuries. Britain, on the other hand, has a long history of emigration, providing a significant portion of the European peoples who settled around the globe. Australia has been labeled a new settler state that promoted immigration and incorporated immigrants into its society and political system.[21]

Britain and France both have systems of "probationary migration" whereby foreigners enter subject to residence and working permits granted for specified periods of time and gain permanent residence rights only after a certain length of stay. Australia emphasizes settler migration, encouraging those who are interested in permanent rather than temporary migration.

Britain and France both had colonial histories and a tradition of freedom of movement within their empires that created specific migratory flows from colonies and former colonies after World War II. Both countries initially had immigration control systems that privileged these migrants within the overall immigrant flow. Australia's colonial experience was limited to the adjacent Papua New Guinea, with restricted migratory flows based on a "White Australia" policy.

The timing and circumstances associated with immigration control also differed. Britain restricted the flow of New Commonwealth immigrants in the early 1960s, when its own foreign-born population was fairly small. France stopped immigration of workers in 1974, when the foreign-born population was more than 7 percent of the resident population. And Australia reduced its immigration intakes in 1972, when approximately 22 percent of its population was foreign born. Moreover, although each nation took steps to reduce immigration control during a period of economic recession, previous periods of economic recession did not induce intake restrictions. Britain failed to introduce immigration control during the economic downturn in 1954–55; France failed to do so after the recession caused by

21. The term "settler" is a benign description of the process by which the new immigrant population displaced the indigenous population, leading to its decline and, in some cases, decimation. Nonetheless, it is a widely used and commonly understood term for a specific set of states and I employ it as such.

the social revolution in May 1968; and Australia retained high immigration intakes during the 1961–62 recession.

Thus the three countries selected for this analysis differ enormously on the various dimensions hypothesized to contribute to immigration policy. But these differences cannot account for the common policy outcome. Only by locating similar policy processes in countries with very different immigration histories is it possible to establish the plausibility of the argument that local political pressures combine with national electoral incentives to determine immigration control policy outcomes.

Chapters 4, 5, and 6 follow a parallel structure. I begin with an overview of immigration control policy, including the national laws and regulations governing the flows, as a complement to the quantitative analysis of immigrant flows. Then, I analyze the political process through which significant immigration laws and regulations were adopted. In particular, I focus on the rise of immigrant pressures, the political organization of anti-immigrant groups, and the set of electoral incentives that structured political decisions to ignore or to adopt local political agendas at the national level. The qualitative analysis of critical turning points in immigration control policy provides an assessment of the process by which local issues are generated and transferred to the national political agenda. Finally, I evaluate the country-specific literature, pointing out where it can be incorporated into the broader framework and where it is inaccurately or insufficiently specified.

Because I focus on the contemporary period and, in particular, immigration control policies during the 1960s and 1970s, the empirical evidence focuses primarily on the geographically concentrated rise and organization of opposition to immigration rather than on the geographically concentrated support for immigration. Although I do provide some indicators of the geographic concentration of support, the evidence provided substantiates most systematically the organization of anti-immigrant interests. Given the limitations of time and space, the symmetry of organization underlying the theoretical framework presented in Chapter 3 is only partially substantiated empirically. Another project, reaching back into the nineteenth century or covering the 1920s or the 1950s, would provide additional evidence supporting the hypotheses developed here regarding the geographically concentrated support for immigration.

In the concluding chapter, I summarize the argument and findings. I return to a main theme in the country-specific literature, that of racism. I argue, based on the evidence presented in the text, that immigrants' most distinguishing feature is their nonmembership in the society. Race is only one of many attributes that differentiate the immigrant from the host population.

This analytical distinction is important if we want to understand the ways in which race may interact with immigration policy in either its control or integration dimensions. I also place my arguments about the distribution of costs and benefits of immigration within the wider literature that evaluates the net national costs and benefits of immigration.

Finally I discuss the policy implications of the model with attention to issues of societal equity. Although substantiated with data from Britain, France, and Australia, the theory is general and is applicable to all wealthy democratic countries whose politicians confront electoral incentives to address immigration control. So too are the policy recommendations. To help retain openness to immigration while ensuring equity among members of the host society, between the immigrant and host communities, and between the host and home countries of the immigrants, politicians should develop policies to reduce the costs of immigration through flexible immigrant intakes and to transfer some of the revenues generated by immigration to cover the costs incurred.

I have defined my research question in a relatively concise and narrow manner. As a result, some aspects of immigration control policy are excluded. For example, I ignore the supranational dimension of immigration control such as the European Union's immigration control policy. I do so for two reasons. First, for the period under review, immigration control decisions were made by nation-states. Even in Europe, members of the European Union adopted a policy permitting the free movement of community citizens but retained control over national borders and alien admissions.[22] A real European Union immigration control policy is a very recent phenomenon that is closely associated with the removal of internal border controls, via the Schengen Agreement.[23] Moreover, some member states have refused to participate, retaining border controls and national sovereignty over immigration policy.[24] The European immigration control efforts are the most fully developed supranational immigration control policies of advanced industrial countries. Other types of supranational cooperation in immigration control issues remain in their infancy. Thus the focus on nation-states is appropriate for the period under review. Second, a clear understanding of the political dynamics of immigration control at the national level can only enhance our

---

22. The European regional organization has undergone several name changes since its inception in the 1952 Treaty of Paris: European Coal and Steel Community, European Economic Community, European Community, and, since 1993, European Union.
23. The Schengen Agreement was originally signed in 1985 by five European Union members, in the city of Schengen, hence the name. The ultimate goal was to eliminate border controls between the member states. The implementation date was postponed on several occasions, and even after it went into effect in 1996, some signatories reneged on its provisions, at least temporarily.
24. The United Kingdom and Ireland are the two notable holdouts.

understanding of immigration control when we turn to the supranational level. This book should provide a solid foundation from which to explore the politics of immigration control at the supranational level.

Also, the research question encompasses only one aspect of immigration policy. Immigration policy is generally viewed as having two dimensions, control and integration. The first includes policies governing admission to a nation's territory and the second, policies governing admission to citizenship.[25] My research question specifically addresses the politics of immigration control. The answer I provide may or may not explain the politics of immigrant integration.[26]

The Policy Significance of Immigration Research

In advanced market economy countries in the late 1990s, the importance of understanding the politics of immigration control may seem self-evident. Immigration is a Janus-faced policy with both domestic and international consequences. Domestically, many politicians are confronting a politically powerful backlash against foreign residents of all types: undocumented and documented; foreign born and foreign by ethnicity; workers and dependents; voluntary migrants and involuntary refugees and asylum seekers. This backlash is sometimes anomic, erupting periodically in race riots or playing out in random attacks on individuals with a foreign appearance. Often it is organized in the form of citizens' initiatives, as in the United States and Switzerland, or in political parties contending elections, as in Austria, the Netherlands, and France. But whatever form the backlash takes, it represents a challenge to the established law and order and to incumbent politicians. At the same time, employers continue to petition for greater access to migrant labor, both skilled and unskilled. Moreover, the domestic political consequences of immigrant streams are not confined to advanced industrial countries. Even among developing countries, the more dynamic

25. "Citizenship" here denotes the degree of equality of immigrants vis-à-vis the indigenous population. Full equality is defined by the grant of citizenship; but there are lesser degrees of equality that nonetheless provide immigrants with a broad array of economic and social services, such as unemployment payments, various types of social security, and education. Immigrants who are "part" citizens without full incorporation in the polity have been labeled "denizens" (Hammar 1990).

26. A cursory review of immigration policy in advanced industrial countries suggests that the two dimensions may not be systematically related. Germany is a nation that has permitted a high level of resident alien admissions but considers that population to be "foreign"; the United States has, on a per capita basis, relatively restricted flows but facilitates incorporation through naturalization. Japan is a nation with low levels of resident aliens and difficult integration; Australia rounds out the possible variations by admitting high levels of resident aliens and facilitating integration.

economies are attracting their own immigrant flows and attendant problems.[27]

Immigration control is also a source of potential international conflict. Conflict arises over disparate interests, such as developing countries' desire for broader emigration versus the preference of advanced industrial countries for limited immigration. A case in point is the attempt by Mexico and other Central American, Caribbean, and South American nations to add immigration policy to the 1994 Summit of the Americas' agenda, an effort that the United States rebuffed. Another dimension of conflict arises when one country develops and implements policies that transfer its control problems to other nations. The 1993 German modification to its asylum policy endorsed the rejection of asylum seekers transiting "safe" countries en route to Germany. This measure reduced Germany's intake of asylum seekers but at the expense of an increase in neighboring countries.

To address these domestic and international political issues, we require a clearer understanding of the determinants of immigration policy. Yet our understanding of the politics of immigration control is limited. The international flow of people has not yet been drawn systematically into the research agenda in international political economy (Haus 1995a). Although the determinants of global patterns of trade, production, and capital flows are now widely studied, immigration remains predominantly in the domain of economists, demographers, and sociologists. The literature on immigration policy formation that does exist tends to be country-specific rather than comparative, making it difficult to sort between idiosyncratic factors and more generally applicable theories. As James Hollifield (1992:17) notes, "Truly comparative works on immigration are few. In the field of migration studies, the tendency has been to collect national case studies, bind them together and call the study comparative. Such compendia are useful sources of information, but they rarely yield theoretical insights." Comparative research on the sources of immigration policy and patterns will add to the research agenda of international political economy by including an important flow of resources across national boundaries.

Although my approach emphasizes certain unique aspects of the politics of immigration control, I believe that the political dynamics of immigration policy are much like those of other international economic policies. My stance varies from that of others who argue that immigration, because it involves human beings who cross borders, is inherently different from other international economic transactions. It is true that migration is an international transaction that encompasses social as well as economic dimensions.

---

27. See various issues of *Migration News* for a good, contemporary account of policies in developing nations, such as Taiwan, Korea, Singapore, and Malaysia, regarding immigrant labor flows.

To paraphrase Michael Piore (1979:7–8), "men are not shirts." Another well-known adage from Europe also emphasizes the social aspects of immigration: "We asked for workers but got people instead." Similar statements could and should be made about other international economic transactions whose social dimensions often are overlooked because the social consequences are concentrated in the receiving countries of the periphery.[28] By systematically incorporating the flow of individuals across international borders into the study of international political economy, we can become more fully cognizant of the similarities of international economic transactions as well as their distinctive attributes.

Research on international migration and the determinants of immigration control policy is not an abstract exercise. Newspapers are filled daily with the dilemmas associated with immigration. A survey in the United States in the closing weeks of 1997 reveals such dilemmas. An African immigrant in Denver, Colorado, was murdered. A Hmong refugee in Fresno, California, committed suicide after failing to pass the naturalization exam. A congressional election in Orange County, California, was contested because of alleged noncitizen voting. An initiative to restrict bilingual education was qualified for the California ballot. The lives of immigrants and those members of the host community who interact with them are dramatically affected by the policy choices of states. If we want to change these policies and their effects, we must first understand how these policies are constructed.

28. The social consequences of international capital flows in developing nations are well documented, as are the social consequences of various product flows, one of the most notorious being infant formula exported to developing nations.

2   *Testing the Hypotheses*

In the modern world system, control over national boundaries is a jealously guarded prerogative of all nation-states. Migration, the movement of individuals across national boundaries, is one element of the broader jurisdiction over national boundaries derived from the concept of national sovereignty. "It is an accepted maxim of international law that every sovereign nation has the power, as inherent in sovereignty, and essential to self preservation, to forbid the entrance of foreigners within its dominions, or to admit them, only in such cases and upon such conditions as it may see fit" (*Nishimura Ikiu v. United States*, 142 U.S. 651, 659).

Politicians and pundits defend immigration control policies in the name of the state, whether on economic or cultural grounds. Jean-Marie Le Pen, the French extremist advocate of immigration control, shouts "*La France pour les français!*" at his rallies and equates the two million foreign workers in France with the two million unemployed French. Enoch Powell, an earlier counterpart in Britain, decried "coloured" immigration as a threat to the British nation, and his Conservative colleagues sought to reduce immigration to avoid a "multiracial state" and to maintain "the kind of Britain we know and love." It is not surprising, then, that analysts of immigration control policy couch their explanations in terms of national attributes. The national culture, the national economy, and the tensions between the economic benefits and cultural costs of immigration are the primary explanatory variables proposed by immigration analysts to explain the level of openness to immigration. In this chapter I examine these various contending hypotheses through a quantitative analysis of national characteristics.

Immigration Control Policy as a Dependent Variable

In any quantitative research, the analysis depends on the ability to capture the theoretical concepts with appropriate quantitative indicators. Often, this is easier said than done. One possible method of capturing the dependent variable "immigration control policy" is to use the laws governing migration. Eytan Meyers (1995) takes this approach and employs an ordinal coding scheme to distinguish among major laws, minor laws, major laws that were introduced but not passed, and no laws. Positive values indicate greater openness to immigration flows and negative values, greater closure.[1] One problem with this method is that it misses administrative controls, especially in countries where these mechanisms are far more important than actual legislation, as in France and Australia. But even if administrative controls were incorporated into the coding scheme, it is still an inadequate method of operationalizing the dependent variable in a cross-national context because it is unable to account for the differences in levels of openness across countries. A coding scheme based on laws incorporates the direction and the degree of change but does not necessarily translate into the overall level of openness to immigration. A parallel may be drawn to the use of nontariff barriers (NTBs) in the analysis of trade policies. Two nontariff barriers are likely to provide more protection than one NTB, but it is unlikely that two NTBs provide exactly twice as much protection as one NTB or that two NTBs in France provide the same degree of protection as two NTBs in the United States. This problem is less acute in a national setting but becomes critical when one attempts to perform cross-national analyses.

Therefore, for the cross-national statistical analysis, I chose to operationalize the dependent variable as the volume of immigrants, that is, the annual per capita gross flow of legal resident aliens.[2] The term "resident" alien is employed to distinguish between short-term visitors such as tourists and business people and those who take up residence in the host country for extended periods of time. Countries normally classify those who stay for less than one year as short term and those who remain for one year or more as long term.[3] The absolute number of resident aliens is standardized across countries by population, producing a per capita comparison of the annual resident alien intake. Unfortunately, this method of operationalizing

1. To be fair to Meyers's presentation, he employed this indicator in a national rather than cross-national context where the problems of comparability are present but less acute.
2. In the detailed country analyses that follow, legislation, executive decrees, and target immigration levels are also employed to evaluate the state's immigration control policy.
3. This definition is not uniform; for some countries, the cutoff is six months. In all cases, however, seasonal workers are not considered long-term residents.

immigration control policy is not without problems.[4] I address each in turn.

As noted in Chapter 1, migratory flows are determined both by push factors—conditions in the migrant's home country that create incentives to leave—and by pull factors—the incentives that draw migrants to a particular country. A critic might argue that variation in immigration flows is caused, at least in part, by push factors; that is, the volume of immigrants is associated with the supply of immigrants rather than with government policy. This criticism might be appropriate for earlier historical periods but is unlikely to affect the analysis in the post–World War II period when the supply of migrants is, for all intents and purposes, unlimited. Even in Australia, where the government pursued a goal of 1 percent (of population) net annual immigration combined with a strong preference for British immigrants, insufficient supply led to a relaxation of admissions criteria, not to decreasing admissions. Similarly, when the supply of Italian migrants to (West) Germany decreased, Germany negotiated immigration agreements with other Mediterranean countries to assure a continuous supply. Therefore, it is reasonable to assume that variation in flows is determined almost exclusively by government policy in the host state rather than by the supply of migrants, at least for the period under review.

Illegal or undocumented migratory flows are not captured directly in this indicator. Undocumented migration contributes to the presence of aliens on national territory; moreover, analysts suggest that illegal flows are increasing relative to legal flows, especially as controls over legal flows mount. As the front door to legal migration is closing, so the argument goes, the back door to illegal flows is being shoved open (Thranhardt 1992, Zolberg 1990).[5] This objection cannot be entirely dismissed but assumes less significance in light of my objective of capturing government policy. Illegal flows are those that escape government control; undocumented migration is extralegal and is not a government policy unless there is evidence that the government tolerates or actively encourages illegal flows. Moreover, illegal flows that the government does tolerate are often included in legal migrant flow data via ongoing or periodic amnesty programs. In France, for example, up through the early 1970s, most immigration was "illegal" but the migrants were sub-

---

4. I received useful feedback on the quantitative analysis from audiences to which I presented earlier versions of my research, including, but not limited to, the International Relations Seminar Series at the University of California, San Diego, the Comparative Immigration and Integration Policy working group sponsored by the Center for German and European Studies, and the Agricultural History Center at the University of California, Davis.

5. According to Thranhardt 1992:38, among others, "Another effect of closing of the 'main gate' of immigration was the enhanced importance of 'back doors,' especially the quest for political asylum and illegal immigration."

sequently legalized or "regularized" and show up in gross migratory flows shortly after arrival.[6] So, despite the exclusion of undocumented aliens, the annual gross flow of legal resident aliens does capture, to a large extent, government decisions regarding the appropriate flow.

The dependent variable is composed of the gross flows of legal resident aliens rather than the net flows, a figure that would indicate the number of permanent settlers rather than the annual intake and provide a better idea of the ultimate costs and benefits of immigration flows. From a theoretical perspective, the inability to employ net flows may be problematic because public and political perceptions vary regarding the permanence of immigrant flows. Even without a clear understanding of return migration rates, countries with guest worker programs assumed that the net flow would be small, whereas countries that accepted migrants as permanent settlers assumed that net flows would be substantial. This problem is connected to the criticism that the data lump together different types of migrants and confound different types of selection rules. The annual flow of legal resident aliens lumps together family reunification migrants with labor force migrants and permanent resident aliens with so-called guest workers.

I agree with others that the distinction between "temporary" guest workers and "permanent" settlers is overstated. As Stephen Castles and Godula Kosack (1973:12) note,

> No rigid distinction between permanent and temporary immigrants is possible. Few migrants actually intend to remain away from their country of origin forever when they first depart, and there is no way of knowing in advance whether an individual will settle permanently or not.... Secondly where most individual immigrants come for a limited period only, immigrants as a group are permanently present. This group, despite its changing membership, may have the same long-term effects on society as a group of permanent settlers.

That is, even guest worker programs that succeed in rotating workers back home after a specified period of time, which are exceedingly rare, acknowledge the permanent presence of "aliens" within the geographic territory of the state. More frequently, guest workers are really "probationary migrants," who gain permanent residence status after a specified length of residence in the host country. Furthermore, family reunification has labor market implications, either immediate—when the spouse enters the labor market immediately—or longer term—when the dependent children reach working age and join the labor force. Moreover, if guest workers are more perma-

6. The details of the French process of regularization are discussed at greater length in Chapter 5. For the most part, those who regularized their status in France entered legally but did not adhere to the provisions of their entry visas by obtaining employment or by overstaying their visas.

nent than their nomenclature implies, settler immigrants are less permanent than their label indicates. Individuals admitted as permanent residents may not settle in the host country but return home after shorter or longer stays.

Aristide Zolberg (1983:36), among others, argues that "categoric distinctions between immigrants and migrants, and between guest workers and undocumented aliens, reflect administrative practices rather than economic and sociological realities." Nonetheless, this critique is the most serious, especially if the analyst suspects that different types of migratory flows are driven by different political processes, that the political dynamics of policy governing "probationary migrants" are distinctive from those governing "settler migrants." Jagdish Bhagwati (1984:694), for example, suggests that the "economic impacts [including the quantity of immigration] can vary interestingly with the specific features of the control regime." He contrasts the high flow of migrants in the German *gastarbeiter* or guest worker system with the low flow of immigrants in the U.S. post-1965 system. Unfortunately, the data often do not distinguish between either gross and net flows or "temporary" and "permanent" resident immigrants.[7]

Nonetheless, we can distinguish between settler states that allow both long-term temporary and permanent settler migration and most European states that grant entry primarily to probationary migrants who gain permanent residence status only after a specified period of residence.[8] If the levels of migration vary systematically based on the general type of migrant, we can test whether there are systematic differences between states that permit probationary migrants and states that permit settler migrants. We can then test Bhagwati's implicit hypothesis that guest worker states are more open to immigration than settler states, or the opposite hypothesis, delineated below, that settler states are more open to immigration. That is, the empirical analysis itself will provide evidence on whether cross-national quantitative analyses are better confined to like groups of migrants or whether we can work around this critique.

Finally, there are various problems of comparability given each country's immigration system, the system that defines, controls, and accounts for

---

7. The quality of the data has improved over time, but the only nation for which both gross and net migration statistics are available for the entire period under review is Australia. More recently, other countries have begun to collect exit as well as entry data, providing the basis for net migration statistics, but several countries, including the United States, do not have exit controls so the data are either nonexistent or unreliable.

8. Britain is the major exception to the European rule; until 1971, when rules governing aliens and Commonwealth citizens were merged, Commonwealth immigrants, once admitted, were granted permanent residence status. Special provisions in France for Algerians and in the Netherlands for colonial and former colonial subjects do not affect the data analysis because the Netherlands is excluded altogether because of missing data and the provisions for Algerians were discontinued in 1964, only two years into the statistical analysis.

legal resident aliens. One important problem is associated with the exclusion of particular groups from control. For example, Irish migrants to Britain are uncontrolled and therefore uncounted; ethnic Germans from Eastern Europe and the Soviet successor states are not considered immigrants even though they often are unable to speak German. Immigration control systems are complex sets of rules and regulations that may classify individuals crossing international borders differently, depending on the border crossed.

These data, then, are not without problems. I have argued, however, that several of the perceived problems—issues of immigrant supply and undocumented immigrants—are overstated and that the potentially serious problem of distinguishing between long-term temporary (guest workers) and permanent (settler) immigrants can be evaluated with the data. Even if the data are imperfect, the analysis does provide at least a broad picture of immigrant flows to advanced industrial countries and allows us to test some hypotheses in a more systematic fashion than has been done previously.

Cultural and Economic Sources of Immigration Control

I group the explanations into three types: those that emphasize cultural traits and national identity, those that emphasize economic interests, and those that explore the tension between cultural values and economic interests. Most explanations delineate the sources of societal preferences and assume that societal demands are translated into political outputs without defining the methods through which demands are filtered through the political process. Inevitably, the series of hypotheses described and tested here will not be exhaustive.[9] There are several reasons for this problem. First, many analyses of immigration policy rely on idiosyncratic, country-specific variables, for which there are no comparative counterparts (Hollifield 1992:17). Second, many hypotheses are insufficiently specified to test, including a large portion of the literature that points to the tension between economic and cultural variables but fails to specify the conditions under which one dimension will outweigh the other. And, finally, in some cases, no cross-national time-series data are available.

I draw on both comparative and national analyses of immigration policy that develop a systematic theoretical framework that can be tested empirically. The literature on the determinants of immigration policy covers a wide

---

9. See, for example, the various factors hypothesized to influence immigration policy in Kabala 1993 and Hardcastle et al. 1994.

variety of dependent variables including many aspects of immigrant integration. I have attempted to incorporate those that could plausibly be applied to immigration control policy. But to test and dismiss those hypotheses with a particular dependent variable does not erode all aspects of the authors' original, hypothesized relationship; the evidence suggests only that the relationship does not hold for immigration control policy. Moreover, in a complex world, even one dimension of immigration policy may not be fully explained without reliance on additional country-specific, idiosyncratic factors. Nonetheless, the analysis should help determine whether there are common tendencies underlying policy formation in all advanced industrial countries.

The primacy of cultural values

Analysts of immigration policy often consider national identity a primary determinant of immigration policy. No modern society permits open access to all comers. This closure reflects a widespread perception that "the central values and ethos that characterize one's society could be diluted by the entry of individuals and groups who do not share them" (Bhagwati 1984:681). Nonetheless, societies appear to have different levels of tolerance for foreigners, and "perhaps the most fundamental factor" in defining that level of tolerance "is how the country regards itself—its own national mythology" (Stalker 1994:138). Analysts who work in this tradition are generally country specialists;[10] those who examine immigration control policy from a cross-national perspective tend to incorporate additional, economic variables into the analysis. Nonetheless, the comparativists provide a good overview of the logic propounded by country experts.

Leitner (1995:262), for example, argues that "dominant racial and national ideologies, defining who belongs and who does not belong to a national community, also influence who is admitted." In other words, nations have characteristics that make it more or less easy for the indigenous population to accept a resident alien population. National character or identity has been defined in a variety of ways. One method is to evaluate the homogeneity of the population, assuming that the more ethnically homogeneous the country, the more the citizens will be threatened by an influx of foreigners. According to Zolberg (1981:16), "Given an equal challenge, the degree of tolerance of cultural diversity may vary as a function of the character of the receiving society. A highly . . . ethnically undiversified nation with a dominant religion and which as a consequence of its insularity has experienced little immigra-

---

10. See, for example, Foot 1965 for an analysis of "racialism" in Britain as the source of immigration restrictions and Higham 1963 for a parallel analysis of "nativism" in the United States.

tion in the recent past, may have a lower threshold of tolerance than a more heterogenous one, whose identity may have come to be founded on political rather than ethnic criteria." To test this hypothesis, *ethnic homogeneity* is measured as *the proportion of the population that shares racial (phenotypical), religious, or linguistic characteristics*. The anticipated direction of the relationship is negative: nations that are more ethnically homogeneous are expected to have lower levels of immigrant flows than nations than are ethnically heterogeneous.

Alternatively, a distinction can be made on the basis of concepts of citizenship. Leitner (1995:262) states that "principles of citizenship, as laid down in nationality laws, are one expression of dominant national ideologies since they define what constitutes a nation and the relationship between state membership and nation membership." Where citizenship is based on a common history and tradition, language, religion, or racial characteristics, there should be a low tolerance for immigrants. On the other hand, where citizenship is defined by political participation, tolerance of migrants should be greater (also see Meissner 1992).[11]

This variable is operationalized in two ways. A basic distinction is often made between the settler states, which were created through immigrant streams and whose members are defined by voluntaristic participation in the polity, and the ethnic states of Europe, whose identity was forged via a common history, language, religion, and racial (phenotypical) similarity. "In contrast to the traditional immigration countries like the United States, Canada, Australia, or New Zealand, [in Europe] historically there was no idea of a 'melting pot' or the feeling of a normality of immigration. . . . Rather, national identities were conceived as rooted in everlasting traditions of the land and its people. In many countries they included biological connotations" (Thranhardt 1992:16). The former settler states are believed to be more open to immigration whereas the latter tend to see migrants as disrupting a cohesive society.[12] This distinction is operationalized as a dichotomous variable with *the settler states of Australia, New Zealand, Canada, and the United States taking on a value of 1, and all other states taking on a value of 0*. The relationship is expected to be positive. This distinction also coincides with the distinction between probationary immigrant versus settler immigrant. If the countries of permanent settlement are systematically dif-

11. Brubaker 1989:7 presents a similar argument to explain rules governing citizenship: "There is a basic difference between nations constituted by immigration and countries in which occasional immigration has been incidental to nation building." He is careful, however, not to extend his argument to an explanation of immigration flows because "questions of membership differ from questions of entry."

12. This hypothesized relationship is exactly the opposite of that posited by Bhagwati; he argues that, because foreigners are excluded from permanent membership, the society will allow larger numbers.

ferent from the nonsettler states, this relationship should be statistically significant.

Yet another way of operationalizing national identity is by the rules governing citizenship at birth. There are two basic principles of granting citizenship to children: jus sanguinis, in which the citizenship of the parents determines the child's status, and jus soli, in which citizenship is based on place of birth (SOPEMI 1995:157). Most countries employ some mix of both principles, but one rule or the other tends to dominate. The *citizenship* variable is operationalized as *an interval level variable, with a minimum of 0, categorizing countries that acknowledge only descent from a national, and a maximum of 1, designating countries that acknowledge all individuals born on their territory as citizens.* In between, at 0.5, are countries that acknowledge birth on the soil for second-generation immigrants, that is, a child born in the host country of a foreign parent also born in the host country is recognized as a citizen of the host country. Finally, there is a group of countries that have modified the principle of jus soli to exclude children born to undocumented aliens or short-term visitors to the country. They have been given a value of 0.8 on the scale of 0 to 1. The anticipated direction of the relationship is positive.

Finally, identity may be historically rooted in a nation's colonial past, where national identity encompasses the larger colonial and postcolonial communities. Analysts suggest that nations with a colonial history have ties and commitments that tend to define a special relationship to former colonies and require them to accept greater levels of immigration than would otherwise be anticipated (Foot 1965, Layton-Henry 1985, Hammar 1985, Paul 1997).[13] That is, "colonial experiences and ideologies shaped immigration decisions primarily, but not exclusively, by making these decisions more liberal than they would have been otherwise" (Freeman 1979:314).[14] This variable is operationalized as a dichotomous variable with the *colonial states of Britain, France, Belgium, and Japan taking on a value of 1, and all other states taking on a value of 0.* The relationship is expected to be positive.

Thus, there are various ways of understanding the significance of cultural variables in relating to an alien population, with some cultural traits encouraging greater openness to aliens whereas other cultural traits promote more ethnocentric views. These views are not necessarily racist in nature but form the basis of social boundaries created in support of the nation-state. As Zolberg (1983:18) argues, "The emergence of a scale of moral value, in rela-

---

13. Colonialism is employed by these authors as part of more complex explanations of immigration control and integration.
14. Freeman himself criticizes much of the theorizing on colonialism and its impact on immigration control.

tion to which particular groups are assessed negatively, is to be understood not merely as the expression of aggregate individual prejudice or xenophobia (that, of course, do come into play), but as the manifestation of an integrative mechanism common to all societies."[15]

None of these hypotheses delineate the methods through which these cultural attitudes are translated into policy. It is plausible to believe that politicians adopt policies either because they hold the same view as their constituents or because they respond in some fashion to public opinion. Some analysts have been more sensitive to the methods by which societal preferences are channeled through the political system, pointing to human and civil rights activists and organizations, churches, and immigrant communities and organizations as petitioners for open immigration policy (Goldin 1993, Keeley 1979). Most authors, however, do not specify the characteristics of the groups or political systems that would enhance or detract from their political influence.[16] The power and preferences of groups defending cultural values are usually viewed as static; variation in outcomes is then attributed to changes in preferences and power of economic actors. Therefore, the role of specific political actors pursuing cultural values cannot be evaluated. More attention has been paid to the preferences and power of economic actors, to which we now turn.

The primacy of economic interests

Because migrants participate in the host economy, another group of analysts seeks the determinants of immigration policy in the preferences of economic actors within the host society. Actors' preferences are attributed to the differential economic impact of immigrants on groups in the host society. One line of analysis emerges from the Marxian tradition (Castells 1975, Castles and Kosack 1973, Petras 1981). From this perspective, migrants represent a surplus pool of labor that helps to discipline the indigenous working classes

---

15. Also see Waever's (1993:23) discussion of "societal security." He acknowledges that his "definition makes it difficult to give any objective definition to when there is a threat to societal security" and recommends "studying the processes whereby a group comes to perceive its identity as threatened."

16. See Goldin 1993 and Wong 1995. Both researchers use the percentage of foreign-born in a political constituency as a measure of immigrant influence on U.S. immigration policy and both discover a positive correlation. This finding is difficult to interpret in light of the facts that naturalization rates are low, rates of voter registration among naturalized citizens are lower than in the native population, and rates of voting among naturalized registered voters are lower than in the native population. Moreover, both studies assume, rather than demonstrate empirically, that foreign-born residents want more immigration. In fact, the causal relationship may be reversed. That is, localized labor shortages lead employers to demand greater openness; their political success leads to a more open immigration policy, and the local labor markets succeed in attracting the newcomers, leading to a high proportion of foreign-born in the population.

and to overcome crises in the capitalist system. But the demand for migrant labor is not constant, especially in welfare states where capitalists have maintained control via the quid pro quo of state-supported benefits to the indigenous labor force. Capitalists need a labor force than can be easily mobilized and just as easily disbanded when conditions warrant. Because "capital accumulation does not proceed at a steady and even pace, . . . capital needs to have this [migrant] labor surplus to use, at its disposal, only to discard it when it is not required for production" (Petras 1981:48). In particular, capitalist demands for immigrant labor follow "labor market fluctuations and specialized needs within the [labor] importing region" (Petras 1981:54).

Another line of analysis focuses on the growing inflexibility of labor markets in advanced industrial countries as a result of union efforts to remove the native workforce from the vagaries of the market. Employers respond by hiring a second tier of workers, unprotected by work rules and union guarantees, thereby creating a segmented or dual labor market (Piore 1979). Immigrants are sought for this secondary labor market to provide the flexibility lost as a result of labor market regulation and to fill the jobs abandoned by the native workforce.

Both Marxian and non-Marxian versions that emphasize economic interests of employers/capitalists suggest that demand for migrant labor is not constant but varies with the state of the economy. In periods of prosperity and economic growth, demand for immigrant labor will be high; in periods of recession, demand will be low. One way of operationalizing the *economic interests of employers* in immigrant labor is the *unemployment rate*. The relationship is anticipated to be negative; as unemployment increases, the demand for immigrant labor decreases; as unemployment declines, the demand for immigrant labor rises.

Another measure of the tightness of labor markets or the organizational strength of labor is the relative wage rate. Where tight labor markets or labor organization have forced employers to bid up the price of labor, the demand for immigrant labor should be stronger. Because labor markets are not fully integrated internationally, firms face different national relative prices of labor. The *relative price of labor* is operationalized as the *standardized hourly real wage rate* and is anticipated to be positive: as the wage rate increases, the demand for immigrant labor increases.

Labor market conditions, however, may not be the only reason why the demand for immigrant labor varies. As Zolberg (1983:37) notes, "Because there is no such thing as an absolute labor shortage, importation is always a convenience rather than a necessity. It will be dispensed with should economic or sociopolitical costs go up, and capital often has the alternative of shifting to more capital intensive production or of moving its operations to low-wage sites abroad." Bhagwati (1984:696) also explains "the differential resort to importation of foreign labor" by the "differential demand factors across . . . industries."[17]

We can think of employers as strategic actors who attempt to maximize profits through different production strategies. Strategies of importing cheap foreign labor are comparable to strategies of exporting capital to cheap foreign labor. But the availability of these strategies is not evenly distributed across firms and across nations (Money 1994b). Some firms, especially manufacturing firms with standardized technology, can select either strategy. Natural resource–based firms, agricultural producers, and service firms (in-person delivery of services) are unable to reduce labor costs through capital exports. Because employers in the primary and tertiary sectors of the economy lack a strategy of capital mobility, they prefer higher levels of immigrants than the "footloose" manufacturing firms that can export capital. The degree of capital mobility modifies the preferences for immigrant labor. *Capital mobility* is operationalized as *the proportion of the gross domestic product in manufacturing*, to capture the proportion of the economy that has the option of exporting capital to inexpensive labor. The relationship is hypothesized to be negative: as capital mobility increases, the demand for immigrant labor decreases.

These three hypotheses suggest that variations in immigration flow result from variations in employers' demands; politicians respond solely to employers' demands because, in Marxian terms, they have privileged access to the capitalist state or, in public choice terms, because employers face fewer collective action problems than do other societal interests (Freeman 1995). An alternative interpretation suggests that employers' interests are invariant. Employers may have a continuous interest in a reserve pool of labor or may become dependent on the immigrant workforce. For example, Dietrich Thranhardt (1992:36) describes a "segmented labor market that even in times of new unemployment would not make foreign workers redundant."[18] If employers' interests are constant, variation in policy outcomes can be attributed to other economic actors who enter the political arena to oppose employers' demands (Leitner 1995, Shughart et al. 1986). In this case, the policy outcome depends not on the varying demands of employers but on the power relationship among the various political actors. According to Leitner (1995:262), "Which interests and concerns come to determine the

17. Bhagwati 1984 looks at the effects of changes in effective protection, the rate of growth of demand, and the capital intensity of industries as factors that may modify the demand for immigrant labor.
18. Also see Cornelius, Martin, and Hollifield 1994:4. They also describe a " 'hardening' of employer demand for foreign labor in key sectors of these countries' economies." Cornelius 1998 describes the effects of immigrant labor as leading to both "distortion and dependence."

nature of admission policies in part is dependent on the power relations between the different interest groups and their capacity to exercise political power."

Who is economically harmed by immigration? Leitner (1995:262) suggests that "labor unions might be opposed on the grounds that this will harm workers' wages and working conditions." Shughart et al. (1986:80) also describe "the desire of organized interest groups to influence domestic wages."[19] One way of testing the impact of indigenous labor on immigrant flows is to assume that because the native workforce is harmed economically by immigrant labor, it prefers less immigration, and that its political power varies in part as a function of the rate of unionization. The *unionization rate* is operationalized as the *proportion of the nonagricultural labor force that is unionized*. If these two assumptions are correct, then the relationship between unionization and per capita immigration is expected to be negative: as the rate of unionization rises, the political power of labor to oppose immigration expands, and the level of immigrant labor declines.

Alternatively, labor is viewed as benefiting from immigration. If the dual labor market hypothesis is correct, immigrant labor tends to complement rather than compete with the indigenous workforce and enhances rather than detracts from the return to native workers. Various empirical analyses indicate that immigration has a nominal effect on indigenous wage rates (Borjas 1994, Simon 1989).[20] Gary Freeman (1995) reports that "the most significant organized counterpoint to [migration] has traditionally been labor unions but they have generally come to support immigration, resigning themselves to defensive rather than restrictive measures." And Leah Haus (1995b) points out that unions may favor immigration as a method of maximizing their interests of increased union membership. If these hypotheses are correct, and unions prefer more rather than less immigration, then the relationship between unionization (as a measure of union power) and immigration should be positive.

In summary, immigrants are economic actors who may have distributional effects on other economic actors in the host country. In general, employers are viewed as uniformly benefiting from immigrant labor, although their demand for immigrant labor may vary with labor market conditions and capital mobility. The theoretical and empirical work on the economic impact of immigration on the native workforce is mixed. Therefore, we test both hypotheses, that labor either supports or opposes immigration and its influ-

---

19. Shughart et al. 1986 also include the business cycle and unemployment rate in their analysis of employers' and workers' preferences for immigration and impact on domestic wages.
20. But Bhagwati 1984 points out that as unemployment increases, immigration is constricted, thereby minimizing its impact on the indigenous wage rate and providing an explanation of the empirical findings.

ence on policy is measured by the rate of unionization. But if indigenous labor benefits from immigration, there may be no political actors who oppose immigration on economic grounds. This view is consonant with Charles Kindleberger's (1964) thesis that Europe's post–World War II economic miracle was largely due to the expanding supply of labor, part of which came from migrant labor.[21] If all members of society benefit economically from immigration, then opposition to the economic benefits associated with immigration must come from the cultural costs generated by immigration.

The tension between cultural values and economic interests

Many analysts point to a fundamental tension between the economic benefits of immigration that accrue to the society as a whole and to most or all members of that society, and the cultural costs that immigration entails by challenging the national and cultural identity of the citizens. Zolberg (1981) was one of the first authors to argue that migrants are both societal and economic actors who generate both cultural and economic responses; the difficulty of determining the position of various political actors stems from this tension. Individuals may be pulled in one direction by economic interests and the other by cultural interests. Zolberg (1981:15) argues that "the conflicting interests of industrial societies—to maximize the labor supply and to protect cultural integrity—can be thought of as a dilemma." His opinion is echoed by Leitner (1995:261), who argues that "the politics of admission and exclusion practiced by the potential receiving countries can be thought of as a struggle with the conflict between economic necessity and nationalism." Yet another researcher (Kubat 1979:xxx) points out that "in a democracy, the politics of migration policies are either a response to pressure for more workers, or a response to pressure to preserve the national identity by limiting in-migration." A survey of several new books on European migration points out that "a basic issue that runs through the subject matter of all the books reviewed is the contradiction between the economic (and perhaps demographic) necessity for international migration on the one hand and the widespread political and social opposition to immigration on the other" (King 1996:176). Although various authors point to this tension, many fail to specify the circumstances under which economic interests are critical and when the state responds to the need to maintain cultural integrity. Here I discuss the three authors who do attempt to specify when cultural concerns will outweigh economic interests and vice versa.

Susan Olzak (1992) outlines a theory of ethnic group competition that links economic conditions to the salience of group identity and collective

---

21. Also see Simon 1989, Bhagwati 1984, and Hamilton and Whalley 1984.

action that may be useful in explaining the rise and fall of anti-immigrant sentiment.[22] She argues that "changes in the levels of ethnic and racial competition for valued resources—such as jobs, housing and marital partners—ignite ethnic collective action." If competition for economic, social, and cultural resources is large, society prefers lower levels of immigration, whereas cooperative or complementary relationships generate neutral or positive attitudes. Competition, however, is not constant but is intensified by a variety of factors. Economic recession decreases the availability of resources and magnifies competition; a rapid increase in the number of immigrants can also increase the competition between the native and immigrant populations. The structural features that generate greater *competition* are operationalized as *unemployment* and *the proportional change in the annual immigration intake*. Both relationships are expected to be negative. As unemployment and immigration rates increase, ethnic competition increases, and the state responds by decreasing the level of immigration.

Olzak's pessimism about societal responses to immigrants under conditions of competition can be contrasted to Hollifield's (1992) more optimistic perspective. Hollifield is one of a growing group of authors who emphasize the liberal nature of the state in advanced industrial societies and the concomitant extension of human rights to residents of these states, whether citizen or alien (Weil 1991, Soysal 1994, Cornelius, Martin, and Hollifield 1995). When market tendencies come into conflict with these human rights, the rights triumph. Hollifield (1992:216) argues that market forces accounted for the rise in immigration in the 1960s and early 1970s. When economic conditions turned sour following the 1973 oil shock, the "protection given to aliens in rights-based regimes" accounted for the persistence of immigration "in the face of economic crises, restrictionist policies, and nationalist (anti-immigrant) political movements." Hollifield points to a single turning point in the post–World War II period, the 1973 oil crisis and the recession that followed. I have attempted to test this hypothesis by evaluating whether the determinants of immigration flows differed in the early, precrisis period and the post-1973 oil crisis period, when, according to Hollifield, the rights-based regime kicked in.

A small but growing cohort of political economists is attempting to incorporate the political process through which societal preferences are channeled (Freeman 1995, Soysal 1994, Ireland 1994). Freeman (1995) argues that immigration creates both concentrated benefits and diffuse costs.[23] The recipients

---

22. Olzak is attempting to explain not immigration policy but ethnic collective action; I extend her argument one step further: when ethnic collective action arises, governments interpret it as anti-immigrant sentiment and respond by curtailing the level of immigration.

23. He draws on James Q. Wilson's 1980 typology of policies based on whether the benefits and costs are concentrated or diffuse, where C = concentrated and D = diffuse; and C = costs and B = benefits. Four policy types follow from this typology: CB/DC = client politics; CB/CC = interest-group

of concentrated benefits include employers, ethnic advocacy groups, and civil and human rights organizations. Because benefits are concentrated, these groups are more easily able to overcome the costs of collective action and organize to press government for openness to immigration. Diffuse costs are spread over the public as a whole, giving rise to anti-immigrant sentiment in popular opinion. But because the costs are diffuse, it is difficult for the public to organize and petition their representatives. Hence immigration policy is based on a clientelistic relationship wherein politicians respond to organized interests and ignore unorganized interests; immigration policy therefore has a liberal bias.

Ultimately, however, the diffuse costs turn to concentrated costs, causing opponents of immigration to organize. Concentrated costs arise as a function of the "immigration cycle, . . . a natural cycle based on the dynamics of migration processes themselves—processes that begin with an initial influx, followed by settlement and secondary migration through family reunion and chain migration processes" (Freeman 1995:886). As the cycle of immigration proceeds, opposition to immigration grows, causing immigration politics to shift from client relations (concentrated benefits and diffuse costs) to interest group politics (concentrated benefits and concentrated costs). Anti-immigrant groups are then sufficiently powerful to convince politicians to shut the national door. Unfortunately, we do not have a very good understanding of the immigration cycle, when it begins in each country, the costs it generates, and how it proceeds. Until these dynamics are more clearly worked out, this thesis cannot be tested.[24]

In summary, there are three categories of hypotheses, those that privilege cultural characteristics, those that focus on economic interests, and those that posit a cycle between the realization of cultural values and economic benefits. Thus the full equation of potential determinants of levels of migration combines these various hypotheses:

$$\text{PCIMM} = \beta_0 - \beta_1(\text{ETHNICITY}) + \beta_2(\text{SETTLER}) + \beta_3(\text{CITIZEN})$$
$$+ \beta_4(\text{COLONIAL}) - \beta_5(\text{UNEMPLOYMENT}) - \beta_6(\text{KMOBILITY})$$
$$+ \beta_7(\text{WAGES}) \pm \beta_8(\text{UNION}) + \beta_9(\text{IMMINCREASE}) + \varepsilon \quad (3.1)$$

where PCIMM is the per capita annual gross level of resident aliens permitted to enter the country; β_0 is the intercept; β_1 is the coefficient indicating the

---

politics; *DB/DC* = majoritarian politics; and *DB/CC* = entrepreneurial politics. Each gives rise to a particular political process.

24. The other two analysts who focus on political institutions, Soysal 1994 and Ireland 1994, deal with immigrant integration policy rather than immigration control policy. But "because these two policy arenas are usually administered by different agencies and organizations" (Hammar 1985), the institutional analyses these authors make are not readily transferrable to immigration control policies.

Table 2.1. Operationalization of hypotheses on immigration control

Variable	Indicator	Hypothesized relationship
Cultural traits of nations		
Ethnicity	Percent of the population that shares racial (phenotypical), religious, or linguistic characteristics	–
Settler states	Australia, New Zealand, Canada, United States	+
Citizenship	Rules governing citizenship of children born in host country of alien parentage; jus sanguinis = 0; jus soli = 1; intermediate values	+
Colonial states	Britain, France, Belgium, Japan	+
Economic (labor market) conditions		
Labor supply	Unemployment rate	–
Cost of labor	Standardized hourly real wage rate	+
Capital exports	Percent of gross domestic product in manufacturing	–
Worker power	Union density	±
Competition between indigenous and immigrant populations		
Labor market competition	Unemployment rate	–
Social competition	Annual rate of increase in immigration	–

influence of national ethnic homogeneity on the level of gross immigration; β_2, the influence of settler state status; β_3, the influence of national concepts of citizenship; β_4, the influence of colonial history; β_5, the intensity of employer demand for immigrant labor or competition between the indigenous and immigrant working classes; β_6, the intensity of employer demand associated with nonmobile firms; β_7, the intensity of employer demand associated with high indigenous labor costs; β_8, the power of the working classes; β_9, competition between the indigenous and immigrant working classes over socially provided goods; and the plus and minus signs indicate the nature of the relationship.

Hollifield's argument that the immigration regime in all advanced industrial countries shifted from a market system to a liberal, rights-based system is tested by dividing the data set into two subsets and applying the full equation to each subset.

Table 2.1 provides a summary of the hypotheses, the methods used to oper-

Table 2.2. Summary statistics of regression variables

Variable	Mean	Standard deviation	Minimum	Maximum
Immigration (natural logarithm)	−0.85	0.95	−3.80	0.90
Ethnicity	72.67	23.12	25.00	99.00
Settler states	0.33	0.47	0.00	1.00
Citizenship	0.47	0.43	0.00	1.00
Colonial states	0.33	0.47	0.00	1.00
Unemployment	4.13	3.17	0.10	13.20
Capital mobility	24.58	6.08	4.00	41.40
Wages	5.64	3.29	0.36	17.55
Unionization	42.35	16.99	10.20	84.60
Immigration increase	0.07	0.75	−0.90	12.91

ationalize the hypotheses, and the hypothesized direction of the relationships. The immigration data were gathered from the national statistical yearbooks for the countries in question and the economic data were drawn from Organisation of Economic Cooperation and Development (OECD) publications, in an effort to assure the comparability of data across countries.[25] All data sources are listed in the appendix to this chapter.

Results of the Analysis

The summary statistics for the dependent and independent variables are presented in Table 2.2. Because the dependent variable was positively skewed, it was transformed into the natural logarithm of the original variable. In general, this specification reduced the problems of nonconstant variance across all models and improved the fit, as indicated by higher adjusted R^2s when compared with the untransformed dependent variable.

The hypotheses outlined above were tested using a time-series, cross-section (TSCS) data set incorporating twelve advanced industrial countries, with an average of twenty-eight annual observations per country beginning in 1962 and ending in 1989.[26] This type of data set may exhibit a series of

25. The OECD also produces annual reports on immigration data in a publication called SOPEMI (Système d'Observation Permanente pour les Migrations Internationales), but the series does not begin until 1973 and only gradually incorporates data from OECD members. Moreover, although there have been efforts to standardize the definitions of immigrants, and therefore the data, they remain noncomparable. Therefore, I relied on the annual statistical abstracts, and the noncomparability of the data is indicated in the appendix to this chapter.

26. They are, in alphabetical order, Australia, Belgium, Canada, Denmark, France, (West) Germany, Japan, New Zealand, Norway, Sweden, the United Kingdom, and the United States. Two countries for which data were presented in Chapter 1 are excluded from the analysis because so few years were available: the Netherlands and Finland.

characteristics that create biased or inefficient estimators using ordinary least squares (OLS) multiple regression techniques (Beck and Katz 1995, Stimson 1985). In particular, the residuals or error terms produced by OLS regression may be temporally or spatially correlated or may exhibit heteroscedasticity, that is, nonconstant variance of the residuals (Beck and Katz 1995:634).[27] Standardizing the dependent variable as annual per capita immigrant intakes decreases the likelihood of panel heteroscedasticity that might otherwise be introduced through differences in the scale of immigration based on country size. To correct for any possible remaining heteroscedasticity, country dummy variables were entered into the equation (Stimson 1985). In addition to reducing the possibility of nonconstant variance of the error terms, the country variables capture country-specific variances that are not explained by the independent variables.

The original OLS with country dummy variables estimation indicated first-order autocorrelation of the error terms. I therefore employed the Cochrane-Orcutt generalized least squares (GLS) estimation to correct for first-order autocorrelation. Three equations were estimated. Model 1 excludes the colonial variable and the country dummy variables; model 2 excludes the settler variable and the country dummy variables. Separate models were estimated because when both variables are entered into the equation simultaneously, they create a residual group of countries for which there is no theoretical basis. The hypotheses indicate that there should be significant differences between settler and nonsettler states and colonial and noncolonial states, not among settler states, colonial states, and all other states. Model 3 includes the country dummy variables and excludes the cultural variables.

The results of the statistical analysis are presented in Table 2.3. Statistically, the introduction of the cultural variables attempts to capture whether these groups of countries intercept the y axis at different points, that is, whether countries with a particular set of characteristics have different levels of immigration on average, even if the temporal changes can be attributed to other factors. Three of the four variables that attempt to capture nations' particular cultural characteristics are not statistically significant. Ethnic heterogeneity, history of immigration in settler states, and jus soli rules governing citizenship do not give rise to higher levels of immigration, nor does their absence indicate lower immigrant flows. The colonial variable is statistically significant but has the wrong sign. That is, rather than opening their doors more widely, presumably to accommodate previously imperial subjects, post-colonial countries tended to close their doors more tightly.

It is particularly interesting that immigrant intakes in settler states are not

---

27. Heteroscedasticity in TSCS data sets can involve the entire data set or individual (country) units, where the variance in error processes differs from unit to unit—panel heteroscedasticity.

Table 2.3. Evaluation of determinants of immigration control in selected OECD countries, 1962–1989 (dependent variable: natural logarithm of per capita immigration)

Variable	Model 1		Model 2		Model 3	
	Coefficient	Standard error	Coefficient	Standard error	Coefficient	Standard error
Ethnicity	−0.001	0.037	−0.008	0.023		
Settler states	1.500	1.565				
Citizenship	−0.900	2.742	0.164	1.440		
Colonial states			−1.458[a]	0.604		
Unemployment	−0.081[b]	0.017	−0.078[b]	0.017	−0.077[b]	0.015
Capital mobility	0.011	0.016	0.013	0.016	−0.011	0.014
Wages	−0.209	0.023	−0.023	0.023	−0.004	0.019
Unionization	0.003	0.011	0.004	0.010	−0.005	0.009
Immigrant increase	0.117[b]	0.012	0.117[b]	0.012	0.115[b]	0.013
Country dummies						
Australia					0.237	0.262
Belgium					0.046	0.311
Denmark					0.215	0.435
France					−1.310[b]	0.281
Germany					0.670[a]	0.319
Japan					−2.950[b]	0.282
New Zealand					0.923[b]	0.351
Norway					−0.394	0.323
Sweden					−0.164	0.482
U.K.					−0.382	0.308
U.S.					−0.958[b]	0.236
Constant	0.035	3.914	0.631	2.606	0.367	0.497
Adjusted R^2	0.29		0.29		0.61	
Rho	0.97		0.95		0.71	
N	282		282		282	

[a] Statistical significance at 0.05 level.
[b] Statistical significance at 0.01 level.

statistically different from those in nonsettler states. This finding suggests that states with probationary immigrants and states with settler immigrants do not have distinctive levels of immigration and partially overcomes the concern elicited by the inability to separate the two immigrant systems.

The various cultural concepts are theoretically similar, especially the "settler" and "citizen" concepts. Statistically, these measures are highly collinear. Therefore, although Table 2.3 presents the cultural variables in the same equation, I also tested to determine whether the individual variables perform better than when entered into the equation simultaneously. Even when entered into the equation individually, however, the variables were never statistically significant.

Two of the three variables reflecting the economic interests or the political power of economic actors in the domestic society—wage rates and unionization rates—are not statistically significant and do not explain levels of immigration. Capital mobility is marginally significant in models 1 and 2 but exhibits the wrong sign: immigration increases with increases in capital mobility rather than the reverse. This variable becomes statistically insignificant in model 3. The only economic variable that is systematically associated with immigration flows is unemployment. It reflects the hypothesized direction: as unemployment increases, immigration decreases.

The competition model is also unsupported by the data. The variables reflecting higher levels of competition between the native and immigrant populations are statistically significant, and the unemployment variable has the correct sign; but increased rates of immigration tend to produce higher rather than lower levels of immigration. One possible interpretation of this result is that initial flows give rise to subsequent family reunification that the state does not limit, an interpretation consistent with the "liberal" model of immigration control.[28] When the data set is divided into two subsets, however, the variable is statistically significant in both subsets; if this result does reflect liberalism, liberal policies appear to have been constant throughout the postwar period.

The liberal model suggests a common pattern among advanced industrial countries, with liberal market forces governing the pre-1973 period of economic growth and liberal human rights governing the post-1973 period of economic stagnation. Because the cultural variables are not expected to change across time, only model 3 was estimated. Both unemployment and immigration growth remain statistically significant, regardless of the time frame, although country dummies change in statistical significance. These findings are not consistent with the expectation of change across the pre- and postcrisis periods.

The intercept in model 3 represents Canada, the country with immigration levels closest to the sample mean. Most of the country dummy variables are not statistically different from this mean. This result suggests that once unemployment rates are taken into consideration, most countries in the data set do not have statistically different immigration levels. Outliers on the low end are France, the United States, and Japan, while New Zealand and (West) Germany stand out on the high end.

To test the robustness of the results, I specified the basic model in a variety of ways. In one model, a lagged dependent variable was entered as a regressor, a method that tends to reduce the serial correlation of the residuals. OLS

---

28. According to King 1993a, family reunification follows fairly rapidly after the initial migration, usually within ten years.

was used to estimate this model. In the second model, the dependent variable was redefined as the absolute change in per capita immigration flows, that is, per capita immigration at year t minus per capita immigration at year $t - 1$. The use of first differences also tends to reduce the problems of serial correlation, and OLS can be employed. In a third model, to test whether the absolute level of immigrants is critical to understanding the political process, the dependent variable was redefined as the absolute flows of immigrants with population entered as a regressor to account for variation in country size; this model was estimated using GLS and country dummy variables. Finally, to evaluate whether policy responds more slowly to economic conditions, the three original models were reestimated with lagged economic variables (per capita immigration at year t as a function of economic variables at year $t - 1$). In all four respecifications, the results were similar to those presented here. Unemployment and rates of immigration increase are the only variables that consistently account for some of the variation in immigration control, although in some model specifications, even unemployment becomes statistically insignificant.

Conclusions

Various specifications of the model produced similar results: the only consistently robust determinants of immigration levels were unemployment and rate of change in immigration flows. Therefore, many hypotheses, both cultural and economic, were not supported by the evidence. Unfortunately, unemployment is a variable that underpins several hypotheses and does not permit us to distinguish among them. Clearly, the rise in unemployment is connected to decreased levels of immigration. What is unclear is the location of societal preferences and the process by which the pressures generated by rising unemployment are filtered through the political system to arrive at decreased immigration intakes. It could be attributed to decreased employer support, increased employee opposition, competition between the indigenous and alien population, or a shift between the primacy of economic interests and cultural values. The interpretation of the proportional change in immigration is problematic as well, given the unanticipated positive direction of the relationship.

These "nonresults" are somewhat puzzling. Certainly the logic underlying the various hypotheses is plausible. Correlation between the variables may be absent because the measures employed here imperfectly capture the concepts and theories developed in the literature, a problem that is more or less severe in all quantitative analyses in the social sciences. Nonetheless, the systematic examination of some of the most straightforward distinctions employed in the literature, such as the settler–ethnic state duality, reveals that they do not shed much light on the varying levels of openness to immigration.[29]

This lack suggests an alternative interpretation of the statistical results, that the use of national-level indicators overlooks one central feature of the immigration process: *immigrants are geographically concentrated in the host country*. That is, the citizens of Wyoming, for example, are unlikely to interact with immigrants because there are very few immigrants in Wyoming, whereas citizens of California are likely to interact with immigrants because 22 percent of California residents are foreign born. The geographic concentration of immigrants makes it much more likely that the indigenous population of California will encounter these immigrants—for better or for worse—than the indigenous population of Wyoming. The same intranational comparison could be drawn in Britain between York and London, for example, or in France, between Toulouse and Paris.

Because immigrants are geographically concentrated, it is not surprising that aggregate national statistics fail to uncover statistically significant relationships among the variables. To detect the economic and cultural impact of immigrants, we need to focus on the spatial distribution of the immigrant population; it is in the local communities where they are concentrated that they come into contact with the indigenous population. Le Pen wants France for the French, but it would be more empirically accurate to rally around the slogan "Paris, Lyon, and Marseille for the French."

The analysis may thus prove more fruitful if it is disaggregated and shifted to the local level. Moreover, this shift forces the analyst to confront the issue of how societal preferences are translated into political outputs. The explicit incorporation of political institutions that funnel societal demands from the local to the national level may also enhance the analysis.

Appendix: Description of Variables and Data Sources

The data set comprises twelve OECD countries—Canada, the United States, Japan, Australia, New Zealand, Belgium, Denmark, France, Germany, Norway, Sweden, and the United Kingdom—and covers the years 1962 through 1989.

---

29. Even the most skeptical reader of the quantitative analysis can rest assured, however, that the theoretical argument and evidence that follow do not depend on these results.

PCIMM, the indicator for immigration control, is measured as total immigration as a proportion of total population (total immigration/total population). Data for both immigration and population totals are taken from individual national statistical yearbooks.

Australian Bureau of Statistics. *Yearbook Australia.* Canberra, various years.

Belgium, Institut National de Statistique. *Annuaire statistique de la Belgique.* Brussels, various years.

Canada, Statistics Canada. *Canada Yearbook: A Review of Economic, Social and Political Developments in Canada.* Ottawa, various years.

Denmark, Danmarks Statistik. *Statistisk Arbog* [Statistical yearbook]. Copenhagen, various years.

Finland, Central Statistical Office of Finland. *Statistical Yearbook of Finland.* Helsinki, various years.

France, Institut National de la Statistique et des Études Économiques. *Annuaire statistique de la France.* Paris, various years.

Germany, Statistische Bundesamt. *Statistisches Jahrbuch für die Bundesrepublik Deutschland.* Wiesbaden, various years.

Japan, Statistics Bureau, Management and Coordination Agency. *Japan Statistical Yearbook.* Tokyo, various years.

Netherlands, Centraal Bureau voor de Statistiek. *Statistical Yearbook of the Netherlands.* Voorburg, various years.

New Zealand, Department of Statistics. *New Zealand Official Yearbook.* Wellington, various years.

Norway, Central Bureau of Statistics. *Statistisk arbok* [Statistical yearbook]. Oslo, various years.

Sweden, Statistics Sweden. *Statistisk Arslook for Sverige* [Statistical abstract of Sweden]. Stockholm, various years.

United Kingdom, Central Satistical Office. *Annual Abstract of Statistics.* London: HMSO, various years.

United States, Department of Later, Bureau of the Census. *Statistical Abstract of the United States.* Washington, D.C.: GPO, various years.

Ethnicity, an index of ethnic homogeneity, is taken from George Thomas Kurian, *The New Book of World Rankings*, 3d ed. (New York: Facts on File, 1991).

Citizenship is a categorical variable distinguishing how citizenship is granted to a child born in the host state (jus soli or jus sanguinis). Citizen equals 1.0 if nationality/citizenship is granted if born on territory (Canada, New Zealand, United States).

Citizen equals 0.8 if nationality/citizenship is granted if at least one parent is at least a permanent resident (Australia, United Kingdom).

Citizen equals 0.5 if nationality/citizenship is granted if at least one alien parent was also born in the country (Belgium, France).

Citizen equals 0.0 if nationality/citizenship is granted if at least one parent is a national citizen (Denmark, Germany, Japan, Norway, Sweden).

Settler is a dichotomous variable, equal to 1.0 if the country is a settler state (Australia, Canada, New Zealand, United States).

Colonial is a dichotomous variable, equal to 1.0 if the country was a colonial state (Belgium, France, Japan, United Kingdom).

Unionization is measured as the union density rate and is taken from two works by Jelle Visser: *European Trade Unions in Figures* (Deventer: Kluwer Law and Taxation Publishers, 1989) and "In Search of Inclusive Unionism," special issue of *Bulletin of Comparative Labour Relations*, no. 18, 1990.

Capital mobility is the percent of GDP in manufacturing. For the years 1962–67 data are from Organisation for Economic Cooperation and Development, *National Accounts of OECD Countries, 1950–1978* (Paris, 1980). For the years 1967–90, data are from the Organisation for Economic Cooperation and Development, *Historical Statistics, 1960–1981* (Paris, 1983) and *Historical Statistics, 1960–1990* (Paris, 1992). For 1991, data are from Organisation for Economic Cooperation and Development, *Quarterly National Accounts* (Paris, 1992) and *National Accounts of OECD Countries, 1980–1992* (Paris, 1994). For Denmark, 1962–65, and for Norway, 1991, data are from the respective national statistical yearbooks.

Wages is an adjusted measure of real wages and is calculated as wage/(price level of consumption/100), where price level of consumption is the purchasing power parity over consumption divided by the exchange rate. Wages are measured as current national currency hourly earnings and are taken from International Labour Office, *Yearbook of Labour Statistics* (Geneva, various years), for all years. Price level of consumption (PC) is taken from table 2 (base country is the United States; base year is 1980) of Robert Summers and Alan Heston, "A New Set of International Comparisons of Real Product and Price Levels Estimates for 130 Countries, 1950–1985," in *Review of Income and Wealth*, ser. 34, no. 1 (March 1988).

Note: In the United Kingdom, 1962–82, and Norway, 1962–72, earnings are for men only; in Australia, 1962–72, earnings are also for men only, and in 1962–64 earnings are by the week, so that hourly earnings were obtained by dividing by the average number of hours worked in a week; in Belgium, 1962 and 1963 earnings are reported by the day, so hourly earnings were obtained by dividing by the average number of hours worked in a day; in Japan, earnings are reported by the month, so that hourly earnings were obtained by dividing by the average number of hours worked in a month. Data on earnings in France, 1962–72, are not available; minimum rates are reported and used instead, although this practice creates a discontinuity, as calculated pre-1973 real wages are substantially lower.

Unemployment is measured as persons unemployed as a percentage of total labor force. Data for all years are taken from Organisation for Economic Cooperation and Development, *Labor Force Statistics, 1965–1985* (Paris, 1987) and *Labor Force Statistics, 1972–1992* (Paris, 1994).

Immigration increase is measured as (PCIMM – Lagged PCIMM) / Lagged PCIMM. For sources see PCIMM.

3 The Political Geography of
Immigration Control

Aggregate national data do not reveal comprehensible relationships between factors that account for societal preferences and immigration control outcomes in advanced industrial countries. There are at least two plausible explanations for these nonresults. First, aggregate national data may not reveal the real conditions under which immigrants and the indigenous community interact. Migrants are spatially concentrated within nations; thus some residents have much more contact with the immigrant community than others. As a result, national indicators of societal preferences may be insufficiently sensitive to capture local societal preferences.

Second, the explanations evaluated in Chapter 2 fail to incorporate any institutional elements that may channel societal preferences through the political system. We cannot assume that politicians weigh all societal preferences equally. One institutional element involves the organization of societal interests. For example, small groups may find it easier to organize politically than large groups (Olson 1965). The second involves the structure of national political institutions. Electoral systems of proportional representation, for example, provide easier access to small political parties than do single-member constituencies. Thus specifying the preferences of societal actors may be necessary but insufficient to explain political outcomes.

In this chapter, I sketch a new model, building on the insights of analysts described in Chapter 2, while incorporating the missing elements: the spatial concentration of migrants in local communities and the translation of local preferences into national policy through national political institutions.

47

The Geographic Concentration of Immigrants

The geographic specificity of migratory patterns, on both the sending and receiving ends, is well known to demographers and sociologists. "Migrants arriving in a particular country do not spread out randomly throughout all possible destinations" (White 1993a:52). Although these patterns are visible in all of the advanced industrial countries, I focus here on evidence from the United States as a basis of comparison with Australia, France, and Britain, the three nations whose immigration control policies will be examined in greater detail.

In 1990, according to the census of that year, 73 percent of the foreign-born population of the United States were concentrated in six states. As Table 3.1 illustrates, California, New York, Florida, Texas, New Jersey, and Illinois attracted the vast majority of the immigrants, and 33 percent of the foreign-born population resided in California alone (Martin and Midgley 1994). A comparison of these states' foreign-born populations with the national average provides another measure of geographic concentration. As a whole, 8 percent of the U.S. population was foreign born, in contrast to California's 22 percent and New York's 16 percent. And the foreign-born were so overrepresented in these few states that other states fell well below the national average.

This pattern holds in Australia as well. There 22.3 percent of the population were foreign born in 1991; this population was concentrated in New South Wales and Victoria, particularly in the cities and suburbs of Sydney and Melbourne (Kopras 1993). Of the 147 parliamentary constituencies of

Table 3.1. Geographic concentration of immigrants in United States, 1990

State	Foreign-born population (thousands)	Percent of foreign-born in state	Foreign-born as percent of population
Total U.S.	19,767	100%	8%
California	6,459	33	22
New York	2,852	14	16
Florida	1,663	8	13
Texas	1,524	8	9
New Jersey	967	5	13
Illinois	952	5	8
Massachusetts	574	3	10
Pennsylvania	369	2	3
Michigan	355	2	4
All other states	4,052	20	3

Source: Martin and Midgley 1994:5.

approximately equal population, the smallest percentage of foreign born was 4.8 percent and the largest was ten times larger at 49 percent. Thirty of the 147 constituencies had foreign-born populations of at least 30 percent; all but seven of these were located in the Melbourne and Sydney metropolitan areas. The "new" immigrant population was similarly concentrated. Immigrant arrivals in the five years preceding the census for the country as a whole averaged 3.7 percent of the national population, whereas twelve constituencies experienced inflows exceeding 10 percent of their population. Of these twelve, eight were among the top twelve constituencies containing foreign born (ranging from 37.8 to 49.0 percent), demonstrating that areas with the highest percentage of foreign born continue to attract new immigrant populations. Table 3.2 illustrates the contrast between the twelve constituencies with the highest foreign-born population and the national average.

A similar concentration of immigrants is found in European states. In Britain, for example, in 1987, 58 percent of the Afro-Caribbeans lived in Greater London as did 80 percent of the black African immigrants (Cross 1993:124). Immigrants from the Indian subcontinent were less concentrated but nonetheless were located primarily in the conurbations of London, the Midlands (Birmingham), and the Northwest (Manchester). In France, in 1987, 40 percent of the foreign population was found in the Parisian basin, with the remainder concentrated in the industrial regions surrounding Lyon, Marseille, and Strasbourg (King 1993a). Within these regions, immigrants were further concentrated in urban areas. Table 3.3 provides data on the

Table 3.2. Foreign born as percent of population in selected Australian electoral divisions, 1991

Electoral division	Foreign born	"New" foreign born[a]
National average	22.3%	3.7%
Wentworth (N.S.W.)	37.8	11.1
Blaxland (N.S.W.)	39.1	9.6
Kingsford-Smith (N.S.W.)	39.3	11.6
Gellibrand (Vic.)	39.4	9.5
Reid (N.S.W.)	39.5	12.4
Maribyrnong (Vic.)	39.7	5.7
Holt (Vic.)	40.4	10.9
Hotham (Vic.)	42.5	11.9
Prospect (N.S.W.)	42.4	9.1
Watson (N.S.W.)	43.6	13.1
Grayndler (N.S.W.)	46.1	15.2
Fowler (N.S.W.)	49.0	15.4

[a] Residence of less than five years.
Source: Adapted from Kopras 1993.

Table 3.3. Foreign born as percent of population in selected British and French cities, 1980s

City	Year	Percent
France	1990	6.3%
Lyon	1982	12.2
Marseille	1982	10.4
Greater Paris	1982	13.9
Strasbourg	1982	10.9
United Kingdom	1986–87	3.2
London	1987–88	16.6
West Midlands	1987–88	12.5

Source: Adapted from White 1993b.

immigrant population in selected cities in Britain and France, compared with the national averages.

In sum, in advanced market economy countries that experienced immigration after World War II, immigrants are concentrated in particular regions and especially in urban areas within those regions. Moreover, that concentration in increasing rather than decreasing. Paul White (1993b:67–68) reports that, at least in Europe, "there is little sign of any dispersion tendency on the interregional scale."

This spatial concentration of migrants has several sources. White (1993a) enumerates the economic, social, political, and geographic forces that affect migrants' destinations in the host countries, the most important of which are the initial economic pull of labor markets and the subsequent reinforcement of concentration via migrant networks or "chain migration" (King 1993a, Massey et al. 1987, Massey 1989).

Economics is the most powerful determinant of migrants' destinations in the initial phase.[1] Whatever their reasons for migration, newcomers need to support themselves, and they seek economically vibrant regions in which to settle and find employment. This decision is reinforced in many cases by employer or state recruitment of foreign workers and their placement in the host country in regions experiencing labor shortages.

The original economic impetus becomes less critical as the social dimension of migration takes hold.[2] The original migrants facilitate the migration process for family and friends who remained in the home country through

---

1. According to White 1993a:52, "At a regional scale, explanations are usually couched in terms of economic and employment factors, with chain migration playing a secondary role."
2. Piore 1979 describes the role of migrant networks in the process of immigrant settlement in the United States. Also see King 1993a:23: "In the literature on European migration, chain migration has been underestimated as a phenomenon conditioning the micro-scale pattern of spatial links between origins and destinations."

migrant networks. Douglas Massey (1989:16–17) defines migrant networks as "sets of interpersonal ties that link together migrants, former migrants, and nonmigrants in origin and destination areas through the bonds of kinship, friendship, and shared community origin." These networks are a source of information to new migrants about conditions in the host country; members of networks provide introductions to potential employers in the host countries and provide living facilities while the new migrants are getting settled. Transportation costs are often sponsored through the migrant network. By helping new migrants "get to know the ropes" in the host country, these interpersonal relations reduce the financial and psychic costs of migration.

At the same time, chain migration sustained through migrant networks helps to ensure the geographic concentration of migrants within the host country even after the draw of economic opportunities has diminished. In Australia, for example, eight of the twelve constituencies with the highest intake of recent immigrants (more than 10 percent between 1987 and 1991) are also among the twelve constituencies with the highest level of immigrants (from 37.8 percent to 49.0 percent foreign born). Six of these twelve constituencies had unemployment rates above the mean of 11.5 percent (in 1991), and three ranked at the top of all constituencies in unemployment rates, ranging from 15.3 to 24.2 percent. Six of the twelve constituencies with high new immigrant intakes were also among the poorest in the nation, ranking at the bottom of all constituencies in socioeconomic status, with between 73.4 and 87.3 percent of the national average income (Kopras 1993). Thus migrant networks generate chain migration and are a powerful factor in reinforcing the concentration of immigrants in particular districts and regions, regardless of economic conditions.

Political and geographic factors play smaller roles in the spatial distribution of immigrants. For example, state housing policies have alternately reinforced the concentration of immigrant communities, as in French social housing, or attempted to disperse the immigrant communities, as in Britain. But even where dispersal is a state goal, policies have been relatively ineffective, and the withdrawal of the government from housing and labor markets only increases the impact of migrant networks in concentrating immigrant communities.

The geographic dimension of migrant flows emphasizes proximity of borders, such as the concentration of Mexican immigrants in the United States on the U.S.-Mexican border, or the concentration of Italian immigrants in France on the French-Italian border. Geography is clearly a significant determinant of immigrants' spatial location in specific cases but assumes much less importance overall given the initial and growing diversity of immigrant flows.

Hence all four factors, economic, social, political, and geographic, are important determinants of immigrants' destinations in the host country. All four work to concentrate immigrants in a few, predominantly urban, locations in the host country.[3] This brief overview indicates that the spatial concentration of immigrants in host countries is well documented empirically and well understood theoretically. But the political significance of this concentration has been widely overlooked. One factor that may diminish the significance of the immigrant community's geographic concentration—and may account for why this aspect of immigration has been ignored in political analyses of immigration policy—is internal migration. Evidence of internal out-migration of the host population from regions of international in-migration is unsystematic and of recent origin. It has been developed most systematically for the United States (Borjas 1994). William Frey (1994), in a provocatively titled report, "The New White Flight," reports that international immigration to the United States between 1985 and 1995 generated internal out-migration from the areas of immigrant destination. The 1990 census reveals that five of the six states that received the largest inflows of international migrants between 1985 and 1990 had net negative outflows of the resident (predominantly indigenous) population (Frey 1996). For the 1990–95 period, the sixth state, California, which had previously experienced net positive internal migration, turned negative as well. Vernon Briggs (1992) argues that the presence of growing immigrant communities in the United States dampens the attraction of those regions to internal migrants.

Malcolm Cross (1993:124) also reports a trend in British internal migration associated with international migration: "The 'inner city' boroughs [of London] with high black concentrations lead the way in terms of out-migration.[4] The fall for Inner London between 1981 and 1991 was −11.1 percent but for three of the five boroughs with black populations of 15 percent or more, the figure was well above that. Previous evidence suggests that this out-migration is unlikely to be black, with the resultant greater separation and concentration of populations." A broader observation on Europe comes from White (1993b:68), who notes the "counter urbanization trends

3. In the post–World War II period, migration to rural areas, where immigrants work as agricultural laborers, is part of the overall flow but does not dominate the flow for two reasons. The first is that a substantial proportion of agricultural work is seasonal and is excluded from the analysis because most seasonal agricultural workers are admitted for less than one year. Second, agriculture represents a declining proportion of the workforce in all advanced market economy countries and is becoming more mechanized, thereby reducing the demand for agricultural labor. Thus most, but not all, immigration is urban.

4. In Britain, the term "black" is used generically to refer to all nonwhite populations, Afro-Caribbeans and Asians as well as Africans. Moreover, since a substantial proportion of immigrants who arrived in Britain after World War II are (black) New Commonwealth immigrants, there is also a tendency to conflate "black" with "immigrant." See Chapter 4 for additional details.

. . . starting for the population at large" that abandon urban areas to the immigrant population.

If these internal migratory trends are systematic and significant, the impact of immigrant concentration is diminished and more widely spread among the indigenous population. Internal migrants spread whatever impact immigrants have on wage rates and unemployment rates (either negative or positive) to the region where they relocate. And the social impact of immigration is reduced by the self-selected out-migration of individuals with the least tolerance for immigrants. But there are two reasons to believe that internal migration does not mitigate entirely the consequences of immigrants' geographic concentration. First, internal migration is never so complete that it entirely separates the indigenous and immigrant communities. Therefore, for better or worse, interaction between the two populations is always higher in some areas than in others. Second, what appears to be a recent trend in internal out-migration may, in fact, intensify relations between the two communities by increasing the ratio of immigrants to the remaining indigenous population.

Ultimately, because immigrant communities are spatially concentrated, the impact of immigration is not evenly spread across the indigenous population. Internal migration may diminish the impact of spatial concentration but does not erase it. So we need to examine the spatial distribution of both the benefits and costs of immigration to understand the politics of immigration control.

Local Political Actors and Interests

I begin with a model of immigration policy as a function of domestic political interests. I assume, following the "regulation school" of politics, that politicians maximize the likelihood of (re)election by promising or producing policies that maximize political support while minimizing political opposition (Peltzman 1976). Although immigration control can be modeled as a function of the support for and opposition to immigrant flows arising from distinct societal sources, I focus on the *local* support for and opposition to immigration, the politicization of immigration in local politics, and its translation onto the national political agenda. I draw on the literature introduced in Chapter 2 but apply it at the local level.

The support for immigration

On the demand side, firms are the primary actors with an interest in immigrant labor and an incentive to lobby government regarding immigration issues. Local support for immigration varies over time in response to employers' labor market needs and is strongest in periods of low unemployment but is mitigated by flexible labor markets and high capital mobility.[5]

Other factors being equal, low levels of local unemployment put pressure on local wage levels. But local labor market conditions may be insufficiently attractive to generate internal migration, giving rise to geographically segmented labor markets and geographically specific corporate demands for immigrant labor. Regardless of conditions in the economy as a whole, tight local labor markets may intensify the demand for immigrant labor.

But other factors are not always equal. Firms with high capital mobility, such as manufacturing firms with standardized technology, can choose to export capital to sites of cheap foreign labor whereas other firms have no alternative but to petition for the importation of labor. Natural resource–based firms, agricultural producers, and service firms (in-person delivery of services) are spatially fixed and therefore unable to reduce labor costs through capital exports. Firms in declining sectors of the economy also lack capital mobility. When levels of unemployment are equal, support for immigration will be strongest among firms with limited capital mobility. Therefore, local demand for immigrant labor will be strongest where firms with limited capital mobility dominate the local economy.

Firms also confront variation in labor market flexibility. Numerous studies demonstrate that migrant labor provides the desired flexibility by participating in the secondary labor market (Piore 1979). That is, immigrants permit the expansion of dual labor markets and increase flexibility of production. Firms confronting inflexible labor markets prefer higher levels of immigration than firms confronting flexible labor markets. Given equal levels of unemployment and similar levels of capital mobility, local demand for immigrant labor is strongest where employers experience inflexible labor markets.

I exclude from this portrait of support for immigration civil rights groups, churches, and immigrants themselves, groups that are often cited as petitioning in favor of immigrants.[6] I do so for two reasons. First, these groups, although often active in immigration policy arenas, are generally oriented toward what I label immigrant integration, that is, policies that affect the treatment of immigrants already in the host country. They usually petition the government to ensure equal treatment and equal protection of asylum

---

5. Smith and Edmonston 1997 report that immigration in the United States has provided lower prices for consumers rather than higher profits for employers. This finding does not refute the contention made here that employers are the primary societal actors supporting immigration. Migrant labor allows domestic employers to compete in domestic and international markets whereas, in the absence of that labor, they may be forced out of business.

6. See Keely 1979, Kabala 1993, Hardcastle et al. 1994, and Freeman 1995, among others.

seekers and illegal immigrants as well as for policies that facilitate integration of legal immigrants. Within the constraints of the immigration control regime, they also claim priority for family reunification. But they rarely focus on the level of immigration per se and, when they do, their preferences are often similar to those of the indigenous population.[7]

And second, even when these groups favor greater openness to immigration, they are often politically powerless. This is especially true of the immigrants themselves, who may be either reluctant or unable to participate politically in the host country. Some countries make political organization of immigrants illegal, as witnessed by laws controlling immigrant associations in France up through the 1970s. Other countries prevent immigrants from voting at either the local or national level unless they become naturalized citizens, which may be difficult or impossible (SOPEMI 1995). Australia actively encourages naturalization, currently requiring a mere two years residence as one minimum requisite. Other countries, such as Britain, in addition to subjecting immigrants to various measures of eligibility, make the grant of citizenship discretionary, preventing some immigrants from ever obtaining citizenship. Ultimately, rates of naturalization vary enormously across nations, and where naturalization is difficult, the political power of immigrants is reduced.

Some countries also prevent the political incorporation of second-generation immigrants into the host polity through the policy of jus sanguinis, granting citizenship only through the ties of parentage, so that "foreigners" live for many generations within their borders. Even countries that facilitate the political incorporation of immigrant offspring through the policy of jus soli, the grant of citizenship as a result of birth on the host country's soil, are starting to limit this grant to legal "settled" residents, prohibiting undocumented residents and temporary visitors from gaining a permanent connection with the host country.[8] The ability of second-generation immigrants to participate politically varies enormously across nations, as does the political power of immigrant communities.

Even where political incorporation is welcomed, the immigrants themselves are often reluctant to participate politically. Many are hesitant to trade their nationality of birth for that of the host polity because of penalties their home country attaches to the acquisition of a new citizenship. In Mexico, for example, until recently, citizens who acquired another nationality lost their Mexican citizenship and, with it, their ability to own property in Mexico. Moreover, the immigrants often consider themselves temporary residents,

---

7. This is a broad generalization to which there are numerous exceptions; nonetheless, the exceptions do not invalidate the rule. See Layton-Henry 1994 for the British case, Wihtol de Wenden 1988 for the French case, and Jupp 1993 for the Australian case.

8. Britain, France, and Australia have all passed legislation limiting in some way the unrestricted or less restrictive application of jus soli (SOPEMI 1995).

ultimately destined to return to their countries of origin. They retain an interest in the politics of their home countries and have neither the time nor the interest to participate in the politics of the host country.

In rare instances, immigrants have been granted rights of political participation without the associated formality of naturalization. In Britain, for example, until 1971, citizens of New Commonwealth countries, as British subjects, were granted many of the rights of citizenship, including the right to vote. Yet, for the reasons cited above, many chose not to participate electorally for many years (FitzGerald 1984, 1987).[9] The same is true for Algerians in France, who were considered French citizens until Algeria gained independence in 1961 (Wihtol de Wenden 1988).

In summary, the local support for immigration varies over time in response to employers' labor market needs. It is strongest in periods of low unemployment but is mitigated by flexible labor markets and high capital mobility. For immigrants to count in the politics of immigration control, they must have preferences that are distinctive from those of the host society, and they must be politically powerful. Because these conditions are difficult to meet, the analysis of support for immigration can exclude them.[10]

The opposition to immigration

I argue that local conditions trigger opposition to immigration through the level of native-immigrant competition. Although this thesis is not original, I clarify the conditions under which competition increases and diminishes, thereby isolating those factors that intensify anti-immigrant sentiment. This competition contains at least three dimensions: labor market competition, competition over state resources, and competition over societal identity.

COMPETITION OVER MARKET-BASED RESOURCES. There is considerable controversy regarding the position of the migrant vis-à-vis the native workforce.[11] Some economists believe that migrants complement the native workforce and actually enhance the returns of the host population by increasing their productivity and hence their wages. Others argue that the immigrant labor force substitutes for the native workforce because they obtain employment at the expense of the native population. For example, where indige-

---

9. For France, see Wihtol de Wenden 1988; she argues that immigrants' political participation follows a rhythm associated with the permanent establishment of the immigrant community rather than with immigrants' preferences on specific political issues.

10. Also see evidence in the empirical chapters demonstrating that preferences of the foreign-born population are often indistinguishable from those of the indigenous population and that few immigrants favor increased volumes of immigration.

11. See Borjas 1994 for an overview of the debate.

nous labor is skilled and immigrant labor is unskilled, immigrants may be employed to increase the productivity of the native workforce, thereby increasing the wages of the latter. In contrast, unskilled immigrant workers may compete with and displace native unskilled workers, thereby reducing their wages. Alternatively, immigrants create their own enclave economies and have little or no effect on the labor market (Light et al. 1997). Because the labor market is never completely segmented, undoubtedly there is some truth to all three propositions. I focus on the variation in labor market segmentation during periods of recession and economic prosperity that modifies the level of competition between the native and immigrant workforces.

The immigrant workforce usually bears the brunt of economic recession, as indicated by higher than average unemployment rates, but the native workforce is not totally protected by the immigrant buffer, as indicated by rising local and national levels of unemployment. The native and immigrant labor forces compete more directly in times of economic recession than in periods of prosperity because workers are often willing to take otherwise unacceptable employment during periods of economic downturn.[12] To be sure, this willingness is mitigated by the presence of a "reservation wage," the remuneration available from nonwork sources such as unemployment benefits and family allowances. To the extent that employment exists at greater than the reservation wage, unemployed workers accept employment that is lower in pay and prestige during economic recession because they evaluate the probability of future employment opportunities differently then than in periods of prosperity. Mathematically, this dynamic can be shown by examining the decision calculus of workers when accepting employment. An individual will accept employment when the offer O exceeds the value of the probability of employment $p(e)$ at the previous (higher) wage pw and exceeds the reservation wage rw, or when $O > p(e)pw > rw$.

In economic recession, the probability of employment, $p(e)$, at the higher wage diminishes, thereby making less remunerative employment more acceptable than in periods of economic prosperity. If these jobs are filled by immigrant laborers, as undoubtedly some are, the competition between the native and immigrant labor forces will rise during economic downturns.[13] In sum, competition for market-based resources—jobs—intensifies during periods of economic recession, leading to the rise of anti-immigrant senti-

---

12. In Olzak's 1992 terms, economic recession enlarges "niche overlap."

13. The immigrant also faces a reservation wage but one that is generally lower than the native worker's. The gap between the immigrant and native reservation wages depends in part on the degree to which benefits offered to the native population are extended to the immigrant population.

ment; in periods of economic prosperity, competition diminishes, leading to the decline of anti-immigrant sentiment.

COMPETITION FOR STATE-BASED RESOURCES. Another vociferous debate centers around whether immigrants contribute more in taxes than they receive in services from the state.[14] Again, I attempt to avoid this debate by pointing out that competition varies as a function of economic prosperity, regardless of the underlying net balance of contributions. The equation above incorporates the reservation wage, that is, services and revenues unrelated to employment. Many of these services and revenues are supplied by the state, but economic recession reduces state revenues while increasing demands on those revenues.[15] The scarcity of resources available to the state for redistribution increases the competition between the immigrant and the native populations over access to these assets regardless of whether immigrant contributions exceed expenditures on them. Moreover, the more access immigrants have to resources, the broader will be the base of competition and hence the more intense the competition. At a more general level, economic recession reduces the reservation wage and aggravates the competition between the native and the immigrant workforces for employment by enlarging the segment of employment opportunities over which they compete.

The competition over state-based resources also increases as a function of the rate at which the immigrant population increases. The state provides public as well as private goods to its residents: clean water, schools, health care, and transportation and communications systems are but a few examples (Zolberg 1992; Freeman 1986).[16] Public goods in the rigorous sense are

14. This debate is summarized in Martin and Midgley 1994; see also Simon 1989 and the citations listed therein. As George J. Borjas 1990 points out for the United States, the dependency ratio is based on the composition of the immigrant intake, among other factors, and that composition changes over time. See Freeman 1986 for an early analysis of the political implications of the welfare state for migration policy. John Roemer 1997 has constructed a formal model that systematically incorporates redistributive policies to evaluate the welfare implications of migration. He concludes that if economic efficiency is the goal, the inclusion of redistributive policies does not alter the prescriptions for open borders. However, if equity is sought, the model indicates that some degree of closure produces more equitable outcomes.

15. The implication is that federal systems or decentralized unitary systems that raise a significant amount of revenues locally will be more sensitive to local economic conditions than highly centralized unitary systems. See Smith and Edmonston 1997 for empirical evidence on the United States. The report suggests that, although short-term expenditures are balanced by long-term revenues, there remain geographic disparities in the distribution of expenditures and revenues. In Smith and Edmonston's model, the federal government received a net benefit from immigration in the long run while states where immigrants were concentrated incurred a net cost, both short and long term.

16. Schools and health care may not always be classified as public goods. To the extent that the state legislates that all children between certain ages must be in school, education may be considered a public good. To the extent that emergency rooms and health care providers cannot turn away noncitizens, health care may also be considered a public good.

characterized by two traits: nonexcludability, which means that once the good is provided to a particular class of individuals, other members of that class cannot be excluded from consuming that good; and jointness of supply, which means that the provision of the good to one person does not diminish the supply available to others. To the extent that public goods are nonexcludable but lack jointness of supply, these goods become subject to crowding, thereby increasing the competition between the indigenous and immigrant communities for them. If the rate of increase in the immigrant community is large, immigrants stretch the capacity of the system to deliver these goods: classrooms become crowded; traffic increases; public transportation becomes overburdened; sewage treatment facilities are overloaded. In the medium to long term, additional public goods may be made available as revenues from the increased population that flow to the state are allocated to the provision of these goods. But in the short term, competition for these goods is exacerbated by a rapid increase in the number of immigrants.

COMPETITION FOR COMMUNITY RESOURCES. When foreigners enter a community, they bring with them an alternative conception of society, thereby presenting competition over the definition of the local community.[17] Rather than being associated with economic recession, this competition is triggered by the sheer number of immigrants in the community. The competition is offset by the process of incorporating the foreign population into the native population, thereby undermining competition from the alternative. The ability of immigrants to assimilate and the length of time required to do so appear to vary across groups, introducing immigrants' characteristics into the equation of native-immigrant competition.[18]

In sum, opposition to immigration is driven by competition between the host and the immigrant communities. The first dimension, labor market competition, is triggered by economic recession. The second dimension, competition over state resources, is triggered by economic recession and the rate of growth of the immigrant community, as well as the level of access immigrants have to publicly provided goods. The third dimension, competition

---

17. Ole Waever 1993: chap. 2 has defined this as "societal security." According to his analysis, members of a society "have a feeling of together constituting an entity: a people, a nation, a community." Societal security is threatened when a community's identity is threatened.
18. The ability to assimilate can be, but is not necessarily, associated with race. In Britain, for example, most observers would argue that European migrants are more easily assimilated than the "coloured" migrants from the New Commonwealth countries. Yet Switzerland has failed to integrate its European (Italian) immigrant population, and in France, black Africans were initially better received than Spaniards, although North African Arabs were the least well accepted. See Castles and Kosack 1973: chap. 10 for a discussion of race and discrimination against the immigrant community. Additional examples come from Germany and Japan, which have ethnically homogeneous immigrants who, having reimmigrated after generations of absence, face considerable discrimination despite a common ethnicity.

over societal identity, is triggered by the size of the immigrant community but is offset by its incorporation into the native population. The argument is conjunctural; that is, opposition to immigration that becomes politically important is triggered by the presence of an immigrant community in conjunction with economic recession. It is aggravated by the degree to which the migrant community challenges the preeminence of the host community.

Playing the Immigrant Card

The local political agenda

Party positions at the local level reflect the underlying preferences of the population for immigration control. As structural conditions that affect support for and opposition to immigration change, the position of the local parties will change as well. Models of collective action suggest that large groups are more difficult to organize than small groups and are therefore less powerful politically. If this is true, then employers should always be more politically powerful than public opinion, and immigration control policy should be similarly skewed toward employers' interests. The geographic concentration of immigrants, however, tends to concentrate the costs of immigration and facilitate the organization of political opposition to immigration at particular conjunctures.[19] Drawing on James Q. Wilson's (1980) policy typology, I argue that under certain conditions the politics of immigration policy shift from "client" to "interest group" politics. The former is characterized by the political participation of groups receiving concentrated benefits and the absence of organized opposition from those bearing the diffuse costs of immigration, whereas the latter is characterized by political activity from pro-immigrant groups receiving concentrated benefits and anti-immigrant groups bearing concentrated costs.

Empirically, societal opposition to immigration sometimes resembles the interest group organization of employers; examples include FAIR (the Federation of Americans for Immigration Reform) in the United States and the Birmingham Immigration Control Association in Britain. It is sometimes represented by political parties, such as the Vlaamsblok in Belgium and the

---

19. The argument is similar to Freeman's 1995 model described but not tested in Chapter 2. In his model, employers' interests are static and they always favor higher levels of immigration whereas my model suggests that employers' preferences change according to specific structural conditions. Freeman suggests that anti-immigrant sentiment is attached to the "immigration cycle" and specifically discounts the business cycle; my argument attaches anti-immigrant sentiment to the business cycle as well as to some dimensions of what may be associated with an immigration cycle. The most basic difference is that I concentrate on the local organization of interests and their subsequent transmission to the national level whereas Freeman's argument is couched at the national level.

National Front in France. It may be more amorphous, such as the initiative movements in California and Switzerland. Or it may be anomic, such as the race riots in Nottingham and Notting Hill, Britain, in 1958 or in Marseille, France, in 1973. Regardless of the form of organization, as the costs of immigration increase, the political salience of the opposition to immigrants increases.[20] This picture is consonant with public opinion surveys in advanced industrial countries that indicate most respondents oppose additional immigration but also believe that immigration is not a significant political problem, most of the time. Thus opposition to immigration periodically becomes organized rather than remaining constantly latent. Political organization can be attributed in part to the concentration of costs arising from immigration associated with the concentration of the immigrant community—a facet that is largely overlooked by those who analyze the politics of immigration control policy.

I suggest that it is the political salience of attitudes that changes in response to the changing context rather than the underlying attitudes toward immigrants in general. Moreover, the change in salience need not be uniformly distributed among the affected population.[21] Unfortunately, public opinion surveys are poorly structured to capture this change in salience.[22] But with or without survey data on individual attitudes, the argument emphasizes the political organization of groups affected by immigration. This political organization makes the salience of immigration issues more visible to politicians who gather information on constituency preferences from a broad variety of sources. Moreover, the indicators of immigrant pressures are themselves sources of information that politicians employ to evaluate the salience of immigration issues.

Thus both support for and opposition to immigration are politically organized and politically significant. Yet support and opposition do not necessarily rise and fall in tandem, that is, when opposition to immigration is at a peak, support can be either strong or weak. Support for and opposition to immigration are connected via unemployment: when unemployment is high, other things being equal, local support will be weak and opposition will be strong. Opposition may rise during a period of economic prosperity in the presence of a large, unassimilated population. And support may be strong in

20. Husbands 1988 makes a similar distinction between "racism" and "political racism," the subset of racism that affects political outcomes.
21. See below for the importance of swing constituencies where only a small change in the number of votes affects election results.
22. Public opinion surveys that do address immigration rarely ask more than respondents' preferences on levels of immigration, so they do not tap the salience of the issue. Moreover, the surveys are structured to address "national" opinion; there is rarely oversampling of electoral constituencies or regions that would permit statements on constituency or regional attitudes.

periods of economic recession if firms face inflexible labor markets or capital immobility.[23]

Driven by electoral competition, local politicians will shift their policy positions in response to changing community preferences, toward either greater openness or greater closure. This depiction of immigration control suggests two hypotheses. First, policy positions of mainstream parties will tend to converge toward the local median voter. Second, as preferences of the population on immigration control shift, the positions of the parties will tend to shift in tandem. I do not suggest that positions of candidates will always be identical and shift exactly the same degree; rather candidates learn that their position differs from constituency preferences through electoral defeat. They respond by changing their position or are replaced by candidates who will. Furthermore, the positions of the parties reflect not the extreme position of some supporters but a balance between the support for and opposition to immigration. But immigration control is determined in the national rather than the local political arena. Therefore, it is crucial to understand the conditions under which local demands are successfully transmitted to the national level.

The national political agenda

Local demands will be addressed at the national level if a majority of the national constituencies demands changes in immigration control. Because both support for and opposition to immigration are concentrated spatially, however, this scenario does not occur frequently. This is one reason that changes in immigration control policies are usually infrequent; it is difficult to obtain a legislative majority to change the status quo (Cornelius, Martin, and Hollifield 1994:4). But under some circumstances it pays national politicians to adopt local constituencies' preferences, even when these do not reflect those of the national median voter. If local politicians respond to the changing distribution of support for and opposition to immigrants in their communities, national politicians respond to different incentives; that is, they respond to the shifts in preferences of those constituencies that are important for building a national political coalition (James 1992, 1995, 1997).[24]

---

23. An example of strong and continuing support for immigration despite economic recession and rising anti-immigrant sentiment comes from California, where agricultural employers clamored for more immigration in the midst of the 1990–94 recession at the same time that groups were organizing the anti-immigrant Proposition 187 initiative. Another example comes from Germany, where guest worker programs are being revived in the 1990s despite unemployment rates of more than 10 percent, presumably because of inflexible labor markets created in part by the high reservation wage of the indigenous population.

24. See James 1997 for a discussion of the importance of national (presidential) coalition building to national regulatory policy positions.

The preferences of immigration constituencies will be accorded greater weight if the constituents have the potential to swing the national election results between parties. Thus local preferences are not translated on a one-to-one basis to the national political agenda. Both the size and the safety of the constituencies factor into the political calculus of national leaders when evaluating the level of electoral competition. Immigration control will tend to be added to the national political agenda when constituencies can swing the electoral outcomes. This will be true for policies broadening opportunities for immigration as well as policies limiting immigration.

The influence of local constituencies on national electoral outcomes depends in part on the size of the constituency seeking to add immigration issues to the national political agenda. In the United States, for example, states vary in the electoral support they can offer the presidential coalition in accordance with the number of their electoral college votes. Large states, such as California, are politically important because a victory there may swing the national presidential election to the victorious party. When immigration policy is important in California politics, it is more likely to be addressed at the national level than if similar concerns were voiced in Wyoming. In Britain, in contrast, each constituency carries equal weight in the House of Commons; there, the number of constituencies interested in immigration control policies must be compared to the winning party's electoral margin.

The influence of local constituencies also depends on the "safety" of the constituencies. If the constituency cannot convincingly threaten defection to the opposing party, its policy preferences are less important to the national coalition. Definitions of safe constituencies vary across countries depending on the electoral system as well as the attributes of the voters. In Australia, for example, constituencies are considered safe when the electoral margin between the parties is more than 10 percent, "fairly safe" when the margin falls between 6 and 10 percent, and swing when the margin is less than 6 percent (Mackerras 1972). In the United States, the cutoff is usually 20 percent. But whatever the definition of safety, it is widely known, and national politicians attempting to gain or maintain national power pay more attention to swing constituencies than to safe constituencies.

National political institutions are crucial to understanding the transformation of immigration from a local to a national political issue; institutional characteristics define the significance of local support for and opposition to immigration in building national political coalitions. Presidential systems will reflect a different dynamic than parliamentary systems; proportional representation systems will reflect a different dynamic than single-member constituency systems. But the common thread running through all nations is the need for politicians to build a national electoral

Table 3.4. Determinants of immigration control policy

Policy preferences	→	Political salience	→	Policy outcome
a. Local unemployment rates		a. National electoral		
b. Local rates of capital mobility		margin		
c. Local labor market flexibility		b. Size and safety		
d. Local rates of immigration increase		of "immigration"		
e. Local proportion of immigrants		constituencies		
f. Incorporation of immigrants				

majority. Immigration control will be added to the national political agenda when that constituency is both willing and able to swing the electoral outcome between parties.

The theoretical framework I have sketched above can be reduced to a series of statements about the relationship between structural and institutional variables and political outcomes. Immigration control is a function of the direction and political salience of societal preferences. In turn, the salience of preferences is a function of the national electoral margin and the size and safety of "immigration" constituencies; and the direction of preferences is a function of local unemployment rates, local rates of capital mobility, local labor market flexibility, local rates of immigration increase, the proportion of immigrants in the local community and their access to social services, as well as the degree to which immigrants have been assimilated into the local community. These relationships are depicted in Table 3.4.

Research Strategies

I have argued that national aggregate statistics are insufficiently sensitive to capture conditions at the local level that generate political pressures to modify national immigration control policies and the national political institutional structures through which those political pressures are funneled. Unfortunately, time-series data disaggregated at the level of local political units are impossible to generate.[25] I therefore employ a systematic comparative case method and examine the politics of immigration control in three countries, Britain, France, and Australia, at important turning points in their

25. For the cases in question, census data by electoral constituency are unavailable for Australia before 1971 and for Britain before 1966. For France, only departmental level data are available, and departments contain from two to thirty-one electoral constituencies. Moreover, because the census data are periodic rather than continuous, it is impossible to obtain disaggregated time-series data on such variables as the unemployment rate. It may be reasonable to interpolate immigration levels from one census period to the next, but it is unreasonable to do so for unemployment rates.

immigration policies (Jackman 1985, Smelser 1976). In the case studies, I focus on the structural conditions generating local political pressures and the institutional conditions that force politicians to adopt immigration control policies or allow them to ignore local constituency demands. By delineating similar processes in three different countries, the analysis substantiates a common political logic of immigration control and provides evidence that is consistent with the model outlined in this chapter.

For each of the countries in question, I develop quantitative indicators of immigration pressure at the constituency level, based on census data. These indicators incorporate, as available, the proportion of immigrants by electoral constituency, the unemployment rate, and recent increases in immigration. These are supplemented by qualitative and quantitative data on labor market conditions, the crowding of public services, and other factors that contribute to local support for and opposition to immigration.

These structural conditions are then tied to the political organization of groups who petition the government for changes in immigration policy. These data avoid the potential for ecological fallacy, that is, for attributing to individuals behavior that is substantiated empirically only through the use of aggregate data. Nonetheless, when opinion polls provide some measure of the political salience of immigration issues, these polls are combined with census data to substantiate the claim that contextual changes are congruent with attitudinal changes in the salience of immigration issues at the individual level.

These local constituency pressures are then evaluated from the perspective of national electoral politics. Immigration constituencies are evaluated in terms of political safety. Nation-specific definitions of electoral marginality are adopted in analyzing the incentives for politicians to cater to local demands. These are then compared with the national electoral balance of power. For each case, I provide examples when local constituency demands were ignored by national politicians as well as examples when politicians adopted local constituency preferences. Where the strategies of politicians are revealed, I am able to describe the "smoking gun," statements by national politicians that indicate policy positions were adopted to attract a particular constituency.

Systematic evidence is thus marshaled across both time and space in support of the hypotheses outlined in this chapter. The underlying similarities of political process in three countries, despite differences in the direction and timing of immigration control, substantiate a common political logic. This political logic takes as its starting point the geographic concentration of immigration and combines this crucial dimension with the appropriate set of national electoral incentives to determine when local demands will be catapulted to the national political arena.

4   *Immigration and Race Relations in Britain*

The British parliament originally introduced legislation to restrict Commonwealth immigration in 1961 and adopted it in 1962, in an era of full employment when economists both within and outside the government were predicting severe labor shortages. Furthermore, the controls were introduced when the proportion of the foreign-born population was small, only around 1 percent, and in contrast to the British tradition of integrating immigrants through a policy of jus soli, the granting of citizenship by birth on British soil. This pattern of restriction contrasts sharply with the policies of other European countries, which were in the process of rapidly expanding their immigrant workforces during the 1960s.

The perceived bipartisan consensus for restrictive immigration control appeared to break down in the 1970s, when the Labour Party failed to introduce additional restrictions during its control of Parliament between 1974 and 1979, despite the rising electoral popularity of the National Front. The Conservatives capitalized on that neglect in 1979. These anomalies can be explained through the political leverage of a small number of electoral constituencies. In the first case, the Labour and Conservative parties competed for votes from constituencies that experienced economic decline in the presence of a substantial immigrant community and therefore opposed continued immigration. In the second, Labour's parliamentary pact with the Liberal Party, undertaken to retain a working majority in Parliament, forced Labour to consider its ally's pro-immigrant constituencies. The Conservatives, on gaining the parliamentary majority in 1979, were not so restrained and introduced additional controls, thereby deflating the electoral appeal of the anti-immigrant National Front.

British Immigration Control Since 1945

The immigration status quo in the United Kingdom after World War II involved two sets of foreign-born populations: Commonwealth citizens and aliens.[1] The first law restricting alien entry was passed in 1905, in response to Jewish immigration before the turn of the century. The law designated particular ports of entry and authorized immigration officers to refuse entry to and to deport "undesirable" aliens—those unable to support themselves and their dependents. The Alien Restriction Act of 1914, enacted under conditions of war hysteria, strengthened and enlarged the provisions of the 1905 act. It required aliens to register with the police and restricted their movement and employment. The 1914 act was revised and extended in 1919 and renewed annually until 1971, when the system of immigration control was revamped. Regulations issued under the act required, among other things, that aliens obtain work permits in order to enter the labor force, the number and type of which were governed by labor market conditions.

The second group, imperial subjects and Commonwealth citizens, was governed by custom that permitted free circulation within the empire, including the mother country, Britain.[2] Until 1945, free circulation had worked in favor of British emigration. Massive numbers of British citizens emigrated to destinations within and outside the empire; between 1846 and 1924, the number of emigrants amounted to 41 percent of the 1900 U.K. population (Massey 1989). The close of World War II began a period of transition from empire to commonwealth and with it a clarification of the rules governing access to the mother country.[3] The 1948 British Nationality Act distinguished between Citizens of the United Kingdom and Colonies (CUKC) and Commonwealth citizens.[4] But Commonwealth citizens, as British subjects, maintained the right to enter British territory freely and retained access to all rights and privileges of citizenship, including voting. Registration for British citizenship required only twelve months' residence.

In the very early postwar period, reflecting both the need to ease labor

1. The classic chronicle of British immigration legislation is by Macdonald 1972, 1983, continued by Macdonald and Blake 1991. Also see Fransman 1982 and Grant and Martin 1982. Layton-Henry 1992 provides a good overview of immigration control in Britain and Layton-Henry 1994 is the source for the most recent legislation.
2. Since gaining independence from the United Kingdom in 1921, Irish citizens have always been treated as a special category whose entry is uncontrolled. Difficulty of controlling the border between the Irish Republic and Northern Ireland is one purported reason for that policy.
3. "The Commonwealth" originally referred to the association of self-governing communities of the British Empire, composed of the "old" Commonwealth countries, the (white) settler states of Australia, New Zealand, Canada, and South Africa. As other parts of the empire became independent in the years after World War II, they joined the Commonwealth, hence the designation "new" Commonwealth nations.
4. This legislation was triggered by the Canadian government's decision to define a distinct Canadian citizenship (Paul 1997).

market shortages and the humanitarian response to persons displaced by World War II, the British government facilitated immigration from the European continent through a variety of measures. The 1947 Polish Resettlement Act aided members of the Polish armed forces, who served under British command in World War II, to settle with their families. The European Volunteer Workers program, also initiated by the Labour government in 1947, was more limited in scope. The program recruited European workers to fill specific labor market shortages and controlled their stay by issuing twelve-month work permits that allowed neither the right of permanent settlement nor the right of family reunification. The European Volunteer Workers program did little to reduce labor market shortages, in part because local unions negotiated controls over conditions of employment (Macdonald 1969).[5] Continued labor market shortages and the inability to attract and employ sufficient numbers of European migrants led employers to tap immigrants from the Commonwealth whose entrance was uncontrolled. The creation of this labor market network was facilitated by the experience of colonial workers in Britain during World War II.

Although the government periodically discussed control over Commonwealth immigration, the first efforts to connect this flow to the vagaries of labor market conditions was initiated in 1957 in response to the deflationary effects on the economy of the Suez crisis (Rose 1969: chap. 16, Layton-Henry 1987). At the behest of the British government, India and Pakistan (as well as African colonial governments) agreed to control departures for Britain.[6] West Indian states were less amenable to British diplomatic pressures, but after the 1958 race riots in the Notting Hill district of London and Nottingham, they agreed to screen and control emigrants with criminal records. These voluntary efforts to control immigration were never very effective and ultimately collapsed in 1960, when the Indian Supreme Court declared exit controls to be unconstitutional (Layton-Henry 1992).

Control over Commonwealth immigration was introduced by the Conservative government in the fall of 1961, in what became known as the 1962 Commonwealth Immigrants Act. This act introduced immigration control for all Commonwealth citizens and CUKCs whose passports were issued outside the United Kingdom.[7] Entry was now subordinated to the possession of an

5. Also see Hepple 1968, who provides documentation of collective agreements that limited the employment of foreign labor, leading employers to turn to an uncontrolled source of labor, Commonwealth citizens. Various other, smaller programs attempted to recruit European workers, with limited success (Paul 1997).

6. These negotiations were begun and concluded before the race riots in the Notting Hill District of London and in Nottingham in the late summer of 1958, the events often said to have triggered immigration control (Rose 1969, *Hansard*, Lords 209:617–18).

7. In the draft legislation, the Irish were initially included as a group subject to immigration control; they were ultimately excluded in the final legislation although they remained subject to the new deportation provisions.

entry voucher, which carried with it the right of permanent residence and family reunification.[8] Three types of vouchers were devised: "A" vouchers were issued to those who had a specific job arranged in the United Kingdom; "B" vouchers were awarded to individuals whose skills were in short supply in Britain; and "C" vouchers were reserved for all other applicants, with preference given to those with war service. The act also defined conditions under which Commonwealth immigrants could be deported. Registration for British citizenship was still permitted, but the residence requirement was extended from one year to five. This change was effectuated, in part, to coordinate citizenship provisions with protections from deportation. CUKCs and Commonwealth citizens were still a privileged class of immigrants when compared with aliens. The voucher was both a work permit and a residence permit granted to a head of household whose family was not subject to additional immigration restrictions. Nonetheless, these vouchers were now subject to quotas. And when Labour came to power in 1964, it reduced the annual quota of vouchers from an average of 30,000 to 8,500.

The movement toward greater control of Commonwealth immigration came in 1968. In response to an influx of East Asians with U.K. passports from Africa, the Commonwealth Immigrants Act of 1968 addressed the status of CUKCs with no direct familial tie to the United Kingdom. The act created the category of "patrial," individuals who are tied to U.K. territory through family or settlement. Thus CUKCs with parents or grandparents born in the United Kingdom, as well as those who had settled permanently in the United Kingdom, were patrials.[9] Only patrial CUKCs remained free from immigration controls; entry of all others was controlled through the issuance of vouchers; an initial level was set at 1,500. Moreover, illegal entry by Commonwealth citizens was now criminalized, whereas before the act, Commonwealth citizens who bypassed entry controls and remained undetected for twenty-four hours could not be prosecuted or deported. These were still privileged entry vouchers because they were awarded to heads of households and carried with them rights to work, to permanent residence, and to family reunification. Moreover, upon arrival, both Commonwealth citizens and CUKCs were treated essentially as full members of the society, with access to all social services, government employment, and voting rights.

To dispel complaints of arbitrary administrative decisions by immigration officers, the Labour government introduced a system of appeals. The 1969 Immigration Appeals Act created a two-tiered judicial review system. Orig-

8. There were also provisions for "independent" entry of Commonwealth citizens who had sufficient resources to support themselves without recourse to the labor market, students, au pair girls, and dependents of individuals settled in Britain.
9. The designation of patriality by settlement required a minimum five years' residence.

inal appeals are heard by a single adjudicator whose decisions can be appealed, in turn, to an immigration tribunal. Thus decisions that are not in accordance with the rules can be overturned on review.

The two classes of immigration control, alien and Commonwealth, were consolidated in 1971, erasing most of the privileges originally offered to Commonwealth citizens. The 1971 act required visas or entry certificates for all nonpatrials, as well as work permits for those seeking to enter the labor market. The prospective employer, in the absence of qualified employees resident in the United Kingdom, applied for an immigrant work permit. The number of available work permits was fixed by the Department of Employment in consultation with employers and trade unions. Work permits, following the system of alien immigration control, were issued for twelve months for a particular job and could be renewed annually. Work permits carried neither the privileges of permanent residence nor the right of family reunification (Layton-Henry 1994). After four years, the immigrant could apply to remove the work permit restrictions and be accepted for permanent settlement. Access to British citizenship was also made more uniform; registration now carried the same requirements as naturalization and became discretionary rather than an entitlement. To apply for British citizenship, the individual must establish residence in the country for at least five years, show good character and knowledge of the English language, declare an intention to reside in Britain, and take a loyalty oath. Commonwealth status still carried some privileges such as access to services, government employment, and voting rights in the first five years of residence, but the differences between Commonwealth citizens and aliens were dissolving.

The sole reduction in immigration controls came in 1972 with Britain's treaty of accession to the European Community (EC, later European Union). Adherence to the Treaty of Rome required, among other things, freedom of movement of the citizens of member states. Although this requirement reduced immigration controls for a specific group of aliens, it cannot be interpreted as a movement toward greater openness to immigration because Britain was not expected to draw European migrants. The increasing wealth of labor-exporting countries in the Community, especially Italy, the attraction of high wages in France and Germany, and comparatively low British wages all combined to suggest that accession to the EC would not bring a flood of immigrants (Böhning 1972, Layton-Henry 1994, Dummett and Nicol 1990).[10]

Some minor adjustments were made to British immigration regulations during the 1970s, but the next major revision was introduced by the Con-

10. As Layton-Henry 1994:285 notes, "European immigration was, after all, unlikely."

servative government in 1981. The British Nationality Act of that year revised the nationality code to correspond to immigration control laws. Three categories of citizenship were established: U.K. citizens, British dependent territory citizens, and British overseas citizens. The latter two categories had no rights of entry or abode. The registration of children born to British citizens on foreign territory was limited to a single generation. And Britain also departed from its tradition of jus soli. Once the provisions of the act came into effect, citizenship to those born on British soil was limited to those born of U.K. parent(s) or settled immigrants. Almost all of the remaining differences between aliens and Commonwealth citizens were abolished; now certain rights, such as voting, were reserved for British citizens.

The movement toward greater immigration control did not stop there. In 1987, the Conservative government passed the Immigration (Carrier Liability) Act, which penalized carriers for transporting aliens who lacked proper papers. The 1988 Immigration Act removed guarantees of family reunification for Commonwealth immigrants settled before the 1973 implementation of the 1971 Immigration Act and restricted entry of polygamous wives. The British Nationality (Hong Kong) Act of 1991 limited access to British citizenship (and entry) to a small percentage of residents of Hong Kong.[11]

Even asylum seekers have come under greater scrutiny. Although the 1992 Asylum and Immigration Appeals Act reaffirmed the right of political asylum, it speeded up procedures for assessing applications and introduced compulsory fingerprinting to reduce fraud. It removed the right of appeal for certain categories of asylum seekers and ended the obligation of local authorities to house them. Finally, it extended the Immigration (Carrier Liability) Act to transit passengers.

British immigration control legislation is summarized in Table 4.1. Although alien movements were brought under control shortly after the turn of the century, Commonwealth migration was uncontrolled until 1962. Since that time, the regime governing Commonwealth migration has been incorporated in terms similar to those for aliens, and all controls, with the exception of immigration of citizens of European Union member states, have been tightened.

The Institution of Immigration Control

In the years following World War II, the British government, under both Labour and Conservative control, considered restricting Commonwealth

11. The government argued that this legislation was necessary to maintain the Hong Kong government's infrastructure until the transfer to China in 1997; 50,000 permits were issued to heads of households (Layton-Henry 1994).

Table 4.1. British immigration control legislation, 1948–1992

Legislation	Year	Provisions
British Nationality Act	1948	Distinguishes between citizens of U.K. and colonies (CUKCs) and Commonwealth citizens; both categories have unrestricted rights of entry and residence in U.K.
Commonwealth Immigrants Act	1962	Subordinates entry of all Commonwealth citizens and CUKCs whose passports were issued outside U.K. to immigration controls and labor market controls; defines conditions for deportation of immigrants in this category
Commonwealth Immigrants Act	1968	Defines, within classification of CUKCs, the category of patrial, consisting of individuals connected to U.K. by parentage or 5 years of settlement, who are exempted from immigration controls; others are now subjected to such controls, with an initial quota set at 1,500 heads of household
Immigration Appeals Act	1969	Sets up appeals process for immigration control and deportation decisions
Immigration Act	1971	Consolidates Commonwealth immigration control into the more restrictive alien immigration control system
Treaty of Accession to European Communities	1972	Permits freedom of movement of labor market participants from EC member states
British Nationality Act	1981	Defines patrials as U.K. citizens, distinct from British dependent territory citizens (BDTCs) and British overseas citizens (BOCs), who are subject to immigration controls; restricts jus soli designation of citizenship to children of British parentage and those of settled immigrants.
Immigration (Carriers) Act	1987	Penalizes carriers for transport of aliens who lack proper papers
Immigration Act	1988	Dismantles rights of family reunification
British Nationality (Hong Kong) Act	1991	Grants 50,000 Hong Kong residents and their families access to British citizenship
Asylum and Immigration Appeals Act	1992	Speeds asylum determination process; introduces measures to reduce asylum fraud; removes certain rights of appeal

immigration (Layton-Henry 1987, Rose 1969).[12] Various studies were completed regarding the impact of "coloured" immigrants on the native population. Report after report indicated that the immigrants were as healthy and industrious as the native population but warned of a potential backlash caused by the presence of a racially distinct population. The government regularly reviewed the question and deemed controls inappropriate. Why, then, did the Conservative government choose to introduce immigration control legislation in the fall of 1961? Why, too, did the Labour Party, after vociferously opposing this legislation during its passage, adopt and strengthen the controls when it gained power in 1964?

The first question is important because Commonwealth immigration control was never entirely absent from the political agenda and public eye during the postwar period, yet control legislation was not introduced until the fall of 1961. Commonwealth immigration was studied by various commissions, such as the Royal Commission on Population (1949) and the Interdepartmental Working Party (1954). The reports issued by these committees were debated at the highest levels of government. Legislation was drafted in 1954 but never introduced (Layton-Henry 1987). Moreover, since at least 1952, Cyril Osborne, a Conservative backbench gadfly, had carried on an active campaign in Parliament to introduce immigration controls, forcing the government to debate the issue with some regularity. Race riots in Nottingham and the Notting Hill district of London erupted in the late summer of 1958, bringing Commonwealth immigration to the attention of the British public in a particularly unsettling way (Pilkington 1988). Yet immigration and immigration control were not issues in the 1959 national election campaign (Butler and Rose 1960, Steel 1969). The government did not support, and therefore forced the withdrawal of, the private member immigration control bill introduced by Norman Pannell (Conservative, Liverpool Kirkdale) in 1960 as well as the parliamentary motion introduced by Osborne as late as February 1961.[13] At its conferences in 1958 and 1960, the Conservative Party passed motions calling for the introduction of Commonwealth immigration control, but the government failed to adopt these resolutions (Conservative Party, various years).[14] The announcement, then, directly after the October

12. This case study draws on, among others, Cooper and Martucelli 1994; Deakin 1968; Dummett and Nicol 1990; Foot 1965; Freeman 1979; Katznelson 1973; Layton-Henry 1994, 1992, 1987, 1985; Messina 1989; Rose 1969; and Steel 1969.
13. The privilege of introducing private member bills and motions is awarded by lot in the British system so the timing of these anti-immigrant measures introduced by backbenchers is random (Griffith and Ryle 1989).
14. Party conferences are usually held annually, but none was held in 1959. The first year in the postwar period when a resolution was adopted by the party conference to control immigration was 1958.

1961 Conservative Party conference at Brighton, that the government would introduce control legislation, was a sudden change in policy.

The second question is significant because the Labour Party, in opposition when immigration control legislation was initially introduced, was a vociferous opponent of Commonwealth immigration control. The party leaders Gordon Walker and Hugh Gaitskell argued eloquently that the proposed legislation undermined Commonwealth relations at a particularly delicate time and, moreover, carried racist undertones. Labour suggested that immigration itself created no problems but served as a scapegoat for the government, allowing it to ignore its responsibilities in providing services to the public, especially housing. Yet, upon coming to power in 1964, Labour actually reduced the quotas for Commonwealth migrants and went on to pass control legislation in 1968.

This startling change of position in both parties is reflected in statements that demonstrate the dramatic turnaround in party position and in legislative outcomes. In 1960, less than a year before the Conservatives introduced control legislation, a party document indicated that "there is enough experience in the Commonwealth to prove that harmony between the races on a basis of partnership is a practical policy. We believe the mingling of culture leads to a richer and better society." In sharp contrast, in March 1965 the Conservative Party "for the moment reject[ed] the multi-racial state not because we are superior to our Commonwealth partners but because we want to maintain the kind of Britain we know and love" (quoted in Foot 1965:124).

The change in the Labour position was equally dramatic. A Labour Party spokesman was quoted in 1958 as opposing restrictions: "We on this side are clear in our attitude towards restricted immigration. I think I speak for my Right Honourable [leader] and honourable friends by saying that we are categorically against [restrictions]." But by 1964 another party spokesman, with a decidedly short memory, opined: "There should be no doubt about the Government's view. The Government are firmly convinced that an effective control is indispensable. That we accept and have always accepted" (quoted in Foot 1965:161).[15]

Why did these parties change their positions so dramatically in the early 1960s rather than earlier or later? As indicated by the theoretical framework set out in Chapter 3, electoral incentives drove first the Conservative Party and then the Labour Party to cater to constituencies in which immigrants were concentrated. These incentives are defined by the nation's electoral and legislative institutions. The United Kingdom has single-member constituencies, where the candidate who receives the largest number of votes,

---

15. These contrasting statements belie Paul's 1997 argument that the political elite was uniformly opposed to "coloured" immigration during the entire postwar period.

even though not a majority, wins the election. This system discourages the development of small parties and tends to produce two major parties that contend for control over the government. In these circumstances, the two parties pay close attention to constituencies where a small swing in votes will shift the outcome from an electoral loss to a victory, and vice versa. Swing constituencies in Britain are defined as those where 5 percent or less of the voters can change an electoral outcome (Norton 1994).[16]

The United Kingdom has a parliamentary government in which the party receiving the majority of seats in the House of Commons forms the government.[17] Elections must be held every five years, but the government may call an election at any time during the five-year period and must call an election if it loses a vote of confidence in the House of Commons, that is, if its own members fail to provide majority support. Because the parties have considerable control over the nomination of candidates for election, individual legislators threaten defection from the parliamentary majority only at a substantial risk to their political careers. Nonetheless, if the government fails to respond to real constituency demands, as represented by legislators, they risk losing those seats in the following election to an opposition party that promises to resolve the issue at hand. But unlike the United States, where elections are part of a fixed two- and four-year cycle, there is no "safe" period for a British government. The safety of the parliamentary majority depends on the breadth of that majority. If the margin is narrow, the demands of a small group of legislators (backbenchers) are important to the maintenance of the government; it the margin is wide, it takes a much larger group of backbenchers to force the hand of government. These, then, are the electoral incentives that structure the government's response to constituencies where immigrants are concentrated.

The rise of anti-immigrant pressures

During World War II, Britain imported colonial labor to supplement its war effort. Although most of these immigrants were repatriated after the war, the poor economic conditions in their home countries prompted them to return to Britain. Jamaican citizens, who were familiar with Britain as a result of their wartime work, began to arrive in 1948. That flow was increased by the passage of the Walter-McCarran Act of 1952 in the United States, which changed the status of Jamaicans from British citizens (who had a large quota)

---

16. Thus swing constituencies are those with less than 10 percentage points difference between the two largest parties.

17. The United Kingdom has a bicameral legislature consisting of the House of Commons and the House of Lords. Various reforms of the House of Lords prevent it from vetoing legislation; it has only the power of delay. Because the upper house is relatively powerless, I exclude it from the analysis. See Tsebelis and Money 1997 for an analysis of relative house power.

Table 4.2. Immigration to Britain from New Commonwealth (NCW) countries, 1955–1962

Year	West Indies	India	Pakistan	Other NCW	Net flows	Gross flows	Gross alien flows
1955	27,550	5,800	1,850	7,500	42,700	76,150	
1956	29,800	5,600	2,050	9,400	46,850	84,780	
1957	23,020	6,620	5,170	7,590	42,400	80,750	
1958	15,020	6,200	4,690	3,990	29,900	67,890	
1959	16,390	2,930	860	1,420	21,600	64,110	
1960	39,670	5,920	2,500	9,610	57,700	116,500	32,218
1961	66,290	23,750	25,080	21,280	136,400	199,550	34,246
1962[a]	31,400	19,050	25,090	19,350	94,890	124,450	31,382

[a] First six months only, before the implementation of controls.

Source: Adapted from Davison 1966 for New Commonwealth figures; Institute of Race Relations 1969:17 for gross alien figures.

to Jamaican citizens, for whom there was a 200-person annual quota (Layton-Henry 1992). Indians and Pakistanis began arriving as well. They settled in London, in the industrial Midlands, and in the Northwest. The usual immigrant networks started to operate, facilitating the passage of both friends and family.

New Commonwealth (NCW) immigrants formed the largest part of the increase in immigration and in the foreign-born population in Britain. Between 1951 and 1966, they accounted for 60 percent of the increase in the foreign-born population in Britain, almost six hundred thousand in all (Jones and Smith 1970: chap. 2). Perhaps more important, for my purposes here, the pace of immigration picked up in 1960 and 1961. As the figures in Table 4.2 demonstrate, after declining from 1956 to 1959, both gross and net NCW immigration expanded on what appeared to be an exponential track in 1960 and 1961. Part of this growth can be attributed to economic expansion associated with the 1959 election year boom; another part can be attributed to the relaxation of exit controls in India, subsequent to its Supreme Court decision declaring exit controls unconstitutional, followed by Pakistan.[18] A significant proportion of the 1962 flow can be attributed to the efforts to "beat" the controls following the introduction of control legislation announced in October 1961. But the bulk of the previous increase could not have been generated by the debate in Britain. As Ronald Bell stated, when speaking for the government, "That campaign has been going on for eight years and I have a Ministerial statement made as long as eight years ago that

18. According to Butler, the home secretary who introduced the immigration control legislation, "the governments of the West Indies, India and Pakistan did their best to control the flow in 1958 and 1959" (*Hansard* 649:692).

the government were on the brink of introducing legislation. Does my honorable Friend think that there have been eight years of anticipatory rush?" (*Hansard* 649:782). In contrast, gross alien admissions during the same time frame were about one-quarter of gross New Commonwealth admissions and demonstrated no upward trend.

New Commonwealth immigration was increasing rapidly, but its impact was unevenly distributed among the British populace because the spatial distribution of the migrants was quite skewed. In the United Kingdom as a whole, the average number of NCW immigrants present in the population was 1.7 per 100, but the range among the 630 parliamentary constituencies was enormous.[19] Many constituencies had no NCW immigrants at all, and more than half of the constituencies had fewer than 1 NCW immigrant per 100 residents. On the other hand, 51 constituencies had NCW populations ranging from 5 to 15 percent.[20] Gordon Walker, in leading the opposition to the Conservative bill, acknowledged the "clotting" of the immigrant population, with 40 percent located in London and an additional 30 percent in the West Midlands. And as he remarked, "The position is worse than the figures show, because the immigrants are concentrated in small areas within larger conurbations" (*Hansard* 649:714). Figure 4.1 illustrates the distribution of the NCW population. Ninety percent of the constituencies had fewer than 3.2 NCW immigrants per 100 residents, whereas the remaining constituencies experienced much higher concentrations.

This "clotting" was aggravated by the tendency of NCW immigrants to settle in areas that attracted other immigrants as well. The proportion of NCW immigrants in the population is correlated at the 0.73 level for Irish immigrants and at the 0.51 level for aliens. Table 4.3 illustrates the concentration of the foreign-born population in London boroughs as well as the rate of increase. At the low end, the borough of Woolwich had 41 foreign born per 1,000 residents in 1951 and 44 in 1961. At the high end, the borough of Paddington had 208 per 1,000 residents in 1951 and 294 in 1961, an increase over the decade of 41 percent. Some boroughs, such as Islington, experienced increases of more than 100 percent, much of it in the most recent years.

Table 4.4 provides statistics for the spatial distribution of foreign-born residents in Britain as a whole, confirming the geographically concentrated nature of immigration. Some electoral constituencies had less than 1 immigrant per 100 residents whereas, combining NCW, alien, and Irish immi-

19. These statistics are drawn from the 1966 10 percent sample census, the first census in which the data were disaggregated by parliamentary constituencies. Given the reduction in immigration after the introduction of immigration control in 1962, these numbers provide a reasonable representation of both the volume and the distribution of the immigrant population in 1961.

20. This total corresponds closely to the fifty constituencies designated as "colour problem districts," selected on the basis of the electoral importance of the immigration issue. See Patterson for details (1969:417–22).

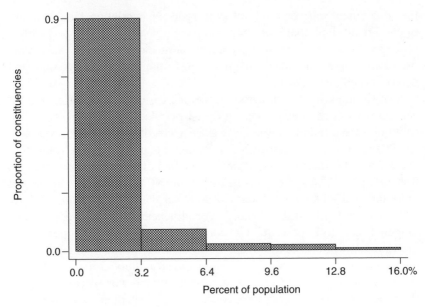

Figure 4.1. Distribution of New Commonwealth immigrants among British electoral constituencies, 1966. (*Source:* Great Britain, General Register Office, 1969.)

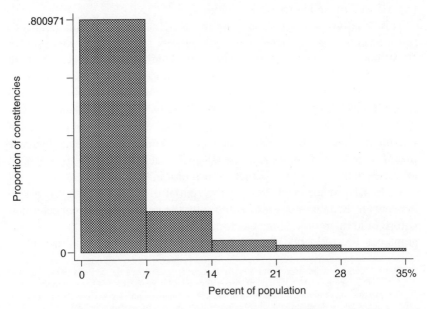

Figure 4.2. Distribution of foreign-born population (inclusive of Irish) among British electoral constituencies, 1966. (*Source:* Great Britain, General Register Office, 1969.)

Table 4.3. Resident immigrants in London, 1951–1961, by borough (per 1,000 population)

Borough	1951	1961	Percent increase
Paddington	208	294	41
Kensington	226	289	28
Hampstead	251	286	14
St. Marylbone	200	220	10
Westminster	187	203	9
St. Pancras	133	200	50
Islington	72	189	163
Holborn	174	197	13
Stoke Newington	105	192	83
Hammersmith	101	190	88
Chelsea	164	187	14
Hackney	88	142	61
Lambeth	70	138	97
Fulham	82	137	67
Stepney	123	136	10
Wandsworth	74	108	46
Finsbury	66	108	64
Battersea	46	101	119
Camberwell	42	84	100
Deptford	33	79	139
Southwark	49	75	53
Bermondsey	28	73	160
Bethnal Green	49	66	35
Poplar	34	61	79
Lewisham	34	58	71
Shoreditch	36	50	14
Greenwich	41	49	20
Woolwich	41	44	7

Source: Adapted from Davison 1966:20.

grants, some constituencies had as many as 35 foreign born per 100 residents, more than one in every three residents. Figure 4.2 shows that the total foreign-born population had the same type of geographic concentration as NCW immigrants alone. Of the 630 electoral constituencies, 106 had a combined alien and New Commonwealth immigrant population of more than 5 percent; at least 33 of these constituencies had a combined alien and NCW immigrant population of more than 10 percent. If the Irish are included, 120 constituencies had foreign-born populations of more than 7 percent.

Thus the British polity was faced with a concentrated and rising immigrant population. The question is how this affected the support for and opposition to immigration. Given the tight labor markets—vacancies continued to exceed unemployment—it is likely that support for immigration did not

Table 4.4. Percent of foreign-born population in 630 electoral constituencies of Great Britain, 1966 and 1981

Category	(1) Mean	(2) Standard deviation	Median	Minimum	(3) Maximum
1966					
New Commonwealth (1)	1.7%	2.5%	0.8%	0.0%	15.8%
Alien (2)	1.7	1.9	1.2	0.2	17.3
Irish (3)	1.9	1.8	1.3	0.1	14.5
Foreign 1 (1 + 2)	3.5	3.8	2.2	0.3	26.7
Foreign 2 (1 + 2 + 3)	5.3	5.8	3.5	0.5	34.8
1981					
New Commonwealth (1)	2.8	4.1	1.2	0.1	30.0
Alien (2)	1.8	1.9	1.3	0.3	20.1
Irish (3)	1.1	1.2	0.7	0.1	10.4
Foreign 1 (1 + 2)	4.6	5.2	2.7	0.4	33.4
Foreign 2 (1 + 2 + 3)	5.7	6.2	3.5	0.7	40.2

Source: Great Britain, General Register Office, *Census 1966* and *Census 1981.*

decline. Support for immigration was significant in Britain. As late as 1965, the government predicted labor shortages of two hundred thousand annually.[21] Declining industries, especially the northern textile companies, relied on immigrant labor to maintain their competitive advantage. And the British government itself was actively involved in recruiting immigrant labor for the London Transport and the National Health Service. The British Hotels and Restaurants Association also actively enlisted Commonwealth immigrants (Layton-Henry 1992).

Initially opposition appears to have been mild.[22] By most accounts, the immigrants were replacement workers; that is, they gained employment in industries deserted by the native labor force because of low wages and poor working conditions. They took up jobs in stagnant manufacturing industries, such as textiles and foundries, and in the service sector, in transport and in the National Health Service, that is, in exactly those industries characterized by low capital mobility. The newly arrived immigrants found housing in inner city areas that was vacated when the native workforce moved to more desirable suburban locations.

Recession, however, triggered opposition in areas of high immigrant con-

21. As reported in Dummett and Nicol 1990:195, "George Brown, Secretary of State at the Department of Economic Affairs, produced a National Plan for economic growth which included a demand for 200,000 extra workers in direct contradiction to the program limiting work vouchers to 8,500 per year."
22. An early sociological study of the relations between the indigenous and immigrant populations indicated limited opposition (Patterson 1963). Also see Layton-Henry 1987, who notes that in the early 1950s, "ordinary people in Britain seemed by no means intolerant of coloured people in their midst." These remarks do not necessarily mean that immigrants were widely welcomed, only that they were not actively opposed.

centration. The downturn in 1958 produced race riots in Nottingham (Birmingham) and London's Notting Hill district. But the 1959 election year economic boom undercut these tensions, and immigration was not actively debated during the campaign.[23] The 1961 recession triggered broader-based opposition. In April 1961, the chancellor of the exchequer introduced counterinflationary measures and supplemented these in July with a rise in the bank rate from 5 to 7 percent and a "pay pause." These anti-inflationary measures generated a recession that was only aggravated by the strikes that greeted the pay pause.

The recession intensified competition between the native and immigrant populations for both social services and employment. Zig Layton-Henry notes that despite very low unemployment rates, there was apparently some competition between the native and the immigrant workforces, a competition controlled in part through racist practices. Interestingly, and in support of the competition thesis, discrimination was strongest against "those with the best knowledge of the English language and the most qualifications— presumably, because they were competing for the better jobs" (Layton-Henry 1992:47).

Industrial restructuring contributed to labor market pressures for particular classes of workers in areas where immigrants were concentrated. Despite overall job creation, London and Birmingham were the only two cities to show postwar decline in manufacturing employment as manufacturers either went out of business or moved to the surrounding counties (Hoare 1983). The pressure was especially intense in Birmingham, where, in contrast to London, the economy was relatively undiversified. Because production was concentrated in consumer durables—automobiles—the region was especially sensitive to downturns in the economy and to the pay pause that reduced product demand. And despite the overall tightness of the labor markets, many of those displaced were those with the least resources, either financial or educational, to move to areas of economic growth. In reference to an inner city district of London, A. G. Hoare (1983:120) reported that 70 percent of the semi- and unskilled workers lived in the community where their plant closed. "Once unemployed, local ex-workers . . . lacked the money and the work skills to enable them to move." Therefore, local unemployment rose in particular districts despite low national unemployment rates.

Unemployment rates by constituency are unavailable. But data indicate that in April 1961, unemployment rates in London were more than double the national average, with a 1.3 percent unemployment rate in the nation as a whole against a 3.2 percent London average for native-born males and 2.5

23. This view is widely held. See Butler and Rose 1960 and Steel 1969.

percent for native-born females. Unemployment rates in London ranged from 4.4 to 7.4 percent for foreign-born males and 2.5 to 7.6 percent for foreign-born females (Davison 1966: chap. 5). Compared with today's unemployment rates, these may seem minuscule, but they were large by the standards of the day.

Labor market competition was aggravated by competition over state resources such as national assistance and council housing (Layton-Henry 1992:73). As a Conservative member of parliament (MP), Robin Turton (Thirsk and Malton), noted, even "where there is the problem of full employment . . . the position will arise in which there will be more people wanting jobs in a particular town than can be accommodated and looked after" (*Hansard* 649:756). This competition between the indigenous and immigrant populations was more fierce for New Commonwealth immigrants (as opposed to other aliens) because they were eligible for all available state services. Because the immigrant community invariably had higher levels of unemployment than the native workforce through the 1960s (Jones and Smith, 1970: chap. 3), constituents complained bitterly about "the number of coloured immigrants receiving national assistance" (Layton-Henry 1987). Tension also arose over housing. Immigrant access to council housing was normally limited by a five-year residence requirement. But slum removal required rehousing of slum occupants in council housing. Immigrants who settled in the city centers and occupied slums therefore leapfrogged over natives on the waiting list for council housing.

Schools, too, became crowded with children, many of whom spoke a foreign language. An Institute of Race Relations (1969) study from the 1960s reported the same concentration in schools as in the population at large.[24] In 9 percent of public primary and secondary schools immigrant pupils exceeded 10 percent of the student population; half of those (4.4 percent) had an immigrant student population exceeding 20 percent. Moreover, most of these students were from New Commonwealth countries. Aliens brought fewer dependents with them than the NCW immigrants, in part because rights of family reunification were not extended to aliens. Between 1960 and 1962, alien dependents were 7.2 percent of the gross flow. No comparable figures exist for NCW immigrants before control, but in the first full year of control when vouchers were relatively plentiful, dependents made up 48 percent of the gross flow (Institute of Race Relations 1969). Thus NCW immigrants availed themselves of a broader variety of state-supplied services. As with housing, education was a service

24. An "immigrant pupil" was defined as a child born outside the British Isles or a child born in the United Kingdom of foreign-born parents who immigrated within the last ten years. Children of "mixed" immigrant/indigenous parents and Irish children were excluded.

in short supply in Britain at a time when the government was reforming education and attempting to increase the number of students in secondary education.

Cultural competition is less amenable to quantitative measures than housing and education. Nonetheless, studies of immigrants, and NCW immigrants in particular, indicate that they had substantially different cultural mores, ranging from race, religion, and language, to food, clothing, music, and marital patterns (Patterson 1963, Pilkington 1988).

The change in structural conditions—high and rising immigration in concentrated areas, combined with local unemployment, immigrant access to social services, and the crowding of public facilities—is reflected in growing opposition to immigration in affected communities. Politicians became aware of this opposition and its political significance through various channels. Politicians in Britain, as elsewhere, focused most attention on marginal constituencies, that is, those that might defect to the opposition if their preferences were ignored. Yet it was often difficult to assess these preferences through public opinion polls because polls were either unavailable or failed to address critical issues until after they had already become politically significant. Moreover, national-level polls often failed to delineate clearly local concerns.[25] As a result, strategic politicians relied on a variety of indicators. One manifestation of constituencies' concerns was the organization of the local communities into political organizations such as the Birmingham Immigration Control Association, established in 1960. Another method of determining constituencies' preferences was communication with constituency representatives to the party, including members of Parliament from marginal constituencies. On immigration issues, Conservative MPs complained of the concentration of immigrants in their constituencies, the rate of increase in immigration, immigrant housing in areas of housing shortages, the rate of employment, and the educational problems (Conservative Party 1961).[26]

That these indicators were a reasonable gauge of anti-immigrant sentiment in constituencies is reflected in a retrospective analysis of public opinion. Public opinion polls in 1964 showed a substantial correlation (0.41) between the structural conditions defining anti-immigrant constituencies and the opinion that immigrants were a "problem" in the respondents'

25. National polls may be ineffective because local concerns do not reach the national level and so are overlooked. But even when local concerns are included in national polls, the polls are structured to evaluate national opinion and, therefore, without changes in sample selection, the statements about national opinion cannot be transferred to the local level.

26. The MPs themselves had several methods of gauging their constituencies' temperament. At least one, Toby Jessel, "organized a straw poll which found only one in ten of his constituents opposed to immigration control" (Foot 1965:137).

neighborhoods.[27] Thus changes in structural conditions are a reasonable indicator in the growth of anti-immigrant sentiment and were employed by the politicians themselves in gauging the political salience of immigration control.

Electoral incentives for immigration control, 1961–1962

In response to the growing recession during 1961, the Conservative Party's standing in the opinion polls dropped precipitously as the year progressed while Labour's standing rose. According to D. E. Butler and Anthony King (1965), "Ever since mid-1961 Labour had led the Conservatives in both Gallup and NOP [National Opinion Polls]." Thus the constituency pressures described above were framed in a broader analysis of Conservative electoral fortunes.

Initially, the backbench lobby in the Conservative Party was too small to represent a political threat to the party leadership. But as the 1959 election year boom petered out and turned to recession, the chorus of Conservative MPs, who represented constituencies with large concentrations of immigrants, grew. In 1950 Sir Cyril Osborne was apparently the lone Conservative voice in Parliament against immigration. He was joined in 1955 by Norman Pannell, Liverpool/Kirkdale, Harold Gurden, Selly Oak (Birmingham), and Martin Lindsay, Solihull (Birmingham). The 1959 elections added more Conservative MPs from marginal electoral constituencies with large immigrant populations (Foot 1965).[28] Examples included Leslie Cleaver of Birmingham, Sparkbrook, which had a 10.3 percent foreign-born population; Cleaver won by an electoral margin of 2.6 percent. John Hollingworth of Birmingham, All Saints, also had a large immigrant population in his constituency and won by a margin of less than 1 percent. In the constituency of Peckham, with a foreign-born population of 6.2 percent, Toby Jessel won the seat with a margin of 4.2 percent. Frank Taylor, representing Manchester Moss Side, with a 12.8 percent foreign-born population, also supported immigration control, although his was considered a safe Conservative seat. Pressure also came from unsuccessful Conservative candidates, such as Barbara Madden, who lost the election in Southhall, which had a foreign-born population of 12.3 percent, by the narrow margin of 5.4 percent. These individuals, both within and outside Parliament, had an impact on the

27. Public opinion data are from the Butler and Stokes (1972) 1964 polls and are combined with the 1966 census data to evaluate the effects of constituency characteristics on public opinion. The 1964 polls are the ones most proximate to the period under review that include questions on the political salience of immigration and residence locators necessary to match constituencies' characteristics with individual respondents. The 1966 and 1970 polls show a similar relationship.

28. See Deakin 1968 for an analysis of Labour backbenchers supporting immigration controls during the 1950s.

Conservative leadership because they represented or sought to represent constituencies that had to cope with large immigrant populations. Their situation is in clear distinction from that of Cyril Osborne, who had 1.4 percent foreign born in his constituency (Louth) and Norman Pannell from Liverpool Kirkdale with 0.7 percent foreign born.

These constituency pressures, combined with the drop in overall public support, correlate with the debate in the cabinet over immigration control legislation during the summer and fall of 1961 (Paul 1997, Spencer 1997). The government's recognition of electoral vulnerability to anti-immigrant constituencies came when, in preparation for the annual Conservative Party conference, 39 of the 576 motions submitted for discussion at the conference proposed immigration control (Foot 1965:136).[29] No longer were Osborne and Pannell alone in their racially biased campaign against Commonwealth immigration—MPs in electorally vulnerable constituencies were also demanding immigration control.

The Conservative Party had achieved a comfortable margin of fifty seats in the 1959 parliamentary elections.[30] But of the 106 constituencies with at least 5 percent foreign-born population, two-thirds were held by Conservative MPs, an indicator that despite accounts to the contrary, immigrants were concentrated in Conservative rather than Labour constituencies. Thus the leaders of the parliamentary Conservative Party, despite a comfortable electoral margin, faced potential opposition within their party that threatened their parliamentary majority.[31] As it turned out, the cabinet decided on 10 October to introduce controlling legislation, one day before the party conference that began on 11 October, but the public announcement awaited the queen's speech announcing the Conservative legislative program for the year (Paul 1997).[32]

Were there fifty seats to be lost to the opposition parties in a national election? In this initial period when the exact dimensions of public opposition were unclear, the margin was close enough so that, when confronting the

29. By comparison, only forty motions on the European Economic Community membership, a hotly disputed issue, were submitted. One lone pro-immigrant motion was submitted.

30. The margin here is the number of seats that would give the (combined) opposition a parliamentary majority. It is therefore one-half the margin described in Norton 1994.

31. This comfortable margin was reduced to a single vote, on a different issue, in March 1963, demonstrating the potential threat to the parliamentary majority (Butler and King 1965: chap. 1).

32. The issue was debated at the party conference, but the government's response by the secretary of state for the Home Department, R. A. B. Butler, indicated that "the final decision must be that of Her Majesty's government" (Conservative Party 1961:33). Nonetheless, he promised conference participants that "the government will pay the utmost attention to your expression of opinion." The Labour Party appeared to be taken by surprise. Gordon Walker, the opposition leader who led the parliamentary debate against the bill, objected to the "unseeming haste in preparation of the bill" (*Hansard* 649:705) as well as the fact that "other Commonwealth governments were informed—not consulted but just told . . . a week or so before the decision was announced to the Brighton conference" (*Hansard* 649:705).

issue, party leaders would be concerned. By conservative estimate, at least 36 of the 106 constituencies were swing constituencies, that is, ones that were highly contested by the Conservative and Labour parties.[33] Moreover, the system of single-member constituencies translated small swings in voting to large swings in parliamentary seats. This was the lesson preached by the Labour leader Hugh Gaitskell following his party's 1959 electoral defeat when he noted that, "on balance, fewer than three electors in every 200 had switched sides" (Butler and Rose 1960:196). This is not to claim that fifty seats were lost on the immigration issue in the following general election. But the potential was there, and the Conservative Party did lose the 1964 election despite its comfortable national electoral margin.

Thus, as a member of the opposition noted in the 1962 parliamentary debate on immigration control, "It may be that there is some electoral advantage in the position that the government have adopted" (Denis Howell, Labour, Birmingham Small Heath, *Hansard* 649:765). The cynical comment of Winston Churchill that "perhaps the cry of 'Keep Britain white' might be a good slogan" for future elections fought without his leadership came back to haunt Conservative leaders.[34] Recognizing the strength of the anti-immigrant lobby and its potential to undermine its parliamentary majority, the queen's speech delivered on 31 October 1961 included immigration control in the legislative agenda. The first reading of the bill was on 1 November, and the government proceeded quickly thereafter, pushing for final passage by 17 February 1962. The Commonwealth Immigration Act of 1962 created controls over Commonwealth citizens for the first time.

The controls were effective. Net NCW immigration in the six months before the implementation of the act was 94,890; for the six months after the act, it was less than one-tenth that level, 8,290. Part of this change was undoubtedly caused by the rush to beat immigration controls. After controls were implemented in July 1962, however, quotas served to limit dramatically Commonwealth immigration. Between July 1962 and December 1964, the United Kingdom received 444,263 applications for work vouchers; only 49,951 voucher holders were admitted (Foot 1965:253).

Electoral incentives for immigration control, 1964

Labour had vociferously opposed this control legislation but shifted its position when the party recognized the political consequences of its pro-immigration stance. The 1964 elections were critical in providing these polit-

33. Norton 1994 defined swing constituencies as those with less than 10 percentage points difference between the two largest parties. This definition has been adopted here although it may be conservative. See below for a Labour defeat in a supposedly "safe" constituency in 1965.
34. As reported in Harold Macmillan's memoirs and cited in Layton-Henry 1980:54.

ical lessons. All three parties, Labour, Liberal, and Conservative, preferred to avoid the immigration issue during the election campaign (Foot 1965, Singham 1965, Butler and King 1965). And most candidates who stood for election excluded immigration controls from their political platforms. Only 8 percent of Conservative candidates mentioned immigration or racial discrimination, as did 14 percent of Labour candidates and 3 percent of Liberal candidates.[35] No doubt the reason for these low percentages was that only 106 of 630 constituencies had immigrant populations exceeding 5 percent of the resident population.[36] Even fewer experienced structural shifts that modified the underlying preferences for immigration control.

The expectation that political positions will converge at the local level is reflected in two sample constituencies; both had concentrated immigrant communities but varied in underlying structural conditions and, therefore, in preferences. In Southhall (London), the Labour candidate was "defending such a slender majority, and having two candidates breathing so closely down his neck, it is, perhaps, not surprising that [he] moved to the right of official Labour policy on immigration" (Steel 1969:75). In Deptford (London), an independent candidate tried to raise the issue. Labour and Conservative candidates issued a joint statement: "We are united in regarding any attempt to incite racial or religious hatred as being utterly opposed to the . . . way of life in our country. We have learned that a third candidate . . . advocates the forcible repatriation of immigrants from the Commonwealth. We regard such a doctrine with the contempt that it deserves" (Steel 1969:77).

There are also examples of political learning. The constituency of Aston (Birmingham) was represented by a principled politician, Beaumont Dark, who refused to respond to the shift in constituent attitudes. He stated: "I have an immigrant problem in Aston, but I have gone out of my way to speak to the coloured immigrant population . . . I would not want a vote from anyone because I was against coloured immigrants. I would rather lose by 10,000, even 20,000 votes rather than be accused of being against immigrants" (Foot 1965:144). Dark lost his seat.

The adoption of an anti-immigrant stance by Labour at the national level can be attributed to the closeness of the election—a four-seat margin—and the potential that future by-elections might be fought on immigration issues. In this regard, the 1964 campaign fought in Smethwick (Birmingham) is instructive. Like other constituencies in the industrial Midlands, the area was undergoing economic restructuring. A recession in 1956 in the motor industry had produced layoffs, but the recently arrived immigrants migrated to other communities for employment. The 1959–1960 election year boom

---

35. As a basis of comparison, 89 percent, 93 percent, and 90 percent of the respective candidates mentioned education. See Butler and King 1965:143.
36. Also see the analysis of immigration issues in the 1964 election in Singham 1965.

induced the immigrant workers to return, this time with their families in tow, to settle permanently. The 1961 recession brought unemployment; by 1962, 10 percent of the immigrants were unemployed.

The 1964 campaign was waged by the Conservative Peter Griffiths on the immigration issue. The Labour candidate who had won the previous four elections, Gordon Walker, was the Labour shadow secretary who helped lead the opposition to the Conservatives' immigration control act. Not only did Walker lose the seat, but the Smethwick constituency experienced the largest swing toward the Conservative party of any constituency in an election when all but twenty-six constituencies swung toward Labour.[37]

With its margin of four seats, Labour vacated a "safe" seat to elect Gordon Walker so that he could join the cabinet. The constituency of Leyton was chosen in part because the electoral margin there was 16.8 percent, registered only a few months earlier. But that election was lost as well, and with it, the Labour margin shrank to two seats.[38] The lesson was learned. Even though immigration had played a marginal role in the overall election, it was important in a small number of constituencies, where by-elections promised to threaten Labour's parliamentary majority. In 1961, two by-elections were fought on immigration issues (Small Heath/Birmingham and Moss Side/Manchester), so this threat was real. It is not surprising, then, that the Labour Party reduced the annual quota of work vouchers from an average of 30,000 to 8,500 and brought out a White Paper endorsing immigration control.

Labour leaders privately acknowledged this electoral pressure. Richard Crossman, a Labour MP from the West Midlands, reported in his diary, "Ever since the Smethwick election it has been quite clear that immigration can be the greatest potential vote loser for the Labour party." Labour had "out-trump[ed] the Tories by doing what they would have done and so transforming their policy into a bipartisan policy" (quoted in Layton-Henry 1980:58). The Conservative Party offered a similar interpretation, one that emphasized the role of marginal constituencies. Their 1965 party conference proceedings recorded that "when [Labour] realized that continued opposition to the [Commonwealth Immigration] measure would probably lose them the election they executed a neat *volte face* and grudgingly supported a policy of control. Now, under pressure from their marginal seats, their recent White Paper includes a discriminatory system of arbitrary controls, in an effort to gain cheap electoral popularity" (Conservative Party 1965:79).

Immigration control periodically resurfaced on the political agenda, with the Labour and Conservative Parties vying to set ever more stringent stan-

---

37. Of the constituencies that swung against the tide for the Conservative Party, no swing was larger than 3.5% except Smethwick, which experienced a swing of 7.2% (Foot 1965).
38. Apparently the second election was not fought on immigration issues; its importance is to the narrowness of the parliamentary majority (Dummett and Nicol 1990).

dards. As unemployment grew, especially after the 1973–74 oil shock, the number of anti-immigrant constituencies grew as well, as did the British National Front. In addition, the pro-immigrant sentiment collapsed as unemployment relieved pressure on British wages. Election contests did not need to turn on four seats for constituency pressures to be felt. The two parties did diverge on integration policy, with Labour taking a more egalitarian position, supporting race relations legislation and nondiscriminatory immigration legislation while the Conservatives supported positions that restricted settled immigrants' rights of family reunion, among others.[39]

Electoral incentives for immigration control, 1974–1979

After a four-year hiatus, Labour returned to power in February 1974 with a minority government and, after obtaining a narrow parliamentary majority in October 1974, retained power for the next five years. Yet the party failed to introduce additional immigration control legislation. The inactivity of the Labour majority on immigration control issues between 1974 and 1979 appears puzzling for several reasons.

First, Labour promised in both its general election manifestos of 1974 to review the issue of immigration associated with British citizenship and to pass appropriate legislation (Craig 1990:192, 197–98). Moreover, the Labour government published in 1977 a Green Paper that developed a restrictive notion of citizenship—a definition adopted in subsequent Conservative legislation on British citizenship—yet failed to introduce the legislation during its five years as majority parliamentary party. Second, despite its narrow parliamentary majority that ultimately disintegrated into a minority government, Labour had implemented most of its "fairly radical" legislative program, leaving only a few election campaign promises unfulfilled (Butler and Kavanagh 1980). Among the few that were not implemented were additional immigration controls promised in the election manifestos.

Third, this was a period in British history when anti-immigrant sentiment was widely perceived to be substantial. One indicator was the rising prominence of the National Front, an anti-immigrant party, culminating in electoral success in the Greater London Council elections of 1977. This was also a period of economic recession and high unemployment generated in part by the oil shock of 1973. The Conservative Party certainly perceived a potential electoral draw, and the recently elected party leader, Margaret Thatcher, delivered her famous "swamping" comments on nationwide television in January 1978; in that interview she offered sympathy for the indigenous white

---

39. Given Labour's position on egalitarian treatment, its position on immigration control should have been even more restrictive than the Conservative position. For Labour, granting a single work voucher implied the immigration of a family unit whereas for the Conservatives, it implied only one immigrant.

population forced to interact with the immigrants, implying additional controls under a Conservative majority.

And, fourth, Labour's electoral margin was razor thin. The February 1974 elections produced a minority Labour government, and the October elections provided Labour with a slim majority of three, the same narrow margin that, I suggested earlier, caused Labour to cave in to anti-immigrant interests concentrated in a small number of constituencies. By April 1976, by-election losses and defections deprived the government of its majority. All of these factors suggest that constituency pressures would be sufficient to persuade Labour to introduce additional immigration controls. The lack of legislation, I believe, was due to a pact with the Liberal Party that enabled the Labour government to remain in power for almost the full five-year electoral term. Because of the Liberals' pro-immigrant stance, however, the alliance prevented Labour from introducing immigration control legislation.

The Liberals' "liberal" credentials on immigration control were well established in 1974 (FitzGerald and Layton-Henry 1986). They fought beside Labour against the original 1962 act and maintained their position in 1968, against the Labour majority, and again in 1971, against the Conservative majority. The consensus on immigration control shared by Labour and Conservatives excluded the Liberal Party. David Steel, elected party leader in 1976, not only led the parliamentary and extraparliamentary campaign against the 1968 act, but he also continued his campaign in print, including a book on Commonwealth immigration and control in Britain (Steel 1969). Both the February 1974 and the 1979 Liberal general election manifestos promised to repeal those clauses of the 1971 act that negated obligations to citizens of the United Kingdom and colonies and "to abolish the discrimination against non-patrials which creates second-class citizens" (Craig 1990:207–8, 310).

Liberals were free from anti-immigrant pressure to a large extent because their electoral constituencies were predominantly rural and contained few, if any, immigrants. Because the structural conditions in parliamentary constituencies are correlated with and provide a reasonable representation of anti-immigrant sentiment, these figures are shown in Table 4.5, which lists majority Liberal constituences in any one of the 1974 and 1979 elections and the percentage of foreign born in both the 1966 and 1981 censuses.[40] In the post–World War II heyday of Liberal electoral success, when the Liberals

---

40. As I suggested earlier, these structural indicators provided a rule of thumb to politicians in evaluating constituency demands. Individual-level data support the contention that these indicators were correlated with anti-immigrant sentiment in the 1960s; appropriate polls, merged with census data, are unavailable for this later period. Appropriate polls must include questions on attitudes toward immigration as well as the political salience of immigration issues. Moreover, the polls must include a residence locator by political constituency. Therefore, I rely on the correspondence between structural conditions and public opinion established in the preceding section.

Table 4.5. Anti-immigrant pressures in British Liberal constituencies, 1974–1979

Constituency	Percent New Commonwealth immigrants		Percent New Commonwealth immigrants and "aliens"[a]		Anti-immigrant sentiment[a]		Swing		
								1974		1979
	1966	1981	1966	1981	1966	1981	Feb.	Oct.	
Isle of Ely/Cambridgeshire Feb., Oct. 1974; 1979	0.2	0.6	1.0	1.5	1.1	16.0	No	Yes	Yes
Truro Oct. 1974; 1979	0.6	0.8	1.6	2.0	1.8	21.0	n.a.	Yes	No
Rochdale Feb., Oct. 1974; 1979	2.5	6.5	5.2	8.5	4.7	144.6	No	Yes	Yes
Berwick, Northumberland Feb., Oct. 1974; 1979	0.4	0.4	1.0	1.2	1.4	11.6	Yes	Yes	No
Isle of Wight Feb., Oct. 1974; 1979	1.0	0.9	2.3	2.3	3.5	27.3	No	Yes	Yes
Colne Valley Feb., Oct. 1974	0.1	2.7	0.8	3.7	0.5	38.0	Yes	Yes	Yes
Cardigan/Ceredigion & Pembroke Feb., Oct. 1974; 1979	0.4	0.7	1.5	1.7	2.7	18.3	Yes	Yes	Yes

(Table continues)

Table 4.5. (Continued)

Constituency	Percent New Commonwealth immigrants		Percent New Commonwealth immigrants and "aliens"		Anti-immigrant sentiment[a]		Swing		
							1974		
	1966	1981	1966	1981	1966	1981	Feb.	Oct.	1979
Inverness Feb., Oct. 1974	0.6	0.6	1.4	1.8	3.4	21.1	No	Yes	Yes
Orkey & Zetland Feb., Oct. 1974; 1979	0.2	0.4	0.6	1.2	1.6	7.7	No	No	No
Roxburgh/Tweeddale, Ettrick & Lauderdale Feb., Oct. 1974; 1979	0.4	0.5	1.8	2.1	1.3	16.0	No	No	No
Hazel Grove Feb. 1974	n.a.	0.6	n.a.	1.4	n.a.	11.4	Yes	n.a.	n.a.
Bodmin/Cornwall Northeast Feb. 1974	0.9	0.9	1.8	1.8	3.1	19.8	Yes	n.a.	n.a.
Cornwall North Feb., Oct. 1974	0.9	0.8	2.4	1.9	1.9	25.4	No	Yes	n.a.
Devon North Feb., Oct. 1974	0.9	0.8	1.8	1.7	2.3	15.9	No	No	n.a.
Montgomery Feb., Oct. 1974	0.1	0.4	0.7	1.1	0.8	9.7	No	No	n.a

[a]Measured by (% New Commonwealth immigrants + Aliens) × Unemployment.

garnered 20 percent of the national vote, the single-member constituency electoral system permitted only fourteen electoral victories at a maximum, most in swing constituencies. All the Liberal constituencies, with one exception (Rochdale), had low levels of immigrants. Because we rely on census data for the constituency-level characteristics, we do not have indicators of unemployment rates for this period. But if earlier and later levels of unemployment are indicative of average unemployment rates, at least half of the constituencies could be considered pro-immigrant and only one Liberal constituency might meet the criteria associated with anti-immigrant pressures (Rochdale, and that only in 1981).

As the Labour majority dwindled during the course of the electoral term, the Conservative Party tabled a no-confidence vote in March 1977. The Labour prime minister, James Callaghan, defeated the vote of no confidence, by negotiating a "Lib-Lab" pact, initially for six months and ultimately renewed for a total of eighteen months, in the middle of the Parliament, from March 1977 to September 1978. The Liberals were to be consulted in advance on all major policy initiatives, providing an informal veto over legislation. It followed that not only was Labour unable to introduce its own legislation on British citizenship, "in April 1978 an All Party Parliamentary Select Committee called for stricter controls on entry as well as internal controls and a quota for the Indian subcontinent, but this was disowned by the Home secretary" (Butler and Kavanagh 1980: chap. 2).

Another plausible explanation for Labour's about-face on immigration control is related to its efforts to cater to the immigrant or black population (FitzGerald 1984, 1987, FitzGerald and Layton-Henry 1986). Public opinion polls, however, suggest that the black population was only slightly more open to immigration than the indigenous population and that less than 10 percent of the population of any race favored greater immigration levels. Table 4.6 illustrates that, in 1983, majorities of both "whites" and "nonwhites" wanted fewer Asian and West Indian immigrants, and the same majorities favored the current level of Australian and European immigration, perhaps corresponding to the empirical pattern of higher levels of immigration of Asians and West Indians (British Social Attitudes Survey 1983). In two of the four cases, attitudes toward immigration were not statistically different. It seems unlikely, then, that Labour was responding to pressures from black constituencies.

I have discovered no statements by Liberal and Labour ministers to the effect that Liberals prevented Labour from introducing immigration control legislation. Nonetheless, the "liberal" impact of the Lib-Lab parliamentary pact is consistent with the absence of immigration control legislation by Labour in this period whereas alternative explanations are unsatisfactory.

Table 4.6. British public opinion on immigration, 1983

Responses to the following question: Britain controls the number of people from abroad that are allowed to settle in this country. Please say, for *each* of the groups below, whether you think Britain should allow more settlement, less settlement, or about the same amount as now.

Indians and Pakistanis	Less	Same	More
White respondents	73%	26%	1%
Nonwhite respondents	50%	43%	7%

$0^2 = 25.2812, p = 0.00$
$N = 1,624$

West Indians	Less	Same	More
White respondents	69%	30%	2%
Nonwhite respondents	52%	39%	9%

$0^2 = 24.0065, p = 0.00$
$N = 1,594$

Australians and New Zealanders	Less	Same	More
White respondents	28%	56%	16%
Nonwhite respondents	21%	67%	12%

$0^2 = 3.6892, p = 0.16$
$N = 1,622$

People from European Community countries	Less	Same	More
White respondents	45%	48%	7%
Nonwhite respondents	36%	59%	6%

$0^2 = 3.4861, p = 0.18$
$N = 1,615$

Source: British Social Attitudes Survey 1983.

Maintenance of the immigration control status quo did not preclude continued Labour support for integration of immigrants. Labour introduced three Race Relations Acts (1965, 1968, and 1976) outlawing racial discrimination in various arenas and providing penalities for discriminatory behavior. Moreover, the Labour government attempted to apply immigration controls more equitably, as when it modified the regulations in 1974 to grant women residents the same rights of family reunification as those available to men.[41] Equitable treatment was a concern of immigrant voters and may explain why they tended to support the Labour Party regardless of its position on immigration control. But these measures were not and should not be understood as efforts to expand British immigration.

Electoral incentives for immigration control, 1979

The constraints binding Labour did not apply to the Conservative Party. The Conservative leader and later prime minister, Thatcher, in particular, actively employed the immigration issue to defuse the electoral threat of the National Front and to attract National Front voters, as well as to claim the loyalties of previous Labour voters. Immigration control has been a consistent theme in Conservative Party general election manifestos since it first introduced control legislation in 1961.[42] The 1979 manifesto included a detailed and draconian eight-point program that limited entry of parents and adult children of settled migrants, revoked equal treatment of partners of women citizens and settled migrants, and proposed a register of Commonwealth dependents entitled to entry under the 1971 Immigration Act (Craig 1990:276–77).

For the Conservative Party, the structural conditions producing anti-immigrant sentiment had only continued to grow over the intervening period, primarily because of the rapid rise in unemployment and the growing concentration of immigrant communities rather than an overall increase in immigrants. A comparison of the 1981 census data with those of 1966 is instructive (Table 4.4). The average New Commonwealth population per constituency rose from 1.7 to 2.8 percent while the average "alien" population rose from 1.7 to 1.8 percent, and the Irish immigrant population actually dropped from 1.9 to 1.1 percent. So the total average foreign-born population actually rose only 0.4 percent, from 5.3 to 5.7 percent of the resident population. But that population tended to become more concentrated, as indicated by higher maximums in all categories, except the Irish, and a doubling of the maximum of NCW population from 15.8 to 30 percent. The unemployment rate skyrocketed from 1.2 percent in 1966 to 11.8 percent in 1981. From the constituency perspective, the unemployment rate varied enormously, with a 4.1 percent minimum and a 36.0 percent maximum.

Because the structural conditions in parliamentary constituencies are cor-

41. These regulations were reversed by a later Conservative government, triggering a suit in the European Court of Justice. In light of the court's finding of discrimination, the Conservative government revoked all rights of family reunification rather than extend equal privileges to men and women alike (Layton-Henry 1994).
42. A minor exception to the Conservatives' rather uniform immigration control policy is the admission of twenty-seven thousand Asians expelled from Uganda in 1972. These immigrants may be understood best as refugee admissions which, until the refugee and asylum crisis in Europe, were governed by different political processes.

Table 4.7. Coefficients of correlation among location of foreign-born population, unemployment, and "anti-immigrant" constituencies in Britain, 1966 and 1981

	NCW	Aliens	Irish	For. 1	For. 2	Unempl.	Anti 1[a]	Anti 2[a]	Anti 3[a]
1966									
NCW (1)	1.00								
Aliens (2)	0.51	1.00							
Irish (3)	0.73	0.52	1.00						
Foreign 1 (1 + 2)	0.91	0.83	0.74	1.00					
Foreign 2 (1 + 2 + 3)	0.91	0.77	0.87	0.97	1.00				
Unemployment	−0.11	−0.18	−0.01	−0.16	−0.12	1.00			
Anti-immigrant 1[a]	0.85	0.40	0.68	0.75	0.78	0.20	1.00		
Anti-immigrant 2[a]	0.77	0.61	0.68	0.81	0.82	0.25	0.94	1.00	
Anti-immigrant 3[a]	0.66	0.48	0.74	0.67	0.74	0.41	0.88	0.93	1.00
1981									
NCW (1)	1.00								
Aliens (2)	0.41	1.00							
Irish (3)	0.71	0.58	1.00						
Foreign 1 (1 + 2)	0.94	0.70	0.77	1.00					
Foreign 2 (1 + 2 + 3)	0.93	0.70	0.84	0.99	1.00				
Unemployment	0.17	−0.17	0.16	0.07	0.09	1.00			
Anti-immigrant 1[a]	0.92	0.29	0.65	0.83	0.83	0.36	1.00		
Anti-immigrant 2[a]	0.91	0.50	0.74	0.91	0.91	0.35	0.97	1.00	
Anti-immigrant 3[a]	0.89	0.50	0.80	0.89	0.90	0.37	0.95	0.99	1.00

[a] Anti-immigrant measures are created by multiplying three measures of immigrant concentration—NCW, Foreign 1, and Foreign 2—by the unemployment rate.
Source: Great Britain, General Register Office, *Census 1966* and *Census 1981.*

related with and provide a reasonable representation of anti-immigrant sentiment, these figures are shown in Table 4.7. Given the close temporal relationship between the 1981 census and the introduction of the British Nationality Act in January 1981, the calculation of anti-immigrant constituencies, focusing on the interaction between the level of immigrants and the rate of unemployment, is feasible. Three measures of anti-immigrant constituencies were calculated, based on New Commonwealth immigration and unemployment (anti-immigrant 1), NCW and "alien" immigration and unemployment (anti-immigrant 2), and total foreign born and unemployment (anti-immigrant 3). All three scores are highly correlated. The anti-immigrant scores based on New Commonwealth and "alien" immigration range from 5 to 693 with a mean of 56 and a median of 25, indicating the same skewed pattern of distribution as the immigrant population. The top one hundred anti-immigrant constituencies had scores of more than 85, or three times the median score; the top fifty anti-immigrant constituencies had scores of more than 170, or six times the median score. Thirty-four anti-immigrant constituencies were also swing constituencies.

The anti-immigrant score is a quite different measure of anti-immigrant sentiment than either the presence of an immigrant population alone or unemployment alone. Unemployment and immigrant concentration are not highly related. As Table 4.7 indicates, there was a slight negative correlation between unemployment and the various measures of immigrant concentration in 1966, a relationship that changed to a slightly positive one by 1981. Anti-immigrant sentiment rises and falls with the unemployment rate but is only moderated related to the unemployment rate. Anti-immigrant sentiment, however, tends to be concentrated in those areas of NCW immigration ($r = 0.89$ to 0.92 depending on measures) and in areas where NCW immigration is compounded by alien and Irish immigration ($r = 0.83$ to 0.91 depending on measure). Thus, on an individual level, it is not surprising that neither unemployment nor the presence of an immigrant community generates anti-immigrant sentiments while the combination of the two can explain that phenomenon.

Given the electoral competition between the Labour and Conservative Parties and the Conservative national margin in the 1979 election of twenty-two constituencies, it is not surprising to find that the Conservative Party quickly moved to implement its promised immigration controls both through changes in immigration rules in December 1979 and in the British Nationality Act of 1981 (FitzGerald and Layton-Henry 1986).

Legislation restricting immigration into Britain was first passed in the early 1960s, in an era of relative prosperity and full employment. I suggest that the pressure for this legislation arose from a localized response to a concentrated immigrant population that threatened employment opportunities and, more important, access to scarce government resources. As the British economy adjusted to international market forces and unemployment became more widespread, anti-immigrant sentiment grew and overwhelmed the dwindling support for immigration. Support for anti-immigrant parties such as the National Front, however, remained geographically concentrated in areas that experienced both high unemployment and relatively large immigrant communities. Mainstream political parties, threatened with the loss of political support on a local level, adopted immigration control policies to retain or gain power at the national level.

Literature on British Immigration Control

The politics of immigration and race have elicited a large literature in Britain, and much of my argument is consonant with those analyses. For example, Paul Foot (1965), Ann Dummett and Andrew Nicol (1990), and Zig Layton-Henry (1980) all point to Labour's narrow electoral margin and the Smethwick campaign to explain the timing of Labour's conversion to immigration control. Nonetheless, this literature differs in both emphasis and theoretical focus from the framework I presented in Chapter 3 and employed to analyze British immigration control policy.

Much of the literature on British immigration policy agrees with the broader immigration literature that immigration controls are introduced in response to public opinion and in defense of national identity, in this case, a national identity based largely on a common "white" ethnicity.[43] Layton-Henry (1985:95), for example, argues that "British policy makers were very aware, from the beginning, of the problems of racial prejudice." According to Foot (1965:230), "Resentment and propaganda is directed almost exclusively against the *coloured* immigrant." Dummett and Nicol (1990) point to "theories of nationhood." But because racism is interpreted as a constant attribute of the British populace, these analysts introduce additional elements to account for an early period of openness to New Commonwealth immigration, the more or less consensual agreement between the Labour and Conservative Parties to regulate and restrict New Commonwealth immigration in the 1960s, and finally the divergence of policy positions between the two parties in the 1970s. I return to the issue of racism below, but first I address the "intervening" variables.

Some analysts attribute a large role to the 1958 riots in Notting Hill and Nottingham as bringing immigration and race to the public eye and catalyzing the issue on the political agenda. For example, Layton-Henry (1985) suggests that "plans for control were shelved until the racial disturbances in 1958."[44] Certainly this perception contains some elements of truth. Yet earlier race riots—in Liverpool in 1948, in Birmingham and Deptford (London) in 1949, and for two full days in Camden Town (London) in 1954—failed to elicit the implementation of immigration controls (Layton-Henry 1992). Moreover, it is difficult to explain why three years elapsed between the riots and the introduction of control legislation in the fall of 1961. Policy lag cannot explain this delay, especially since the Conservative government presented clear statements of its opposition to immigration control as late as February 1961.

Analysts also point to Commonwealth relations as a reason for postponing control legislation (Foot 1965, Layton-Henry 1985, Hammar 1985, Freeman 1979). Certainly, the Labour Party opposition was couched in terms of the effect of immigration control on Commonwealth relations (*Hansard* 649:687–820). Yet there is nothing that distinguishes 1961 from any other year that makes it appear a more opportune time to introduce Commonwealth immigration controls. Moreover, the Conservative government could have smoothed Commonwealth relations through a process of consultation: that

43. See references in n. 12.
44. See also Cooper and Martucelli 1994.

opportunity had been available earlier in the year at the spring conference of Commonwealth ministers or could have been made available by postponing the introduction of the legislation. But the political imperatives proved too strong.

Britain had concurrently entered negotiations for membership in the European Economic Community, a move that was closely discussed with Commonwealth members. But there is nothing to suggest that these negotiations affected the timing of immigration control. Membership would have meant openness to migrants from Europe, and Italy was still an exporter of labor to northern Europe. But even if the bid for EC membership had been successful, there would have been an extended period of harmonization, delaying immigration from the Continent.[45] And there is no indication that Commonwealth immigration was subject to treaty negotiations. At the time, both France and Germany were negotiating bilateral labor agreements with Mediterranean countries to increase their supply of immigrant labor and may have welcomed additional sources of immigrant labor. In any event, Charles de Gaulle vetoed Britain's application in 1962, so these negotiations could not have played into the Labour decision to adopt immigration control. It is true that since World War II, Britain gradually shifted its economic and political focus away from the Commonwealth and toward Europe. But this observation provides little on which to hang the 1961 shift in Commonwealth immigration controls.

Others have argued that Britain was more sensitive to the social costs of migration and therefore less receptive to the economic benefits of migration than other nations (Freeman 1979, Layton-Henry 1985). If this is true, the question then moves one step back to the issue of why Britain was more sensitive than other countries. The theoretical framework presented here provides an answer. This answer is not racism per se but the difference in immigration streams generated by Commonwealth migrants and their access to public goods. Unlike some of the guest worker programs that were common on the Continent, Commonwealth migration brought in families who had access to the British infrastructure of health, education, and other public goods. In the longer term, immigrants' economic contributions to the provision of these services offsets their use, but, in the short term, crowding may occur and increases the competition between the indigenous and immigrant populations. German guest workers during the 1960s were single men housed at the worksite in company housing and thus represented much less of a strain on the German public infrastructure. In this case, my argument is consonant with the sensitivity thesis but provides a comparative basis for analyzing the level of sensitivity.

---

45. Even the original members were not scheduled to complete the transition to free labor movement until 1968.

My analysis also differs from studies such as those of Ira Katznelson (1973) and Anthony Messina (1989) that argue that the mainstream parties depoliticized immigration and race policy during the 1960s. These authors observe that a "tacit agreement [existed between the Conservative and Labour Parties] to exclude certain issues from the national political agenda" and label immigration policy "a conspiracy of silence" (Messina 1989:10). Messina (1989:173), in particular, addresses the political incentives for politicians to exclude controversial issues from the agenda: "It is primarily the drive and realistic opportunity for political office in highly electorally competitive circumstances which motivates potential parties of government to ignore small and potentially divisive cross-cutting interests." My argument also hinges on electoral incentives but points out the conditions under which it pays to address these issues as well as the circumstances that would allow parties to ignore them.

Where Messina and Katznelson observe depoliticization, I observe a policy consensus. Although often similar in appearance, these two characterizations of politics can be distinguished empirically. The real question is whether immigration policy was debated as a public issue in Britain. It is hard to avoid an answer of yes. The evidence presented here suggests that the issue was debated regularly in the cabinet, in Parliament, and in the press. The 1968 Commonwealth Immigrants Act elicited parliamentary and extra-parliamentary opposition and debate. Enoch Powell, despite his ejection from the shadow cabinet, remained in the public eye. The 1970s brought the rise of the National Front as well as the Anti-Nazi League organized to combat the National Front. Moreover, these pressures and counterpressures were not ignored but balanced by the governments of the day in devising immigration control policies, although, in accordance with my theoretical framework, each voice was not equally weighted. In comparison to Europe during the same time frame, immigration issues in Britain appear highly politicized.

Where Katznelson and Messina observe repoliticization, I observe a second and distinctive immigration issue dimension. Although the Labour and Conservative Parties did share a consensus on immigration control, they differed on issues of immigrant integration. Labour was a proponent of government intervention to ensure equality of treatment whereas the Tories opposed such intervention. Thus the repoliticization during the late 1970s and 1980s noted by Messina can be attributed to policy disparities on immigrant integration and racial discrimination rather than to differences over immigration control. For example, Labour's platform to reform the 1971 Immigration Act was not oriented toward more permissive entrance but toward nondiscriminatory treatment of immigrants.

My argument comes down on the side of those who, like Donley Studlar

(1978, 1980), argue that public opinion had been neither manipulated nor ignored by the political elite. But this does not mean that there is a one-to-one correspondence between public opinion and policy outputs. Rather, societal preferences are filtered through the political system that weighs support for and opposition to immigration according to local and national conditions. In 1961, the rapid influx of Commonwealth immigrants—with families in tow—combined with economic recession to create a significant number of anti-immigrant constituencies. The Conservative government responded with increased restrictions despite a comfortable electoral margin. In 1964, as controls fell into place to reduce the flow of migrants in an era of economic growth, the number of anti-immigrant constituencies diminished. But the narrow national electoral margin forced the Labour government to weigh a small number of constituencies much more heavily. Principled or unprincipled, politicians respond to the particular set of electoral incentives created by the geographic concentration of immigrants and the national political institutions. Moreover, in the absence of these conditions, we should expect the political saliency of immigration to diminish, so that Nicholas Deakin's (1969) analysis that immigration did not play a role in the 1966 general elections should come as no surprise.

My explanation differs from those of analysts who point to the political elite as the source of immigration control policy by manipulating both policy and public opinion to achieve particular personal or political ends (Bulpit 1986, Foot 1965, Freeman 1979, Hammar 1985, Katznelson 1973, Layton-Henry 1985, Messina 1989). In particular, two books that propound an elite-centered thesis were published in 1997, based on newly available archival material. The fact that the two books interpret these sources differently suggests that the archival material does not lead to a definitive intepretation.

Kathleen Paul (1997) provides the more intriguing argument, that the political elite were trapped between a hope of maintaining British power and international prestige through the reinforcement of empire and Commonwealth and a racist desire to prevent coloured immigrants from entering Britain. The conflict was resolved, Paul argues, by manipulating public opinion to generate opposition to immigration that could be employed to justify the imposition of controls.

Paul provides an interesting account of the different types of "Britishness" maintained under the theoretical equality of British subjects, noting the long-standing distinctions based on sex and class, as well as race. After World War II, these distinctions were maintained for Irish, European, and New Commonwealth immigrants, as well.[46] Moreover, she has provided documenta-

---

46. The distinctions between the treatment of European and NCW immigrants are exaggerated through the presentation of noncomparable data, gross intakes for Europeans and net intakes for NCW immigrants. Paul is correct in pointing out the unique treatment of the Irish.

tion that the political elite were racist in their concern over coloured immigration to Britain. Nonetheless, if elites manipulated public opinion, they were singularly ineffective. If, as Paul suggests, concern arose when the first NCW immigrants arrived in 1948, it was some fourteen years later that public opinion was deemed sufficiently prepared for immigration control.

In the absence of public opinion data, it is difficult to prove (or disprove) that the elite attempted to and was successful at manipulating public opinion. But it is possible to point out the diversity of elite opinion: the elite chorus was singing more than one tune. The cabinet, the Conservative Party, the Labour opposition, and the media presented conflicting messages about the problems and promises of NCW immigration, as Paul herself documents. These conflicting messages suggest that the link between the political elite and public opinion is very tenuous. In contrast, I have provided measures of the pressures created by the influx of immigrants, both NCW and alien. These measures correspond temporally to the organization of anti-immigrant groups and to the increase in the number of MPs who placed immigration control high on the political agenda. Thus there is clear evidence that ties the shift in organized public opinion more closely to concrete events than to an amorphous, decade-long effort to generate racist, anti-immigrant attitudes among a "liberal" population.

Ian Spencer's (1997) argument is more straightforward. According to his line of reasoning, the political elite was sensitive to the number of NCW immigrants arriving. As the number grew in 1955, control legislation was drafted, only to be shelved when the volume of NCW immigrants subsided. The surge of immigration in 1960 and 1961 was larger and perceived as more permanent because of the breakdown of administrative controls over immigration in the NCW countries. Therefore, the rise in numbers triggered the introduction of controls, although, in contrast to my emphasis, the legislation anticipated anti-immigrant sentiment rather than responded to it. Here again, the evidence I present suggests that immigration pressures were real although confined to a small number of constituencies and that MPs and, ultimately, party leaders responded to these real pressures rather than anticipated ones.

More generally, I do not refute the existence of elite preferences. Rather, I specify the set of political constraints within which politicians must work in order to retain power. It is only when those preferences run counter to electoral incentives that politicians must choose between responding to electoral incentives and losing office. One measure of the value of a theory is its ability to subsume competing explanations in a single, overarching framework. The framework presented here is a way of reconciling the disparate observations of analysts who emphasize public opinion and those who emphasize political elites as the determinants of immigration control policy. It specifies the set of conditions under which both elite and societal preferences, both pro- and anti-immigrant, are translated into policy outcomes.

Finally, I remind the reader that my framework may not shed light on all the controversy surrounding the politics of immigration control in Britain. Part of the remaining puzzle deals with the role of racism. Whether taking the societal or elite approach, much of the literature on British immigration policy adopts the thesis of the broader immigration literature that immigration controls are introduced in defense of national identity, in this case, a national identity based largely on a common white ethnicity.[47] And the legislation discussed here was racist in the sense that it obstructed coloured immigration from Commonwealth countries. But it was also, and I believe primarily, anti-immigrant. The epithet, "black Irish!" hurled at New Commonwealth immigrants as early as 1956, captures the dual nature of the issue. New Commonwealth immigrants were resented because of their color but also resented as a growing immigrant presence. This was because coloured rather than white immigration was expanding and because it was more concentrated than the white immigration. The 1961 parliamentary debate on the Commonwealth Immigration Act describe similar opposition to white immigration in an earlier era well remembered by participants in the debate. Gordon Walker (Smethwick), a leader of the opposition debate, recalled that "in Oxford all the things that are now said about immigrants were said about the Welsh" (*Hansard* 649:715). James MacColl (Labour, Widnes) remembered a time in Paddington, "where we had all the problems of migration, the problems of the Irish and of the Welsh coming into areas and creating the same kind of difficulties that we have today" (*Hansard* 649:772). These statements suggest that color is only one of the attributes of immigrants and may not be the most prominent source of resentment and that, as Layton-Henry (1992:8) notes, "the response to alien and colonial immigrants has been remarkably similar."

Furthermore, most white immigration was more strictly controlled than Commonwealth immigration and the volume was smaller. For example, aliens were already subordinated to work vouchers and quotas under the 1953 Aliens Order of the 1919 Aliens Immigration Act (Macdonald and Blake 1991). The 1962 act modified policies of Commonwealth immigration—which was completely uncontrolled—to match more closely those pertaining to other aliens. The only relaxation of immigration legislation was for European Community citizens after British accession in 1973. The lack of controversy over this relaxation of immigration controls can be attributed to the small potential flow of EC immigrants given Britain's status as one of

---

47. See references in n. 12. For an opposing argument that attributes problems to immigration, not color, see Patterson 1963.

the poorer EC member states. Clearly race and immigration are intertwined and racism is a problem in most, if not all, societies, but it would be useful to untangle the relationship between racism and immigration rather than to obscure the relationship by treating the two concepts as identical.

Conclusions

The framework presented in Chapter 3 provides a systematic analysis of *when* and *why* British immigration control policy changed without denying the racial component of immigration control in Britain. The analysis focuses on the underlying structural conditions that modify the level of support for and opposition to immigration and the translation of local political concerns to the national political agenda. My account is largely consonant with a large part of the literature, and I have drawn on many of the insights in this literature to build a systematic framework for analyzing immigration control on a comparative basis. I confess to emphasizing the variables significant to my framework and ignoring other factors that appear to play some role in immigration policy. I did so in an effort to develop a comparative framework that explains a large portion of the variance within and across countries. To then embroider on this framework with factors unique to the specific country undoubtedly provides a more complete picture.

Finally, and more generally, national political institutions are important in determining when local concerns about immigration control are translated into the national political agenda. Even widespread and rabid anti-immigrant sentiment may be ignored at the national level if those constituents are unnecessary to building or maintaining national political coalitions, whereas immigration controls may be rapidly erected when a small anti-immigrant constituency is politically significant to the national coalition. And the formation of national political coalitions depends on the institutional structure within which they operate. That is, the British may be no more, nor less, racist than the Dutch, the Swedes, or U.S. citizens. But the dynamics of political competition funneled through British political institutions catapulted immigration controls onto the national agenda much earlier there.

5   Immigration in the French
Fifth Republic

France has an unusual immigration history relative to other European countries. Rather than serving as a source of emigrants who populated the New World during the nineteenth and early twentieth centuries, France actively recruited foreign workers to fill its factories during the process of industrialization. During the 1920s, on a per capita basis, France was one of the countries receiving the largest number of immigrants (Wihtol de Wenden 1988). Naturalization was relatively easy, and children of aliens born on French soil and resident in France became French citizens upon reaching legal majority. Although efforts to reduce immigration were initiated during the Depression of the 1930s, active recruitment of immigrants resumed at the end of World War II. Yet France began to restrict immigration before the energy-economic crisis of 1973–74, stopped labor market immigration almost completely in 1974, and has since continued to enact ever more restrictive controls over entrance, culminating in the adoption of a zero-immigration policy in 1993. Thus, despite historic patterns of openness to immigration and traditions of assimilation, France ended up adopting a policy of control and closure similar to those of Britain and other European nations with very different immigration histories.

Unfortunately for those attempting to untangle the determinants of these policies, the French case is more opaque than the British case. Immigration restrictions in the early period of control were enacted through executive orders and decrees rather than legislation; immigration was a public issue, but there was limited debate in public forums, making it difficult to trace the various political pressures. The second problem arises from the difference between the issuance of regulations (and ultimately legislation) and their implementation. Examination of the regulatory framework alone overlooks real policy choices affecting the level of immigration. Nonetheless, there are clues that allow us both to discern the shift in government policy and to locate political pressures within the society. A careful analysis of both immigration regulations and their implementation reveals a distinct shift in immigration control from openness to relative closure beginning in 1972.

Because controls were initiated through executive orders without parliamentary debate, analysts of French immigration policy usually attribute this initial shift to a state insulated from public pressures. Yet these same analysts often refer to the role of anti-immigrant sentiment and electoral calculations by politicians when explaining immigration control in the 1980s and 1990s (Schain 1985, 1988, Ogden 1987, Lewis-Beck 1993). This latter perspective can be traced to the rising electoral popularity of Le Pen's anti-immigrant National Front Party, first in the 1983 French municipal elections and then more broadly in the 1984 European Parliament elections, a popularity that has since been replicated in national legislative and presidential elections. I believe that an electoral dynamic was present in the early period as well as the later one although, because anti-immigrant sentiment was less widely spread and concentrated in the political opposition, it was not as visible in national politics as in the later period. Electoral calculations of the Gaullist party allowed it to ignore demands for immigration control after its overwhelming legislative victory in 1968, generated by a conservative backlash to the social disorders in May and June of that year. But the run-up to the 1973 legislative elections modified the ruling party's electoral calculations and created an incentive to reduce levels of immigration despite continued economic growth. And electoral competition in the 1974 presidential election was central to the "immigration stop" of that year.

Immigration Control since World War II

In the immediate postwar period, pressure came from many quarters to relax the immigration restrictions implemented during the Depression.[1] "Populationists" promoted the idea of French demographic growth through immigration to overcome both war losses and low rates of population growth. Alfred Sauvy, head of the newly created National Institute of Demographic Studies (the Institut National des Etudes Démographiques, or INED) proposed a figure of 5.3 million permanent immigrants. The national planning commission (Conseil Général du Plan, or CGP), considering the demands of postwar recovery and employers' interests, focused on labor market requirements. The first plan, for the 1946–51 period, projected a need for 1.3 million

---

1. Among the good sources on French immigration policy are CES 1964 and 1969, Minces 1973, Tapinos 1975, Wihtol de Wenden 1988, Noiriel 1988, Weil 1991, and Lequin 1992. In English, Freeman 1979 provides the earliest systematic overview; also see Hollifield 1992 and 1994, Silverman 1992, the chapter in Hammar 1985, and SOPEMI annual reports.

foreign workers, or more than 200,000 net entrants per year. These favorable attitudes were reflected in the political arena as well. De Gaulle, as head of the provisional government, was an "ardent adherent of this [expansionist] perspective" (Freeman 1979:69). Although neither the populationist nor the labor market faction clearly won the day, the consensus for greater immigration was translated into the creation of the National Office of Immigration (Office National d'Immigration, or ONI), via the ordinance of 2 November 1945. The ONI was granted a monopoly over recruitment of immigrant workers while potential concerns over labor market competition between the immigrants and the indigenous workforce were mitigated through the inclusion of union representatives on the ONI administrative board.[2] The populationist side of the equation was reflected in the 1946 Law 46-550 that allowed workers with the appropriate residence and work permits and with adequate housing to be joined by their families, again through the auspices of the ONI. Thus this initial period of consensus created the organizational framework for overseeing immigrant flows within an expansionist immigration policy.

In theory, when confronting a labor shortage, employers were to request foreign workers from the ONI, either by name or by job classification. The ONI would recruit workers in the country of origin, evaluate their health and skill levels, and send approved workers to the employers endowed with the appropriate work and residence permits, the first authorized by the Ministry of Social Affairs, the second by the Ministry of the Interior. Employers' requests could be rejected by the ONI based on labor market conditions so as to provide the native workforce with employment priority. The law of 10 August 1932 remained on the books, allowing the government to set quotas on immigrants by region and labor market sector, although it was not invoked systematically until 1972.

In their scramble to obtain an adequate labor supply, however, employers found the ONI recruitment system cumbersome and time-consuming. They therefore revived their prewar practice of recruiting workers directly from source countries or hired resident foreigners who lacked the appropriate permits. Thus a laissez-faire system of immigration was inaugurated. This practice was actively accommodated by the state through the establishment of a process whereby immigrants with employment contracts but without the proper work and residence permits were "regularized." Adopted in a piecemeal fashion, the process of regularization was formally extended to all categories of employment by a ministerial circular of 10 February 1961 ("Régularisation" 1968). Furthermore, the state negotiated bilateral agree-

2. This safeguard was removed in 1947 when the French Communist Party (PCF, Parti communiste français) was ejected from the government; thereafter, the administrative board was composed of representatives from the affected ministries (Gani 1972).

ments with several countries to facilitate the flow of labor from third countries. Agreements were negotiated with Italy in 1946 and 1951, West Germany in 1950, Greece in 1954, and Spain in 1961. Because an adequate supply of foreign workers was still lacking, the government reached farther abroad to Portugal, Morocco, and Tunisia in 1963 and to Turkey and Yugoslavia in 1965 (Kennedy-Brenner 1979). The ONI installed missions in many of these countries but remained unable to keep up with the demand for labor; most workers flowed to France outside these channels. By 1968, more than 80 percent of all immigrants legally installed in France during that year had been regularized (Tapinos 1975). In essence, a system of permanent amnesty was implicitly declared.

French immigration analysts usually designate 1968 as a turning point in immigration control (Tapinos 1975, Freeman 1979, Wihtol de Wenden 1986). In fact, a reorganization of the administrative apparatus had been initiated two years earlier, with the creation of the Office of Population and Migration under the auspices of the Ministry of Social Affairs. During this period, the government attempted to increase the incentives for employers to participate in the administrative structure created by the state. An *arrêté* of 15 July 1967 required employers to register foreign workers within twenty-four hours of hire. Ordinance 67-707 of 21 August 1967 required partial reimbursement by employers of certain social security expenditures, if the foreign worker in question had failed to obtain the proper medical examination. And Decree 68-399 of 24 April 1968 required employers to provide proof of medical examinations when registering foreign workers. On 29 July 1968, following the "May events" that almost brought down the French government, the Ministry of Social Affairs issued a circular letter that forbade, in principle, the regularization of workers ("Régularisation" 1968). The combined effect of these decrees, circulars, and *arrêtés* was a substantial decrease in the level of regularizations, from a high of 82 percent in 1968 to 44 percent in 1972.

Yet there are four reasons to believe that, although the government appeared to be bringing immigration under control, the real effort was not to reduce the number of immigrant workers but to select them more carefully. First, the government provided three broad exceptions to the new regulation. Thus for Portuguese immigrants, domestic workers, and skilled workers, regularization remained available. Second, the government continued to recruit immigrants actively through the ONI. That is, the ONI continued to expand its capacity to recruit workers, including unskilled workers, in nontraditional countries of immigration, including the installation of a mission in Turkey in 1969 that contributed to the expanded flow of immigrants from the Mediterranean. Third, the General Planning Council continued to project a need for foreign workers amounting to 75,000 (net) immigrants per year throughout the Sixth Plan, running from 1970 to 1975, a net annual increase of 10,000 from the 1965–70 projections ("Le VIe Plan" 1971).[3] And fourth, expulsion of aliens increased, making organization of foreign workers more precarious, another indicator that French employers and the French government wanted docile foreign workers who would not participate in labor disputes, as many had during the May events.

This evaluation was confirmed by Joseph Fontanet, the minister of social affairs, in 1971, three years after the issuance of the 1968 circular. "It remains a fact," he said, "that the refusal by the French to do certain jobs coupled with demographic stagnation means that the need for foreign workers is crucial" (quoted in Silverman 1992:48). On average, therefore, the absolute number of alien workers admitted annually continued to expand, accompanied by the expansion of family migrants as well as seasonal migrants. Figure 5.1 illustrates the continued rise in immigration flows across all three categories of migrants after 1968.[4] Analysts of the period also agreed that "the new direction, we have just seen, has not prevented new records [in immigration] from being broken. It wasn't even attempted. Its goal was not to move against the [immigration] current, but to channel it and thus to place it under the overall government policy" (Singer-Kérel 1976:40).[5]

While this flow of immigrants expanded, an effort was made to regulate and ultimately reduce the number of immigrants from some, but not all, of France's onetime colonies. One significant source of immigrant labor was Algeria. The law of 20 September 1947 transformed all Arabs in Algeria into French citizens, freeing them from entry and exit controls (Kennedy-Brenner 1979). The Evian Accords of 1962, which granted independence to Algeria, retained the principle of freedom of movement and residence, an arrangement dictated in large part by the concern over French colonists returning to France. But this anticipated exodus of the *rapatriés* was followed by a growing immigrant stream of Arab Algerians to France. The French government quickly attempted to bring this flow under control, and an agreement was signed with Algeria in 1964 subordinating entry to medical controls and work contracts; quotas were unilaterally set at an average of 12,000 Algerian immigrants per year (Kennedy-Brenner 1979). But because Algerian tourists remained free to travel to France, this initial control effort was

3. This projection implies annual gross flows at about twice the level of net flows: for the Fifth Plan, gross flows were estimated at 130,000; for the Sixth Plan, at 150,000 (Tapinos 1975).
4. The flow of permanent workers peaked in 1970 and of families in 1971. The drop in the number of permanent workers in 1971 can be attributed to a decline in economic growth and a relaxation of the tensions in the labor market in 1970 (Singer-Kérel 1976), whereas the drop in 1972 can be attributed to the implementation of immigration controls in a period of economic expansion (Tapinos 1975). The regional statistical report confirms that, for 1972, "the reduction in foreign labor force immigration therefore does not reflect the evolution of the economic situation" (INSEE, *Régions* 1973:xxii).
5. This passage and all other quotations from French sources are translated by the author.

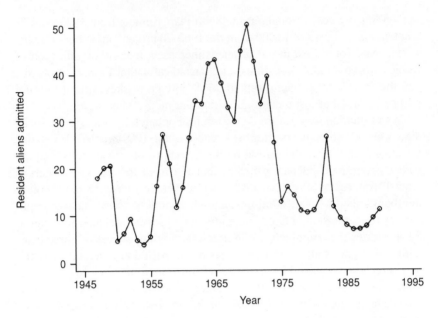

Figure 5.1. Number of resident aliens admitted to France per 10,000 residents, 1947–1990. (*Source:* OMISTATS 1994.)

inadequate. Thus a second agreement was signed in December 1968 requiring residence permits and creating a quota system that limited Algerian labor migration to France to 35,000 workers per year. These individuals had nine months in which to find employment and, in the case of failure, were required to return to Algeria. To help enforce the quota limit, a law (70-1303 of 31 December 1970) was passed clarifying the wording of the Labor Code that forbade the employment of undocumented aliens specifically to include Algerians.[6] In 1972, a third agreement was signed, reducing the annual quota from 35,000 to 25,000 annually.

Another group of immigrants who originally retained privileged access to France were individuals from Francophone Africa. Immigration from these areas was quite limited; few migrant networks existed. Nonetheless, immigrants from three Francophone African countries—Mali, Mauritania, and Senegal—began to arrive in France to seek employment (CES 1964). The government also attempted to control this flow through the negotiation of agreements in 1963 and 1964 that subordinated workers' entry into France

---

6. Per Tapinos 1975, the wording was changed to make it illegal to employ those who lacked a "permit authorizing salaried work in France" rather than just those who lacked a "work permit" ("*un titre l'autorisant à exercer une activité salariée en France*" rather than "*carte de travail*"); the only groups of immigrants who fell in this category were Algerians and Francophone Africans of other nations.

to medical control, a work contract, and financial guarantees for return. But because tourists from these countries could still enter freely, these controls were easily bypassed (CES 1969). Nonetheless, the flows remained limited and similar controls were extended to all of Francophone Africa between 1970 and 1971.

Yet efforts to control immigration from Algeria and Francophone Africa did not extend to other countries with distinct ethnic, religious, or linguistic groups. In 1963, France negotiated agreements with Morocco and Tunisia in which immigrant workers received a work contract before departure, were granted travel expenses, and arrived at reception facilities in France. And in distinction from the Portuguese with whom a treaty was negotiated the same year, Moroccans and Tunisians could bring their families (CES 1969). Similar agreements were negotiated with Yugoslavia and Turkey in 1965. If government policy were driven solely by considerations of racial homogeneity, it seems odd that, at the same time Algerian immigration was restricted, other North African Arab immigration was encouraged, including family reunification.[7] In any case, both the administrative features of control and the actual numbers of immigrants indicate continued openness and expansion of annual immigrant intakes.

The picture changed somewhat in 1972 and definitively in 1974. In early 1972, the government issued two circulars that reduced immigration flows, despite an expanding economy (Tapinos 1975). The Marcellin Circular of 24 January united procedures for granting residence and work permits within the prefecture of police. More significant was the Fontanet Circular of 24 February that subordinated recruitment of foreigners to domestic labor market conditions by requiring employers to advertise available positions for a minimum of three weeks at the National Employment Agency (Agence Nationale pour l'Emploi, or ANPE) before requesting an immigrant worker from the ONI. It also required proof of adequate housing in order to obtain a residence permit. Failure to comply was penalized by expulsion of the immigrant. Although the Fontanet Circular was suspended in the summer of 1973 as an informal amnesty for workers who had failed to meet its provisions, a new circular was issued on 26 September 1973 that excluded all possibility of regularization beginning 1 November 1973. Thus it took almost thirty years to return to the basic provisions of the 1945 ordinance (Tapinos 1975).

Evidence that the government finally meant business comes from the Law 72-617 of 5 July 1972, which doubled employer penalties associated with infractions of immigration laws. Moreover, Decree 72-985 of 24 October

---

7. Tapinos 1975:105 confirms the express policy of the government to enlarge the part of non-Europeans in the immigrant flow when he states that "the expansion of Moroccan immigration confirms the concern of French authorities to expand the part of Morocco among our suppliers of labor."

reapplied the industry quotas originally established in the 10 August 1932 law and provided financial penalties for firms that deviated from those quotas. And the ONI actually began to reject requests for regularization; these amounted to almost 25 percent of those requested in 1972 (Tapinos 1975:103). Thus, despite an expanding economy in 1972 and 1973, immigration of workers was reduced.[8]

Although the picture changed in 1972, it is clear that the measures taken in 1974 dramatically modified the immigration regime in France. In July 1974, the newly appointed secretary of state for immigration, André Postel-Vinay, announced a temporary stop on all worker immigration, a ban that was extended permanently in October of the same year. Concern for immigration was such that the government also suspended family reunification migration, although the ban was lifted the following year. The effectiveness of these bans is reflected in the steady decline in worker and family migration. In 1974, permanent immigration (of workers and families) was reduced by 35 percent despite the midyear implementation and again by an additional 50 percent in 1975. The decline in immigration can be traced through the annual flows of permanent, family, and seasonal immigration detailed in Table 5.1.

Several dimensions of the Marcellin and Fontanet decrees were overturned by the French administrative high court, the Conseil d'Etat. But the government was not deterred from promulgating a new series of regulations to control immigrant flows (Wihtol de Wenden 1988). A decree of 15 January 1976 expanded the conditions under which residence permits could be withdrawn. The right of family reunification was reduced in 1977 to a right of family visitation, although admission was possible if the worker's family agreed to refrain from entering the labor market. And in 1977, a voluntary repatriation scheme was initiated, followed by the 1978 announcement that France sought to reduce its foreign population by 200,000 individuals per year. These decrees were also challenged by the Conseil d'État. But the central issue in the court's decision was not the principle of immigration restriction. Rather, the court ruled that the minister was empowered only to carry out decisions, not to make policy (Wihtol de Wenden 1988). Policymaking was the domain of the parliament. Therefore, the government was obliged to take its proposals to the National Assembly and the Senate.

Because the government sought to reduce the number of new immigrant workers, to encourage (or force) return migration, and to enjoin family reunification, the legislation was anything but uncontroversial. The Stoleru pro-

---

8. The rise in 1973 can be attributed to the informal amnesty associated with the temporary suspension of the Fontanet Circular during that summer.

Table 5.1. Annual inflow of aliens in France, 1946–1993

Year	Permanent workers	Seasonal workers	Families	Total	Total permanent
1946	30,171	11,542	n.a.	n.a.	n.a.
1947	68,223	19,442	4,930	92,595	73,153
1948	57,039	21,801	25,822	104,662	82,861
1949	58,785	20,050	26,594	105,426	85,376
1950	10,525	15,915	8,782	35,222	19,307
1951	20,996	25,713	5,283	51,992	26,279
1952	32,750	33,784	6,616	73,150	39,366
1953	15,361	34,175	4,882	54,418	20,243
1954	12,292	29,874	4,101	46,267	16,393
1955	19,029	35,276	4,647	58,952	23,676
1956	65,428	48,731	5,951	120,110	71,379
1957	111,693	56,969	8,851	177,513	120,544
1958	82,818	63,529	11,510	157,857	94,328
1959	44,179	63,797	8,832	116,808	53,011
1960	48,914	109,798	23,693	182,405	72,607
1961	78,927	96,956	43,454	219,337	122,381
1962	113,069	95,093	47,028	255,190	160,097
1963	115,523	101,274	43,580	260,377	159,103
1964	153,731	120,950	47,293	321,974	201,024
1965	152,063	131,571	55,429	339,063	207,492
1966	131,725	124,270	54,145	310,140	185,870
1967	107,833	113,971	54,479	276,283	162,312
1968	93,165	129,858	55,812	278,835	148,977
1969	167,802	132,871	57,333	358,006	225,135
1970	174,243	135,058	80,952	390,253	255,195
1971	136,004	137,197	81,496	354,697	217,500
1972	98,074	144,492	74,955	317,521	173,029
1973	132,055	142,458	72,647	347,160	204,702
1974	64,461	131,783	68,038	264,282	132,499
1975	15,591	124,126	51,824	191,541	67,415
1976	26,949	121,474	57,337	205,760	84,286
1977	22,756[a]	112,116	52,318	187,190	75,074[a]
1978	18,356[a]	122,658	40,123	181,137	58,479[a]
1979	17,395[a]	124,715	39,300	181,410	56,695[a]
1980	17,370[a]	120,436	42,020	179,826	59,390[a]
1981	33,433[a]	117,542	41,589	192,564	75,022[a]
1982	96,962[a]	107,084	47,396	251,442	144,358[a]
1983	18,483[a]	101,857	45,767	166,107	64,250[a]
1984	11,804[a]	93,220	39,621	144,645	51,425[a]
1985	10,959[a]	86,180	32,545	129,684	43,504[a]
1986	11,238[a]	81,670	27,140	120,048	38,378[a]
1987	12,231[a]	76,647	26,769	115,647	39,000[a]
1988	13,594[a]	70,547	29,345	113,486	42,939[a]
1989	18,646[a]	61,868	34,594	115,108	53,240[a]
1990	26,200[a]	58,249	36,949	121,398	63,149[a]
1991	29,682[a]	54,241	35,625	119,548	65,307[a]
1992	46,174[a]	13,597	32,665	92,436	78,839[a]
1993	28,432[a]	11,283	32,435	72,150	60,867[a]

Note: Algerian families included beginning in 1969; Algerian workers included beginning in 1986; Francophone Africans included beginning in 1969; families of EC/EU workers excluded beginning 1975.
[a] Includes APT workers (*autorisations provisoires de travail*—workers with temporary contracts for more than 12 months but less than two years).
Source: OMISTATS 1994.

posal introduced in the National Assembly in 1978, to enlarge the conditions for the nonrenewal of residence and work permits, was ultimately withdrawn, but the Barre-Bonnet proposal to reduce the tourist–undocumented worker connection was passed by the legislature in 1980. As a result, tourists were now required to demonstrate adequate resources to provide for their stay in France, a partial guarantee against their entry into the labor market. In any event, administrative latitude in the interpretation of rules led to a continuous decrease in the number of legally admitted immigrants across the board. Figure 5.1 shows that the continuous rise in immigration, even after 1968, was followed by a dramatic decline pursuant to government efforts initiated in 1972.

By this time, public debate on immigration issues was widespread. In the run-up to the 1981 presidential election, the candidate of the left, François Mitterrand, promised to maintain tight controls over new and illegal immigration. To ameliorate the conditions of immigrants already in France, however, the Socialist platform promised to introduce policies to improve the status of foreign workers in France while retaining immigration controls. Once elected, Mitterrand remained true to his promises and devised an amnesty for workers who entered before 1 January 1981 along with an amnesty for the firms that employed them. Ultimately more than 140,000 undocumented aliens received permission to remain in France.[9] But this amnesty was combined with increased efforts to enforce border controls and the conditions of entry established by the Barre-Bonnet law of 1980 were expanded and reinforced.

The conservative coalition's return to power in the National Assembly between 1986 and 1988 and again in 1993 led to ever greater restrictions on immigration in France. The 1986 Pasqua law again increased conditions of entry while the 1993 Pasqua law made family reunification conditional on the immigrant's legal residence in France for a minimum of two years. Efforts to restrict access to French citizenship that had failed to pass the National Assembly in the late 1980s were successful in 1993, when the revision of the French Nationality Code withdrew automatic access to French nationality by some groups and limited access to French citizenship for other groups. Thus, in the language of the minister of the interior in 1993, Charles Pasqua, France adopted a "zero immigration" policy.

The various circulars, decrees, and laws governing immigration are outlined in Table 5.2; Table 5.3 describes the country-specific immigration regimes. Ultimately, both the Algerian and Francophone African regimes

---

9. This figure suggests that the net undocumented worker entry was about 21,000 per year. Given the reduction of permanent worker entries from a high of 174,243 to less than 20,000 per year, even when undocumented migration is taken into account, French immigration dropped dramatically.

Table 5.2. Major immigration control legislation and decrees, France, 1945–1993

Control measure	Date	Provisions
Ordinance	2 November 1945	Establishes National Office of Immigration (ONI) to control migratory flows; with exception of special regimes, every alien must have both a residence permit (*carte de séjour*) and either a work contract approved by Ministry of Social Affairs or a work permit (*carte de travail*); art. 64 of Labor Code (bk.2) forbids hiring of a foreign worker without a permit
Law 46-550	1946	Permits workers with appropriate residence and work permits and with adequate housing to be joined by their families.
Bilateral agreements		
Italy	1946–47, 1951	Facilitates immigration of workers
West Germany	1950	Facilitates immigration of workers
Greece	1954	Facilitates immigration of workers
Spain	1961	Facilitates immigration of workers
Morocco, Tunisia, Portugal	1963	Facilitates immigration of workers
Yugoslavia, Turkey	1965	Facilitates immigration of workers
Ministerial circular	10 February 1961	Extends process of regularization to all categories of workers
Arrêté	15 July 1967	Requires employers to register foreign workers within 24 hours of hire
Ordinance 67-707	21 August 1967	Requires employers to reimburse social security funds for alien workers injured on job who do not have appropriate health certificates; applies to workers hired after 1 July 1968
Ministerial circular	29 July 1968	Forbids regularization of workers in sectors with surplus labor, established at least quarterly by each department; regularization forbidden for all unskilled and semiskilled workers (*manœuvres* and *ouvriers spécialisés*); all such workers must be retained through ONI recruitment services
Law 70-1303	31 December 1970	Makes it illegal to hire or retain an alien without the appropriate work permit or for work not specifically authorized in work permit; extends sanctions on undocumented workers to Algerians
Marcellin circular	24 January 1972	Unites procedures for granting residence and work permits within the prefecture of police
Fontanet circular	24 February 1972	Subordinates worker immigration to national labor market conditions and adequate housing
Law 72-617	5 July 1972	Specifies penalty for improper hiring of aliens as imprisonment for 2–12 months and fine of 2,000–10,000F, or both; penalty doubles for second offense and court may order temporary or permanent closure of firm; penalty for labor trafficking specified as 2–5 years' imprisonment and fine of 10,000–100,000F.

Table 5.2. Continued

Control measure	Date	Provisions
Gorse circulars	1973	Grants amnesty to immigrants who entered France before 1 June 1973; sets 1 November 1973 as last date for regularization
Law	6 July 1973	Penalizes labor traffickers; forbids employers to obtain reimbursement for ONI charges and travel advances from immigrants
Ministerial circular	3 July 1974	Temporarily suspends worker immigration; 19 July, family immigration ends; 9 October, suspension of new immigration extended indefinitely; adopts new program re national-local cooperation; family immigration resumes 21 May 1975
Council of State action	1975	Voids parts of Marcellin and Fontanet circulars
Decrees, circular	November–December 1977	Suspend immigration of family members who enter labor market, permit only family visits; permit incarceration of individuals pending expulsion
Council of State action	1978	Voids part or all of measures taken in 1977; decision based on limited powers of executive to make policy and need for legislation rather than executive decrees
Bonnet Law	1980	Modifies conditions for entrance into France; conditions include public order and adequate resources for stay; provides for incarceration of immigrants under expulsion orders in nonpenitentiary setting
Law	17 October 1981	Increases penalties for employing illegal aliens
Circular	11 August 1981	Grants amnesty to illegal aliens who entered France before 1 January 1981 and who are currently employed
Law	25 October 1981	Reinforces conditions for entry into France established under the Bonnet Law
Law	17 July 1984	Creates single residence/work permit for some categories of immigrants, issued for 10 years and automatically renewable
Council of Ministers statement	10 October 1984	Increases requirements for family reunification: adequate resources, prior authorization, and adequate housing; reorganizes program for voluntary repatriation
Pasqua law	1993	To secure French citizenship, children of foreigners born on French soil must make active delaration of citizenship between ages 16 and 21, after continuous residence of at least 5 years

Table 5.3. Special immigration regimes, France, 1947–1986

Area and year	Provisions
European Community	
1957	Treaty of Rome admits principle of free circulation of workers among member states
1960	Plan to lift barriers over 10-year period
1968	Full implementation of 1960 agreement
Francophone Africa	Free circulation
1963–64	Bilateral agreements with Mali, Mauritania, and Senegal: citizens must be in possession of a passport or identity card and must have resources to guarantee return to home country; to work in host country, individual must possess health certificate and work contract approved by Ministry of Labor
1969	Francophone immigration is brought under ONI auspices
Algeria	
1947	Free circulation
1962	Algerian independence maintains free circulation between France and Algeria under Evian accords
1964	Recruitment placed under control of French medical authorities in cooperation with Algerian National Labor Force Office (ONAMO)
1968	Agreement requires residence permit to seek work; 35,000 residence permits to be issued annually
1971	Quota reduced to 25,000
1973	Algeria suspends emigration to France
1986	Algerian worker immigration brought under auspices of ONI (family immigration has been under ONI auspices since 1969)

were joined under the auspices of the ONI, renamed in 1987 the Office of International Migration (Office des Migrations Internationales, or OMI). Only the members of the European Union remain under a special regime of free circulation. But the tables by themselves tell only part of the story. It is only by matching the various decrees with the actual immigration flows depicted in Figure 5.1 that a true picture of French immigration control becomes visible.

The Institution of Immigration Control

As for Britain in 1962, the question in this chapter centers around the major shift in immigration control initiated in 1972. The answer is located in the rise of anti-immigrant sentiment in specific electoral constituencies and the political importance of those constituencies. But the set of electoral incentives in France is more complex than in Britain. In Britain, the electoral system of single-member constituencies favors the creation of two large parties. In combination with the parliamentary system, in which the majority party in Parliament becomes the executive, the focus in Britain can remain exclusively on parliamentary elections and the relative power of the majority and the opposition.

France is distinctive in two ways. First, under the Fifth Republic, the French readopted a two-round electoral system that encourages the formation of multiple parties contending elections in the first round of balloting and then the creation of electoral alliances in the second round.[10] Single-party majority governments are the exception, parliamentary coalitions the rule. Thus legislative electoral incentives are a function of both the relative strength of the majority coalition and its opposition and of the relative strength of the parties of the majority coalition. Second, the French system is characterized as semipresidential. For our purposes, it is enough to know that the government is responsible to the lower house of the parliament, the National Assembly, so that National Assembly elections are crucial for determining the national parliamentary majority.[11] But the president has the constitutional right to dissolve the National Assembly, and therefore, presidential elections may also be crucial to determining the national parliamentary majority.[12] Presidential influence has been considerable. De Gaulle dissolved the National Assembly a year early in 1962 and then again in 1968, only one year after the 1967 legislative elections. The issue was actively debated in the 1974 presidential election (*Textes* 1975), and when the socialist, François Mitterrand, finally won the presidency in 1981, he also took advantage of his electoral victory to dissolve a National Assembly in the third year of a five-year legislative term and did so again upon reelection in 1988. These strategies confirm the significance of presidential elections to the maintenance of a national parliamentary coalition.

In light of these electoral incentives, I contend that the pressures building to contain immigration flows during the 1960s were resisted by the Gaullist majority after its overwhelming electoral victory in June 1968. This victory meant a parliamentary majority for the Gaullists even without their center-

10. To mitigate electoral disaster in the 1986 National Assembly elections, in 1985 the socialist government switched to a system of proportional representation. The conservative coalition that formed the government in 1986 reinstituted the two-round system.
11. The Senate is an indirectly elected body that also votes on legislation. If the Senate disagrees with lower house, however, the government can ask the National Assembly to vote the legislation alone, reducing the power of the Senate over the outcome. See Tsebelis and Money 1997 on the relative power of the French Senate. Because the Senate's power is limited, the focus here is on National Assembly elections. Nonetheless, a full account of French immigration control would include a consideration of senatorial electoral considerations as well.
12. The president is constrained by the fact that he cannot dissolve the newly elected National Assembly for a minimum of twelve months.

right coalition partners and the complete decimation of the left. The unusual events leading to this victory, however, were recognized as transitory, and the approach of the 1973 legislative elections put pressure on the government to recognize and resolve some of the issues surrounding immigration. Gaullist efforts to retain a parliamentary majority led the government to make concessions to constituencies held by its center-right electoral and parliamentary allies as well as to swing constituencies where electoral defeat would mean an opposition victory. The unscheduled presidential election, triggered by Georges Pompidou's death in April 1974, was even more hotly contested and contributed to the ultimate decision to stop immigration, whether for work or for family reunification. Human rights safeguards, meted out through the courts, prevented the complete control of immigration streams. Nonetheless, the French government has managed to achieve an impressive level of control over immigration.

The rise of anti-immigrant pressures

Immigration in the 1950s and 1960s purposefully escaped government controls. Although deputies in the National Assembly began questioning the government's immigration policy as early as 1958, immigration flows continued to be driven by labor market needs to the exclusion of all other dimensions (Freeman 1979). In 1963, the prime minister, Georges Pompidou, defended the employment of foreign labor as necessary for continued economic growth. In his words, immigration "creates a detente in the labor market and the resistance to social [trade union] pressure" (quoted in Minces 1973:37). An even clearer illustration of the priority given to labor market needs is the statement of a minister in Pompidou's cabinet, Jean-Marcel Jeanneney, who argued, on 21 March 1969, that "illegal immigration is not unhelpful, because, if we adhered to the strict application of the international rules, we might possibly lack workers" (quoted in Minces 1973:136).[13]

But the consequences of this laissez-faire immigration regime were readily visible to anyone who chose to look. The immigrant networks and the active recruitment of immigrants during the 1960s led to rapid expansion of the immigrant population. In 1962, 3.9 percent of the resident population in France was foreign; this figure rose to 5.3 percent in 1968 and to 6.5 percent in 1975, while the number of naturalized citizens declined as a proportion of the population.[14] As in Britain, the immigrant population was heavily con-

---

13. The date of this statement is yet another indication that the 1968 circular was not the real turning point in immigration control policy.
14. The absolute number of naturalized citizens rose slightly, from 1,266,680 in 1962 to 1,319,984 in 1968 and 1,392,010 in 1975, but because the population of France was increasing more rapidly than the number of naturalizations, the proportional figure actually declined.

centrated. Data on the immigrant population and unemployment are available only by department rather than by electoral constituency. Nonetheless, these are the figures that are readily available to politicians and therefore serve as reasonable indicators of politicians' perceptions of anti-immigrant pressures. As one analyst notes, "The department, even more than the parliamentary constituency, remains in France the preferred geographical subdivision for broad analytical purposes" (Frears 1977:181). That is, politicians evaluate problems at the departmental level and then weight the political significance of the issues according to the number of electoral constituencies per department.

Departments have a minimum of two National Assembly constituencies; since 1964 the department with the largest number of constituencies is Paris, with thirty-one.[15] Figure 5.2 illustrates the same type of immigrant concentration visible in Britain, although, because there are fewer units—95 departments rather than 630 electoral constituencies—the distribution does not look as skewed. If constituency-level data were available, they would likely reflect the concentration visible in micro-level analyses. For example, two constituencies in central Paris had immigrant populations of more than 20 percent although, on a department-wide basis, immigration levels reached only 10.2 percent in 1968 and 13.6 percent in 1975 (Peach 1987).[16] Overall, in 1968, 34 percent of the departments had fewer than 29 immigrants per 1,000 inhabitants while about 14 percent of the departments had more then 83 immigrants per 1,000 inhabitants.

Because France has a long history of immigration, it is interesting that the immigration dynamics of the 1960s followed a different pattern than in earlier periods. Whereas traditionally immigrants settled in the border regions of the industrialized east and the Mediterranean littoral, immigrants in the 1960s were drawn to the industrial centers in the Paris region (Île-de-France) and the Lyon region (Rhône-Alpes). A comparison of Tables 5.4 and 5.5 reveals this new dynamic. In 1962, the departments with the largest immigrant populations were in the Mediterranean littoral (Alpes-Maritimes, 13%; Bouches-du-Rhône, 7.3%; Pyrénées-Orientales, 13%; Aude, 7.9%; Hérault,

---

15. Before the creation of these new electoral divisions in 1964, the Île de France (Paris) region contained three departments: Seine with 51 constituencies, Seine-et-Oise with 18 constituencies, and Seine-et-Marne with 5 constituencies. Redistricting produced 8 departments in the same region: Paris with 31 electoral constituencies; Seine-St-Denis, 9; Hauts-de-Seine, 13; Val-de-Marne, 8; Val-d'Oise, 5; Yvelines, 8; Essonne, 4. Seine-et-Marne, with 5 constituencies, remained virtually unchanged. The combined constituencies in Île de France constitute 83 of the 487 National Assembly constituencies (17%), so one can easily understand the attention paid to the concerns of the voters in these constituencies.

16. The report analyzed the level of immigrants per arrondissement in Paris; these administrative units are close to but do not necessarily coincide with electoral constituencies. Also see Gokalp and Lamy 1997, who analyze the Île de France region based on the 1968 census and show communes with an immigrant population as high as 26.2%.

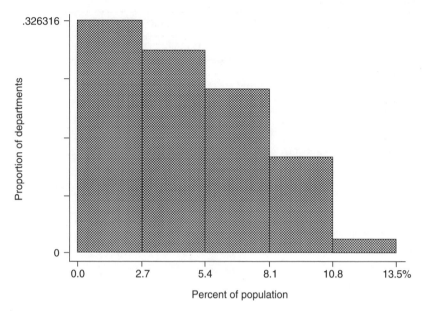

Figure 5.2. Distribution of foreign-born population among French departments, 1968. (*Source:* INSEE, *Recensement général*, 1968.)

7.7%; and Vaucluse, 7.5%) and in the Lorraine mining and steel region (Moselle, 13.6%; Meurthe-et-Moselle, 8.3%). By 1975, in contrast, 6 of the twelve departments with the largest immigrant populations were in the Paris region and three in the Rhône-Alpes region, surrounding the provincial capital of Lyon. Only three of the 1962 top immigrant departments remained in the top twelve, many having actually lost immigrants both absolutely and as a proportion of the resident population. Table 5.5 demonstrates that, of the twelve departments with the largest proportional increase in immigration between 1962 and 1975, eleven were in the Paris or Rhône-Alpes regions.[17]

Thus there were four distinctive areas in France that confronted large or growing immigrant populations: regions of new immigration, the Paris (Ile

17. The figures in Table 5.3 come from the 1962, 1968, and 1975 censuses and represent departmental administrative units, of which there were ninety in metropolitan France in 1962, ninety-five in 1964, and ninety-six in 1974. Twenty-one administrative regions were created by legislation in 1960 and group between two and eight departments (a twenty-second region was created for Corsica in 1970, previously included in the Provence–Côte-d'Azur region). National Assembly constituencies are nested inside departments on the basis of population, although the range of voters per constituency is large. To my knowledge, no data are aggregated at the level of the National Assembly constituencies, at least in this time frame (Ogden 1987). The basic unit of local government is the commune; as there are more than 30,000 communes, aggregation is a time-consuming task.

Table 5.4. Immigrant populations of French departments with greatest concentration of immigrants, 1962–1975 (percent)

Department	1962		1968		1975	
	Percent	Rank[a]	Percent	Rank[a]	Percent	Rank[a]
Seine-St-Denis	6.9%	15	10.4%	3	14.5%	1
Paris	6.9	15	10.2	4	13.6	2
Hauts-de-Seine	6.9	15	8.5	7	11.6	3
Pyrénées-Orientales	13.0	2	13.5	1	11.5	4
Rhône	6.9	15	8.5	7	11.1	5
Val-de-Marne	6.9	15	7.9	16	11.1	6
Moselle	13.6	1	11.4	2	11.1	7
Isère	8.5	4	9.3	6	10.5	8
Val-d'Oise	5.3		8.5	7	10.3	9
Yvelines	5.3		7.5	19	10.2	10
Haute-Savoie	6.2		8.2	14	10.0	11
Alpes-Maritimes	13.0	2	10.1	5	9.8	12
Bouches-du-Rhône	7.3	10	8.1	15	8.5	13
Hérault	7.7	7	8.5	7		
Vaucluse	7.5	9	8.5	7		
Aude	7.9	6	8.4	13		
Meurthe-et-Moselle	8.3	5				
Gers	7.6	8				
Savoie	7.3	10				

[a] Rank in immigrant population among the 94 departments (Corsica excluded).
Sources: INSEE, *Recensement général,* 1962, 1968, 1975.

Table 5.5. Increase in immigration in French departments with largest increases, 1962–1975 (percent)

Department	1962–1968		1968–1975		1962–1975	
	Percent	Rank[a]	Percent	Rank[a]	Percent	Rank[a]
Seine-St-Denis (Paris region)	3.5%	1	4.1%	1	7.6%	1
Paris	3.3	2	3.4	2	6.7	2
Val-d'Oise (Paris region)	3.2	3	1.8		5.0	3
Yvelines (Paris region)	2.2	5	2.7	8	4.9	4
Hauts-de-Seine (Paris region)	1.6	11	3.1	4	4.7	5
Ain (Lyon region)	2.0	7	2.6	10	4.6	6
Rhône (Lyon region)	1.6	12	2.6	9	4.2	7
Val-de-Marne (Paris region)	1.0		3.2	3	4.2	8
Doubs (east)	1.2	14	3.0	5	4.2	9
Haute-Savoie (Lyon region)	2.1	6	1.8		3.9	10
Loire (Lyon region)	2.0	7	1.9		3.9	11
Territoire de Belfort (east)	0.6		2.8	7	3.4	12
Essonne (Paris region)	1.0		2.4	11	3.4	13

Note: To calculate the 1962–68 increases, after the creation of new departments in 1964, the average level of immigration in the Seine Department was attributed to the new departments of Paris, Seine-St-Denis, Val-de-Marne, and Hauts-de-Seine; the average level of immigration for Seine-et-Oise Department was allocated to Val-d'Oise, Yvelines, and Essonne.
[a] Rank in level of increase among the 94 departments (Corsica excluded).
Sources: INSEE, *Recensement général,* 1962, 1968, 1975.

de France) region and the Rhône-Alpes region, and areas of older immigrant streams, the Lorraine and the Mediterranean littoral (the Provence–Côte-d'Azur region in the east and the Languedoc-Roussillon region in the west).

Although employment drew immigrants to France, their arrival presented social problems. Hiring undocumented foreigners and regularizing them allowed employers to avoid the responsibility of providing housing, required when workers were recruited via the ONI. Therefore, as in Britain, after locating employment, one of the initial issues confronting immigrants was adequate housing. But housing shortages and lack of access to social housing forced immigrants to create their own shantytowns (*bidonvilles*) on the outskirts of the various industrial cities where their labor was needed. These shantytowns were most visible in the regions of new immigration, Paris and Lyon, but were also ubiquitous in and around Marseille, a city that experienced both "old" and "new" immigration flows.[18] The largest portion of shantytown residents were new Portuguese immigrants, rather than North African immigrants, another indicator that the total volume of immigration was at issue rather than (or in addition to) the ethnic composition of the immigrant streams (Kennedy-Brenner 1979). The *bidonvilles* were unique in Europe and were recognized as a problem early on; the National Assembly passed legislation in 1964 to suppress them and to rehouse the immigrants elsewhere. But the government failed to allocate adequate resources to resolve the problem, and a survey in 1966 revealed the continued presence of 46,827 shantytown residents in the Paris region alone (White 1987).

Moreover, the construction of public housing as a solution to the shantytowns tended to create new problems. Partly in response to the May 1968 events, the stock of social housing expanded rapidly and, with it, immigrant use of "low-rent housing," *habitation à loyer modéré*, or HLM. Subsequent legislation reserved a minimum of 6.75 percent of these units to house the immigrant population. As a result, the proportion of immigrants in social housing expanded rapidly. In France as a whole, the proportion of immigrant families in HLMs grew from 5.9 percent in 1968 to 15 percent in 1975 and 23.5 percent in 1982 (Frybes 1992). In Île de France (Paris region) between 1968 and 1975, the proportion of immigrant families in social housing doubled, from 4.4 to 9.2 percent. Moreover, the actual number of immigrants in public housing is larger than the family-based figures show because immigrant families are larger than French families on average. For particular national groups, the figures are telling. Compared with the French popula-

---

18. One reason for the smaller number of shantytowns in regions such as the Lorraine and Languedoc was that the nationalized coal firm Charbonnages de France provided housing to its workers, foreign and indigenous.

tion, twice as many Algerians (29%) and almost three times as many Algerian women (44%) depended on public housing. Moreover, immigrants tended to be concentrated even within the stock of public housing. In Venissieux, a suburb of Lyon, for example, 62 percent of the inhabitants of the public housing project, Les Minguettes, were immigrants (Schain 1985).

The irony of government policy to suppress the *bidonvilles* and rehouse the immigrants is that the stock of public housing is primarily concentrated in working-class neighborhoods and, in particular, cities that are governed at the local level by the French Communist Party (Parti Communiste Français, or PCF).[19] The concentration of immigrants in public housing meant their concentration in working-class suburbs. As of 1975, of the 217 cities in France with populations over thirty thousand, 73 had immigrant populations of more than 10 percent, of which seven had more than 20 percent. Only 18 percent of these cities were governed by parties of the right, whereas 56 percent were governed by the PCF and 26 percent by the noncommunist left (Schain 1985, Ogden 1987).

This concentration, when combined with the acquiescence to, if not encouragement of, family immigration, generated additional problems. As the statistics in Table 5.1 illustrate, about one-third of the permanent immigrant stream in any year was composed of family members.[20] Moreover, once spouses were reunited, the population of foreign children born on French soil grew at rates double and triple that of the native French population.[21] Many schools where immigrants were concentrated drew half their children from immigrant families (Ashford 1982). As a result, as in Britain, parents began complaining about the education system (Schain 1985, 1988). Deterioration of public housing was blamed on the concentrated population of immigrants, as was the rise in crime rates (Schain 1985, 1988).[22]

The cultural dimension of immigration is more difficult to quantify. Nonetheless, sociological surveys indicated that French residents in close proximity to immigrant populations complained of different cultural habits, including the smell of cooking, attitudes toward cleanliness, noise, and, for the Gypsy population in particular, criminal behavior (Wieviorka 1992). Initially, at least, there was little or no mention of the religious differences of the North African Muslim population.

19. The PCF accused the government of knowingly channeling the immigrant population into working-class districts.
20. This proportion was reversed after the implementation of controls in 1972 and 1974.
21. These children remained "foreign" until the age of 18, at which time, if they met certain residence requirements, they automatically became French unless they actively renounced French citizenship. This automatic access to French citizenship was withdrawn in 1993.
22. Total estimated costs to the state for social services provided to immigrants was about 4 billion French francs per year (Ashford 1982).

In addition to the common problems described above, each region confronting a large immigrant population also faced unique problems. Lacking general indicators of these problems, such as departmental unemployment rates that became available only beginning in 1978, a brief overview of these problems is in order.

The Paris region is fortunate to be the political and economic center of France, an oasis in the "French desert." As a result, it attracted migrants from the rural areas of France, in addition to the steady stream of international migrants. In the twenty-year period between 1954 and 1975, the population of the metropolitan area increased by 35 percent from 7.3 million to 9.9 million (Parodi 1981). Pressures on public services and private facilities were thus aggravated by the demands of the newly arriving native population. Moreover, efforts to "deconcentrate" the population within the perimeters of the city proper forced massive population growth on the surrounding suburban areas, which had little infrastructure to cope with the growth. Communities that were little more than villages doubled and tripled their populations in short order (Clout 1972).

At the same time, the central government developed ever broader plans to decentralize the economic base, theretofore concentrated in Paris, to the provinces. Beginning as early as 1945, and expanded in 1955 and again in 1965, the government created penalties for firms establishing or expanding facilities in Paris and incentives for firms relocating to the provinces (Thompson 1973). These schemes achieved varying degrees of success, with the outcome reflected in declining employment opportunities in the Paris region. Between 1968 and 1975, the Ile de France region suffered a 1.7 percent loss in industrial employment, reducing industrial employment below 1954 levels when the population of the region had been 35 percent smaller (Tuppen 1980:103). Thus internal migration, deconcentration, and decentralization aggravated the competition between the immigrant community and the indigenous population for social services and employment. Parisians were thereby confronted with a double whammy: increased population, putting pressure on public services, and the loss of industrial jobs.

In the Lorraine, economic problems centered on decline of the heavy industrial base and the traditional textile industry. The Lorraine had experienced rapid economic growth during the 1950s and early 1960s, attracting large numbers of immigrant workers to fill its coal and iron ore mines and to work in its burgeoning steel industry. But as early as the mid-1960s, the region began to experience competition from imported low-cost ores and updated steel mills (Tuppen 1980:166–67). Industrial employment was reduced by more than 13,200 jobs between 1962 and 1968; net job loss in the traditional industries of the region surpassed 60,000 between 1962 and 1975. Inadequate transportation between the various employment centers, nestled in the mountain ranges, aggravated unemployment problems. Here, high immigrant concentrations combined with industrial decline and economic stagnation to aggravate the tensions between the immigrant and indigenous populations.

The Provence–Côte-d'Azur region also suffered from problems of unemployment and underemployment for a variety of reasons (Thompson 1975, Tuppen 1980). The region had been traditionally underindustrialized, with the main locus of economic activity centering around the port and transit activities in Marseille. By the 1960s, Marseille confronted a rapidly changing environment: a decline in ship passenger traffic caused by the rise of the airline industry; a dramatic decrease in colonial trade over which it had maintained a monopoly position; and the 1967 closure of the Suez Canal, cutting off traffic from the east. These problems were aggravated by the technological transformation of the shipping industry to larger vessels and containerization.

The city of Marseille, in conjunction with the national government, responded to these changes by opening a new port facility at Fos. But the capital-intensive restructuring of the port generated few jobs. This problem was compounded by the fact that Marseille and the surrounding Provence–Côte-d'Azur region were the most important destinations of French *rapatriés* after the independence of Algeria in 1962. Thus, although the Bouches-du-Rhône department experienced net employment growth, the population grew even more rapidly, 18 percent between 1954 and 1962 and another 15 percent between 1962 and 1968 (Thompson 1975). In the east Mediterranean littoral, a tradition of underdevelopment, combined with industrial restructuring of its major industry and compounded by the influx of the *rapatriés*, aggravated the tension between the immigrant and indigenous populations.[23]

Thus, for diverse reasons, three of the four regions with high immigrant concentrations also experienced job losses or unemployment, especially in particular sectors of the economy. The fourth region presents a happier economic picture. The Rhône-Alpes area benefited from governmental efforts to construct *métropoles-d'équilibre*, urban industrial centers in the provinces to offset the dominance of Paris. As a result, at least certain departments in the region (in particular the Rhône Department, with its provincial capital of Lyon) experienced sustained job growth between 1962 and 1975, with industrial employment expanding by 0.8 percent on average annually

---

23. The political significance of this underdevelopment is confirmed by the report in *L'Humanité* in the midst of the 1971 municipal elections: "For 13 years, the deindustrialization of the region has been accentuated. Marseille already counts more than 20,000 unemployed. . . . The projects at Fos, by themselves, . . . will not be able to offer sufficient employment" (*L'Humanité*, 10 March 1971, 6).

between 1962 and 1968 and by 0.6 percent between 1968 and 1975 (Tuppen 1980). Building on a long history of commercial and industrial development, "Lyon [became] France's most important provincial decision-making centre" (Tuppen 1980:133). Some areas in the region, such as Grenoble, experienced even higher growth, with industrial employment expanding by 13.9 percent between 1968 and 1975. Other areas were less fortunate; St. Étienne, in the Loire Department, experienced the same throes of industrial restructuring as the Lorraine, with a resulting decline in industrial employment of 4.3 percent between 1968 and 1975 (Tuppen 1980:142).

Immigration pressures were nonetheless high. Between 1946 and 1975, the Rhône-Alpes welcomed 775,000 foreigners—13 percent of all foreigners— plus some 315,000 *rapatriés*. Between 1968 and 1975, this immigration amounted to 41 percent of the regional demographic growth (Labasse et al. 1986:46). The result was a sense that foreigners overwhelmed the indigenous population. Observers reported that, "in a region where demographic growth is not glaring, the Rhônalpin has the impression—and he is not wrong— that from nursery schools to public housing, from the soccer team to the clientele of driving schools, from the Saturday night dance to the Courts, the youth is 'foreign'" (Labasse et al. 1986:48). Thus even regions experiencing economic growth are not invulnerable to pressures created by the rapid influx of immigrants and to the anti-immigrant sentiment that may accompany it.

As these pressures built, opposition to immigration began to organize politically. Feeling the brunt of the burden of the immigrant population, the parties of the left and, in particular, the French Communist Party addressed the issue. As early as 1963, the Political Bureau of the PCF issued a statement concerning the role of foreign workers in the economy. And in 1964, the communist trade union, the CGT (Confédération Générale du Travail), held a conference on the situation of Algerian workers; other *journées d'études* were held regularly thereafter.[24]

But the regional-specific pressure was even more clearly visible when, in 1969 and again in 1972 and 1974, the communist mayors of the Paris region issued statements condemning the concentration of immigrant workers in their neighborhoods (Vieuguet 1975). The 1969 declaration criticized the "immigration policy designed to provide large capitalist companies a cheap workforce—to increase their profits—and to put pressure on the salaries of all workers" (Vieuguet 1975:216). After complaining of the forty-six thou-

---

24. The PCF/CGT position is sometimes labeled ambiguous (Silverman 1992:45). But their position is clear: all immigration should be subordinated to union control so that "national interests" can be protected (Gani 1972). One means of protecting workers' interests is the equalization of salaries, benefits and other services between the immigrant and indigenous working classes to avoid labor market competition and to reduce demand.

sands individuals still living in 117 *bidonvilles*, the statement came to the crux of the problem: "Essentially, immigrant workers are concentrated in communist municipalities. They seek social aid. . . . But their massive presence in these communities comes also from the fact that it is toward them that the government systematically directs the new immigrants. The result for our cities is the insupportable charges [on government services] for which solutions cannot be found at the local level" (Vieuguet 1975:216–17). As Douglas Ashford (1982:283) described it, "Communist mayors began to encounter racial hostility, and the mounting costs of social services for immigrants limited what they could do for their own voters." Thus the communist mayors demanded the "equitable distribution" of foreign workers among municipalities. The October 1969 declaration was followed by demonstrations in various municipalities, including Champigny-sur-Marne, Nanterre, Argenteuil, Gennevillier, and Ivry (Vieuguet 1975:163).[25]

These regional-specific protests coincided with indicators of anti-immigrant pressure generated by the size of the immigrant population, the rates of immigration growth, and the level of local unemployment. Several departments scored high on all three indicators of anti-immigrant pressures, which are all based on the proportion of immigration in each department; the first indicator incorporates the level of unemployment, the second the growth in immigration, and the third combines both the growth and unemployment figures. Paris, Seine-St-Denis, Val-de-Marne, and Hauts-de-Seine were all departments within the Paris region heavily affected by immigration and loss of employment. The Loire Department also scored high, reflecting the influx of immigrants associated with the economic growth in the Lyon metropolitan area but the locally poor economic conditions associated with industrial restructuring. Departments on the Mediterranean littoral are prominent on the first dimension of anti-immigrant pressures (Pyrénées-Orientales, Alpes-Maritimes, Bouches-du-Rhône, Hérault, Gard, and Var) because of their undiversified economic bases. Moselle, in the Lorraine, is in a similar situation. The two other indicators of anti-immigrant pressures point to additional departments in Paris (Val-d'Oise, Yvelines, and Essonnes) and in the Rhône-Alpes region (Isère, Rhône, Ain, Haute-Savoie) that experienced rapid increases in immigrant populations. Table 5.6 enumerates the various departments affected by immigration and pressures created by the presence of immigrants.

Much of the recent literature on immigration in France, paralleling that for Britain, focuses on race and the changing composition of the immigrants from mostly European stock to a substantial proportion—although less than

---

25. To give the communist mayors their due, they recognized the needs and aspirations of the immigrants as "legitimate" but argued that their communities should not bear the burden.

Table 5.6. Scores of anti-immigrant pressures in French departments with greatest pressures, 1962–1975

Department	Anti-immigrant 1[a]		Anti-immigrant 2[b]		Anti-immigrant 3[c]		Number of constituencies	
	Score	Rank[d]	Score	Rank[d]	Score	Rank[d]	Swing	Total
Paris	96.4	1	90.5	2	643	2	19	31
Seine-St-Denis	88.4	2	110.0	1	671	1	4	9
Pyrénées-Orientales	81.9	3					0	2
Bouches-du-Rhône	70.6	4			85	18	3	11
Alpes-Maritimes	70.3	5					3	6
Hérault	64.7	6					3	5
Moselle	62.1	7					1	8
Loire	59.8	8	33.0	11	235	4	2	7
Hauts-de-Seine	56.9	9	54.5	3	267	3	9	13
Gard	54.9	10					2	4
Val-de-Marne	54.4	11	46.5	6	228	6	5	8
Var	54.3	12					3	4
Isère	48.3	13			96	15	6	7
Rhône	47.6	14	46.2	7	199	7	3	10
Val-d'Oise			50.8	4	229	5	4	5
Yvelines			50.1	5	180	8	5	8
Haute-Savoie			39.5	8	134	12	0	3
Ain			39.4	9	110	13	1	3
Doubes			36.9	10	163	10	1	3
Essonne			30.1	12	144	11	4	4
All departments								
Mean	28.4		9.8		47			
Mode	23.5		3.5		18			

[a] The 1975 proportion of immigrants in the department multiplied by departmental unemployment rate in 1978 (the first year in which department unemployment rates are available).

[b] The 1975 proportion of immigrants in the department multiplied by the overall increase in immigration between 1962 and 1975.

[c] The 1975 proportion of immigrants in the department multiplied by the departmental unemployment rate in 1978 and the overall increase in immigration.

[d] Rank in anti-immigrant pressures among the 94 departments (Corsica excluded).

Sources: INSEE, *Recensement général,* 1975, and *Statistiques et indicateurs des régions françaises,* 1984.

50 percent—non-European stock, mostly from North Africa. The 1962, 1968, and 1982 censuses enumerate the Algerian population. If we take these figures as indicators of the North African immigrant population more broadly, we find that the presence of Algerians is highly correlated with the presence of other immigrants and with indicators of anti-immigrant sentiment, as is the case in Britain with NCW and other immigrants. The data in Table 5.7 demonstrate that the proportion of resident Algerian immigrants in 1968 is correlated with the presence of Algerians in 1962 ($r = 0.90$) and with the total foreign population in 1962 (0.62), in 1968 (0.75), and in 1975

Table 5.7. Coefficients of correlation among location of Algerians, foreign-born population, unemployment, growth in immigration, and "anti-immigrant" departments in France, 1962–1982

	1	2	3	4	5	6	7	8	9	10	11
1. Aliens, 1962	1.00										
2. Algerians, 1962	0.67	1.00									
3. Aliens, 1968	0.93	0.75	1.00								
4. Algerians, 1968	0.62	0.90	0.75	1.00							
5. Aliens, 1975	0.81	0.79	0.93	0.82	1.00						
6. Aliens, 1982	0.70	0.79	0.86	0.83	0.96	1.00					
7. Algerians, 1982	0.58	0.86	0.72	0.96	0.81	0.84	1.00				
8. Change, 1962–75	-0.08	0.36	0.24	0.48	0.52	0.60	0.54	1.00			
9. Unemployment, 1978	0.17	0.08	0.12	0.13	0.00	-0.04	0.11	-0.25	1.00		
10. Anti-immigrant 1	0.81	0.75	0.90	0.78	0.89	0.84	0.76	0.33	0.40	1.00	
11. Anti-immigrant 2	0.08	0.49	0.37	0.62	0.61	0.72	0.66	0.92	-0.17	0.46	1.00
12. Anti-immigrant 3	0.06	0.46	0.33	0.59	0.55	0.66	0.64	0.86	-0.05	0.48	0.97

Sources: INSEE, *Recensement général*, 1962, 1968, 1975, 1982, and *Statistiques et indicateurs des régions françaises*, 1984.

(0.82). It is also moderately to highly correlated with all three anti-immigrant scores (r = 0.78, 0.62, and 0.59 respectively).

What is interesting and may help explain the emphasis on North African immigration in the literature is that the anti-immigrant scores are more closely correlated with the presence of Algerians than with the presence of aliens as a whole in this early period. For example, although the proportion of aliens in 1962 is highly correlated with the first anti-immigrant score, it is virtually unrelated to the second and third anti-immigrant scores (r = 0.81, 0.08, and 0.06 respectively). The same holds true for the presence of aliens in 1968 (r = 0.90, 0.37, and 0.33 respectively) because the presence of Algerians is more closely associated with new areas of immigration than with the old. Figure 5.3 demonstrates the same skewed distribution of the Algerian immigrant population that was visible for NCW immigrants in Britain. And the presence of Algerians is a better indicator of anti-immigrant pressures than the presence of the overall immigrant population because Algerians are located in regions of recent immigration, a relationship illustrated in Figure 5.4. The role of Algerians as indicators of new areas of immigration drops off by 1982, when the correlation between the presence of foreigners is very similar to the relationship between Algerians and anti-immigrant sentiment, as in Britain. By 1982, the new patterns of immigration created an immigrant distribution that more closely resembles the concentration of immigrants in Britain. Unemployment alone is only slightly correlated with the presence of immigrants or Algerians and with anti-immigrant sentiment, but the presence of Algerians and immigrants more broadly is strongly correlated with indicators of anti-immigrant sentiment.[26]

Thus, indicators of anti-immigrant pressures converged with the public expression of this sentiment, especially in the Paris region, where the PCF mayors were the most vocal critics of the regime, to a large extent because immigrants were concentrated in those municipalities. These regional-specific demands were reflected in national political forums as well. In the National Assembly, the left opposition demanded "a special 'status' for immigrant workers guaranteeing the same rights and duties for all workers" (Freeman 1979:91). This proposal reflected accurately the position of the PCF, that immigration should be controlled and that one method of control was raising the cost of immigrant workers to the level of indigenous workers. It was thus compatible with a policy of restricted immigration but was based on "economic rather than racial criteria" (Freeman 1979:91).

More broadly, other groups became involved in the issue of immigration. The Economic and Social Council (Conseil Économique et Social, or CES),

26. See Lewis-Beck 1993 for an analysis of the National Front vote. He finds a similar relationship: the National Front vote was unrelated to the level of unemployment alone but was strongly related to unemployment in combination with a strong presence of immigrants.

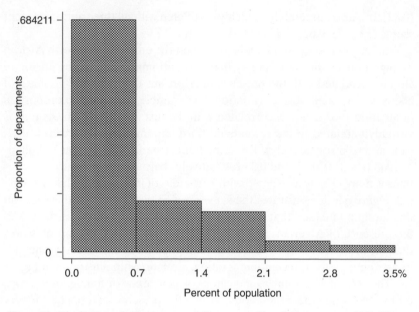

Figure 5.3. Distribution of Algerian population among French departments, 1968. (*Source:* INSEE, *Recensement général,* 1968.)

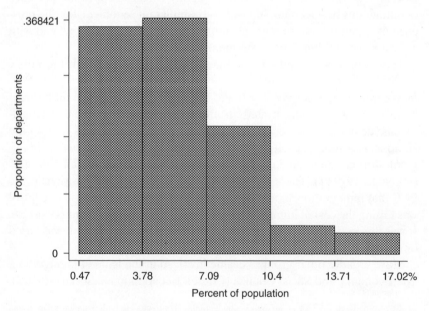

Figure 5.4. Distribution of immigrant population among French departments, 1982. (*Source:* INSEE, *Recensement général,* 1982.)

an advisory body to the government composed of various societal representatives, issued an initial report on Francophone African immigrants to France as early as 1964 (CES 1964). But a second, broader look at the issue was not long in following. In May 1968, before the May events, the CES requested a detailed study of immigration in France, which was completed in 1969. The report noted that immigrants generally made higher use of social services than the native population (CES 1969). A survey conducted by the Ministry of Social Affairs in April 1968 revealed that 14.5 percent of those receiving public aid (unemployment payments) were foreign, whereas foreigners constituted only approximately 8 percent of the workforce. A year earlier, the Ministry of Social Affairs released a report that estimated an 18 percent unemployment rate among Algerians. In light of such facts, the council called for a "real immigration policy," one that emphasized control and selectivity. This report was supported by all representative groups to the CES, with one exception: the representatives of private employers.

Thus the division was not partisan, with parties of the left lining up against parties of the right, but one that juxtaposed those bearing the costs of immigration against those garnering the benefits.[27] Although immigrants were concentrated primarily in communist municipalities, complaints were similar, wherever they were concentrated, regardless of whether the mayor was communist, socialist, or associated with one of the parties of the far right. In fact, the efforts on the left side of the political spectrum were matched by those on the right. November 1969 marks the formation of the extreme right group, New Order (Ordre Nouveau), which adopted a two-pronged strategy of direct action in the streets and contention for political power in elections. It was the leaders of New Order who took the initiative to organize the National Front (Front National, or FN) three years later, in October 1972, to unite the various right-wing splinter groups under a single political party. Both groups preached an anti-immigrant policy (Marcus 1995).

Today, many authors point to this period as one of relative quiescence on the part of the public. But the authors of the era perceived the environment quite differently. Juliette Minces, whose book was published in 1973, dates the public debate on immigration to 1967. According to her observations, it was "in the last five years that immigration has become a phenomenon about which everyone is talking: public authorities, political and union organizations, personalities, the press, etc." (1973:29).[28] This picture of growing

---

27. The nonpartisan reaction to immigration is noted by Schain 1985:174 as well in his discussion of the housing problem: "While politically charged, [it] has not been an issue of partisan contention."
28. Also see Grosser 1975 on the self-imposed censorship of the media, attributed either to government or "monopoly" control that reduced the level of investigative reporting on politically sensitive issues such as immigration.

concern among various societal groups is confirmed by the few public opinion polls on the subject. The French had a remarkably positive opinion of the contributions that immigrants made: 68 percent of those responding to a 1971 questionnaire felt that immigrants provided a service to the country and 63 percent believed that immigrants conducted themselves as they should (Girard 1971). Nonetheless, a clear majority of the French population thought that the immigrant population was too high and that annual inflows of immigrants were also too high. Further, negative attitudes toward immigrants were associated with contact with them (Girard 1971).[29]

Public concern over immigration is also confirmed by numerous press reports on the conditions of immigrants, including the publicity arising from the deaths of five African workers, asphyxiated in their hovel in Aubervilliers (a suburb of Paris), in January 1970. That these tensions were politically important is demonstrated by the arrival on the scene of the prime minister, Jacques Chaban-Delmas, to promise additional resources to rehouse the immigrants.

Electoral incentives for immigration control, 1968–1972

Pressure was thus building. Could the government, as Jeanne Singer-Kérel (1976:49–50) suggested, "possibly be influenced by immediate preoccupations, that is electoral [preoccupations], such as the xenophobia of part of the French?" The immediate answer was no. The Gaullist majority could afford to ignore the calls for a more restrictive and selective immigration policy. Its position in the National Assembly was strong. The May events of 1968, which combined a student revolt with a widely based strike among the working classes, led to an electoral backlash in June 1968 that ensconced the Gaullist majority firmly in the National Assembly—296 seats of 487—with an additional margin of 64 seats from its allies, the Independent Republicans (Frears 1991). No concentration of immigrants in left electoral constituencies could threaten this majority. Nor could the complaints of the Gaullist coalition partners. The only question was how long this state of affairs would last because all recognized that this exceptional outcome would be transitory. In any event, National Assembly elections would not have to be called until the spring of 1973, at the end of the five-year legislative term.

The first challenge came in 1969, when President de Gaulle called a referendum on Senate reform (and on regionalization). On this issue, the right was split, with an important electoral and parliamentary ally, Valéry Giscard d'Estaing, supporting a "no" position.[30] The failure of this referendum led to

---

29. The analysis was bivariate and therefore did not control for various other factors, including economic conditions. No tests of statistical significance were reported.
30. Giscard d'Estaing was the leader of the Independent Republicans.

de Gaulle's resignation and a presidential election. But the left remained in disarray following the May events, and Pompidou, the longtime Gaullist prime minister, ran against a centrist candidate, the president of the Senate and interim president of the republic, Alain Poher. Either candidate would have retained the sitting National Assembly, so these presidential elections did not threaten the Gaullist majority.[31]

Electoral incentives for immigration control, 1972

The next indicator that allowed the Gaullists to gauge the political winds was the 1971 municipal elections. Municipal elections are important for two reasons. First, many national political figures begin their careers as local politicians and retain their local offices as a means of enhancing national electoral support. As a result, winning or retaining local electoral office is central to retaining national electoral office and hence the National Assembly majority (Frears 1977). Second, the municipal elections are often seen as a harbingers of the National Assembly elections. That the 1971 municipal elections were "regarded nationally and internationally as a dress rehearsal" for the 1973 parliamentary election is confirmed by a member of the centrist opposition (Frears 1977:235). The PDM (Progrès et démocratie moderne) deputy and mayor of St. Étienne, Michel Durafour, noted in early 1971, "For several weeks the Government seems to have decided to give these local elections a political twist. One realises why. It thinks that the elections foreshadow the parliamentary elections of 1973 and especially the presidential elections of 1976" (Hayward and Wright 1971:285).[32] Thus the Gaullists came out in force to run for local offices: among the candidates were 36 of the 41 ministers of government. More generally, 379 of the 487 deputies and 191 of the 283 senators, as well as a large number of senior civil servants, sought local office, demonstrating the significance of municipal elections to national legislative elections (Hayward and Wright 1971).

As a result, unlike local elections in the United States, turnout is high for municipal elections. The French vote in higher numbers in municipal elections than in any others, save presidential contests. Even National Assembly elections rank lower in importance because "the municipal election takes

---

31. Poher's position was not readily apparent, and he therefore reassured the voters that he would not dissolve the National Assembly should he be elected president (Charlot and Charlot 1970). Pompidou's position was, of course, taken for granted.

32. The municipal elections are also important for Senate elections because the 468,000 local councillors predominate in the electoral colleges that choose the senators. Thus, according to Hayward and Wright 1971:285–86, "the failure to eliminate the Senate as an Opposition bastion in the April 1969 referendum has left intact the underrepresentation of the [Gaullist] UDR in the Second Chamber and increased the need for more seats on local councils."

place in a well-known context, where one lives and where the ballot has a decisive influence on the quality of life" (Ysmal 1990:72).

And immigration was an electoral issue. Just days before the first round of the March elections, the government granted New Order permission to hold an election rally at the Palais des Sports in Paris. *L'Humanité*, the PCF daily newspaper, described the rally as "proof of a growing insolence in its antisemitic campaigns and its efforts to mobilize the population against immigrant workers through insults and menaces" (3 March 1971, 1). The issue continued to generate headlines when the rally resulted in a coun-terdemonstration by MRAP (Mouvement contre le racisme et pour l'amitié entre les peuples) that degenerated into street fighting and ended only with the arrival of the riot police. At least according to the left, the conservative parties of government were implicated in New Order's anti-immigrant posi-tions because they readily granted this extremist group access to public facilities.

But the right was not the only part of the political spectrum concerned with immigrants. In addition to the concerns raised by the Paris PCF mayors, party members were also asking questions. In the days leading up to the municipal elections, *L'Humanité* ran an article in response to readers' ques-tion, "Is there competition between French and immigrant workers?" (6 March 1971, 7). The response was "In part, yes." In essence, the PCF main-tained that if employers were required to pay the same wages and benefits to immigrant workers as to French workers, there would be no demand for immigrant workers.[33] Until this happened, immigrants would continue to flood into France and compete with French workers for jobs and make claims on social services.

The 1971 elections thus served to inform the government of both sensitive campaign issues and electoral standing. And although the results of the municipal elections were mixed, they suggested that the honeymoon with the Gaullist majority was over (Hayward and Wright 1971). The left increased its share of mayoralties in the 193 biggest towns from 37.6 to 39.8 percent (Hayward and Wright 1971:310). The Gaullists' results were "satis-factory," but the electoral losses of their right-center electoral and par-liamentary allies potentially threatened the national parliamentary coalition. These center parties lost nine of sixty-three mayoralties (Lancelot 1988: 116).

Gaullists therefore began to plan a parliamentary electoral strategy to con-front "the next decisive test [that] will come with the general election of

33. In the words of the PCF's daily newspaper, "To the degree that employers are obligated to give immigrant workers salaries identical to those of the French, that the government is required to provide housing, to open schools, to develop real professional training, the outrageous, frenzied immigration policy will no longer have any reason to exist" (*L'Humanité*, 6 March 1971, 7).

1973" (Hayward and Wright 1971:311). This perception of electoral threat coincides with various contemporaneous electoral analyses. D. B. Goldey and R. I. W. Johnson (1973:321) noted that "as in 1967, but now after 15 years of consecutive Gaullist rule, the majority seemed threatened by a swing to the left, by the feeling that it was 'time for a change.'" Moreover, "among the 370 strong majority, 90 to 100 sitting members were almost certain to lose their seats at the next election; twice as many were afraid they would be the victims." John Frears notes that "what makes 1973 particularly interesting is that it was the first election in the Fifth Republic which the opposition was thought to have a chance of winning" (1991:175). But the left opposition was not the only concern of the Gaullists. Anticipated Gaullist losses enhanced the need for parliamentary allies of the center-right, even, or perhaps especially, in those constituencies where the opposition left was not an electoral threat.[34]

French politicians, like those elsewhere, tended to focus their strategies on the swing voters who could affect the outcome of the election.[35] This focus was reflected at the 1972 Gaullist party conference, where Robert Boulin, the minister in charge of parliamentary relations, worried that "the numbers demonstrate that the upcoming elections, just like all those that have taken place these last years, will be carried by the movement of 4 percent of the votes. The success of a popular front can not be dismissed. The result will play on these marginal masses" (quoted in Le Gall and Riglet 1973:86).[36] These concerns grew as the election approached. The general secretary of the Gaullist Union pour la défense de la République (UDR), Alain Peyrefitte, calculated that "in 188 constituencies that remain to be decided, the results depend on less than 200 votes" (*Provençal*, 8 March 1973, 17). And the day before the election, the prime minister, Pierre Messmer, urged supporters to go to the polls, noting that "Sunday, seats will be lost or won by only a few votes" (*Provençal*, 10 March 1973, 19).

Because the 1968 legislative elections were widely perceived as an inappropriate indicator of future results, analysts turned to the 1967 legislative

34. Another indicator of declining electoral support comes from the April 1972 referendum called by President Pompidou, on enlargement of the European Community. Although 68% of the voters supported the referendum, the widespread abstention and spoiling of ballots—47% of the registered voters—led analysts to see this as a defeat (Goldey and Johnson 1973).

35. Modifying electoral institutions represents an additional and complementary strategy for ensuring a parliamentary majority. For example, de Gaulle modified the rules for qualifying for the second-round ballot to improve the possibilities for electoral victory (Goguel 1983). And the main reason for calling for direct presidential elections was the lack of electoral support in the presidential electoral college (Penniman 1975).

36. Lancelot describes "the play of the majoritarian system, [which] . . . permitted the parliamentary majority, with a few thousand more votes, to find itself almost as numerous as after the election of 1962. But several thousand fewer votes would have been sufficient for electoral failure. This is a phenomenon that recalls in many ways certain characteristics of the British political system" (quoted in Goguel 1983:491).

elections as a more accurate harbinger of the 1973 contest.[37] In 1967 the Gaullist coalition retained the slimmest of parliamentary margins, 245 seats in a 487-seat parliament—201 Gaullist deputies allied with 44 Independent Republican deputies. The concerns over swing constituencies were magnified by the trends visible in 1967, when the left's electoral gains were most prominent in regions of high immigrant concentration. The noncommunist left had progressed in the Marseille, Lyon, and Bordeaux areas, two of which were high immigrant areas. The PCF also made large gains in the Paris region, the industrial north, and Languedoc, all three with substantial immigrant populations. And in a mirror image, Gaullist losses were largest in these areas, especially in the Paris region (Frears 1977, Goguel 1983). It was in this atmosphere that the government began to address immigration control seriously.

These trends are confirmed by a more detailed analysis of swing constituencies in anti-immigrant regions. Gérard Le Gall and Marc Riglet (1973) demonstrate that the largest number of seats that changed parties between the 1967 and 1968 elections were those where the difference between the two parties in the second round was 10 to 16 percent, that is, where 5 to 8 percent of the voters switched sides and changed the outcome of the election.[38] Moreover, three-quarters of the 142 seats lost by the left to the right in 1968 had swings of 16 percent or less, although some constituencies experienced swings of more than 40 percent. Therefore, I employ the 16 percent difference as the cutoff in designating swing constituencies.

Referring back to Table 5.6, we can see that a significant number of the electoral constituencies in the anti-immigrant departments were swing constituencies. In particular, seven of the eight departments in the Ile de France region ranked high on two or three indicators of anti-immigrant pressures. Together, the electoral constituencies accounted for 78 of the 487 National Assembly seats (16%), and of these, two-thirds (50) were swing constituencies. These figures confirm the speculations of analysts who argue that the 1964 departmental and electoral redistricting of the Paris region followed a political dynamic, slicing traditionally left working-class districts in order to make the right more competitive (Boyer et al. 1986).[39] Swing constituencies

37. According to Le Gall and Riglet 1973:91–92, "It is likely that the reference to 1968 is considered too hazardous by the victors themselves, the political conditions presiding over that success having little chance to be replicated in the next elections and, in contrast, the general political connections on the one hand and the state of [electoral] alliances on the other call irresistibly for a comparison with the 1967 legislative elections." Also see Goguel 1983:22.

38. Frears 1977:184 argues that "the more politics in France becomes polarized between the *Union de la Gauche* and the *Majorité*, the more one can use second ballot Left–*Majorité* duels for purposes of comparison."

39. The prefect of the Paris Department at that time claimed that his superiors had ordered him to "break the red [communist] suburbs" by "drowning" them "with areas farther away, going toward the provinces." See Cazeaux 1997:iv.

from the Paris region alone, if compared with the 1967 elections, were sufficient to swing national electoral outcomes. And Parisians were vocal in their concerns about the level of immigration.

Concern over the electoral safety of other regions would only add to the pressure from the Paris region. The parties of the center-right had strong electoral bases in several departments affected by immigration in the Rhône-Alpes region (Ain, Loire, Isère, Haute-Savoie, and Rhône) and in Moselle (Goguel 1983). Schain (1985, 1988) documents the nonpartisan nature of the issues elicited by the immigrant populations. The fact that these concerns were not publicly voiced by local politicians of the center-right, in a manner similar to the communist mayors of Paris, suggests not the absence of concerns but the links with the parliamentary majority that funneled these demands in a less public manner to avoid embarrassment to the ruling majority.

This picture of swing constituencies conflicts with several portraits of French electoral stability. But Le Gall and Riglet (1973) suggest that traditional views on electoral fiefs are not substantiated by the data. Moreover, the French are not averse to split tickets, voting in municipal and national legislative elections for one party and at the presidential level for another. As Colette Ysmal (1990:77) notes, "An elector can vote for a solidly implanted deputy of the right and for a president of the left; for a long known and appreciated deputy of the left and a conservative president." In the 1965 presidential election, for example, de Gaulle polled well "even in working-class industrial districts in northern cities like Lille and communist suburbs of the Paris 'red belt' like Nanterre and Montreuil" (Frears 1977:196; Goguel 1983). Thus various departments were potential electoral prizes that elicited a proactive strategy of responding to perceived local problems.

It is not surprising, then, that the government implemented policies that attempt to relieve these problems. This proactive strategy was an attempt to convince swing voters in constituencies experiencing immigrant pressures that the problem was resolved. The Fontanet and Marcellin circulars of 1972 addressed labor market competition between the indigenous working classes and immigrant workers by requiring that employers advertise available positions locally for three weeks before requesting an immigrant worker. They also reduced the strain on infrastructure by requiring proof of adequate housing for immigrant workers. This strategy reduced pressures on the state by shifting the problem onto employers or, more likely, onto the immigrants themselves. The requirement to provide housing, in an environment of severe shortage, was also a powerful method of reducing levels of immigration.

These proactive strategies were complemented by campaign promises in the 1973 legislative elections by both the government and the opposition.

Immigration was not a major campaign theme at the national level, in large part because most French citizens were unaffected by immigration.[40] But it did play a role in specific constituencies and is reflected in the thriving regional press, in which local news and local campaign coverage form the "core content" (Charon 1991:17).

For example, *Le Provençal*, the newspaper of Marseille and the surrounding region, reported on difficulties associated with the government's immigration policy and asked the candidates to respond (9 March 1973, 5). Campaign speeches by individual legislators promised to "solve" the immigrant problem. Charles-Emile Loa, a candidate in the second constituency of Lyon, claimed to have championed the reduction of *bidonvilles* in the city (*Provençal*, 1 March 1973). In Marseille, "once again election time brought the customary promises by the [socialist] municipality and the [opposition] Gaullists to rebuild the . . . *bidonvilles* which house foreign workers" (Bell 1973:343). *L'Humanité* reported the Gaullist UDR candidate's appeals to anti-immigrant sentiment in the Paris suburb of Argenteuil, which had a immigrant population of 25 percent (4 March 1973).

Campaign platforms promised immigration reform. The PCF program had always contained an element of control whereby "the entry of immigrant workers shall be modulated and regulated" ("Spécial: Élections" 1973:6). This element of control was taken up in the combined left's campaign platform, the Common Program (*Programme Commun*), negotiated with the Socialist Party (Parti Socialiste, or PS) in 1972.[41] The Gaullist UDR also incorporated an immigration control dimension in its platform arguing for a "reinforcement of the state's control over migratory flows . . . to avoid the creation of an 'under-class' at the margins of our life that elicits xenophobic reactions" ("Spécial: Élections" 1973:1).

And the National Front began to participate in the electoral process. The newly formed party fielded around one hundred candidates. Its focus was regionally specific, with two-thirds of the candidates standing in constituencies in the Parisian basin (Marcus 1995). Their minimal electoral success may have been less a function of immigration as an issue than the fact that mainstream parties of both the left and the right themselves promised to "solve" the immigration problem (Kitschelt 1995).

Thus, as Singer-Kérel (1976:51) puts it, "The government could not ignore indefinitely the press campaigns describing the life conditions of the immi-

---

40. A parallel may be drawn to California's governor Pete Wilson, who used immigration and the anti-immigrant Proposition 187 to help retain his governorship in 1994; he employed the same issue in his presidential bid in 1996 but failed miserably, at least in part because immigration failed to attract the same attention nationally as it did in California.

41. This element of control was also taken up by the trade unions. Although they rejected the Fontanet and Marcellin circulars, the unions "favored halting all new immigration" (Ashford 1982:277).

grants, the slums, the *bidonvilles*, the *marchands de sommeil*.[42] Above all, it could not remain indifferent to the xenophobic, racist campaigns, leading to *ratonnades* (beatings) and to assassinations. This is the moment when it again became fashionable to talk of 'thresholds of tolerance.' "

In the election itself, the Gaullist coalition retained its parliamentary majority, but only by the slimmest of margins. After the first-ballot results, the Gaullists realized that the combined Gaullist and Independent Republican forces were unlikely to reach a majority. Therefore, they hastily negotiated an electoral alliance with the members of the center opposition, the CDP (Centre Démocratie et Progrès), assuring them of the 30 seats needed to form a parliamentary party in exchange for their support in parliament. Thus the ultimate electoral outcome was a fragile coalition composed of 183 Gaullists, 55 Independent Republicans, and 30 CDP members, for a majority of 268 in the 490-seat legislature.

Electoral incentives for immigration control, 1974

If the efforts to diminish the costs of immigration contributed to the maintenance of the Gaullist majority, they did little to reduce the controversy over the issue. Although the Fontanet and Marcellin circulars reduced immigration substantially, they made the situation of immigrants in France more precarious. The immigrants themselves, sustained by trade unions and parties of the left, began to protest their conditions.[43] In March 1973, a strike of foreign semiskilled workers broke out in the Renault factories. Although it was not the first strike of immigrant workers, by paralyzing production it brought home the central role of foreign workers in the French economy and, produced a counterreaction. Three months after the strike, public authorities again authorized a meeting of New Order to protest against *l'immigration sauvage* (uncontrolled immigration) (Singer-Kérel 1976:46). Street demonstrations that pitted the forces of the extreme right against the left in Paris that June led the government to ban New Order (Marcus 1995). Some citizens decided to take matters in their own hands by attacking North Africans in immigrant neighborhoods of Paris. A Portuguese immigrant worker was killed in the Paris suburb of Vitry in July (Weil 1991).

By August 1973, anti-immigrant riots broke out in the streets of Marseille, triggered by the death of a streetcar driver at the hands of a mentally ill Algerian. The violence continued as retribution was exacted on the resident

42. The literal French translation of this phrase is the colorful "merchants of sleep," applied to slumlords who rented rooms by shift to immigrant workers.
43. The support of the parties of the left is consonant with their position of controlling the influx of immigrants while providing resident immigrants with conditions equal to those of the indigenous working classes.

Algerian community, with violent attacks and murder, resulting in eleven Algerian deaths (Weil 1991). The conditions were sufficiently horrific to elicit a visit by President Pompidou and the Algerian government's suspension of emigration to France. Finally, the oil crisis of late 1973 brought high inflation, a plummeting franc, and a slow rise in unemployment rates, triggering increasing labor market pressures.[44] In the absence of electoral pressure, the government took no immediate steps to restrict immigration further, and it actually relaxed the conditions of the Fontanet Circular during the summer of 1973. But Pompidou's death in April 1974 and the unanticipated presidential election that followed triggered a response.

The presidential campaign is unlike the legislative elections because there is but one, national, electoral constituency and no swing constituencies per se. Nonetheless, geographic electoral analyses are ubiquitous. Electoral analyses are routinely presented by department, electoral swings among the various parties are traced at the departmental level, and presidential campaigns are organized at the departmental level (Penniman 1975, Colliard 1979, Berne 1981, Goguel 1983). Mitterrand's electoral team, for example, consisted of the national and federal secretaries of the PS and ninty-five departmental delegates to organize and support the departmental campaigns (*Provençal*, 8 May 1974, 18).

Because departments are central to electoral strategies, the picture of anti-immigrant departments sketched above provides an indication of the level and location of anti-immigrant pressures. These departments were still reeling under the impact of large immigrant flows. The vocal reaction to these pressures again came from the communist mayors of Paris, who issued statements in 1972 and again in 1974.

Immigration control remained an issue despite continued pressure from economic sectors most in need of immigrant labor. In 1969, employers' representatives had unanimously rejected the recommendations of the Economic and Social Council for a "controlled and selective" immigration policy (CES 1969). In the construction industry, among others, labor markets remained tight, and the Parisian Building Federation negotiated with the administration to facilitate continued access to foreign workers (Henneresse 1979). At the annual conference of the National Council of French Employers (Conseil National du Patronat François, or CNPF), employers' strategies retained a concern with the availability of immigrant workers. Employers called for the provision of unmarried immigrant workers while developing contingency plans in case of shortages: "revaluing" manual labor and transferring capital abroad (Henneresse 1979).[45]

---

44. The 1973 oil crisis probably also increased anti-Arab sentiment.
45. Carmel 1976:382 also argues that the CNPF's change of heart was the result of competition among European countries for immigrants and the fear of a shortage of immigrant workers. Unless

Although pressures against immigration had grown, as in the 1973 national legislative elections, immigration was not a major presidential campaign issue at the national level. The election literature sent at government cost by the candidates to the electorate was uniform, by law (*Textes* 1975). Immigration, as an issue of local concern, did not appear.[46] But the local forum provided an arena in which politicians could address local concerns. An example comes from Le Pen, a presidential candidate in 1974. He "did his best to stir up the Xenophobic anti-immigrant vote" (Hayward and Wright 1974:211), yet none of his national campaign literature or his nationally televised speeches incorporated an anti-immigrant platform (*Textes* 1975:49–52, 77–78). Thus national platforms are not always the best method of gauging the power of local electoral concerns.

Yet the issue remained a burning one in the period directly preceding the 1974 presidential election. *Le Monde* surveyed immigration issues in its 22 January 1974 edition. The article noted four new phenomena, including "the apparition of racial and political tensions between immigrants and certain fringes of the autochthonous population." It concluded that "this panorama would not be complete if the recent degradation of the climate of relations between France in general and her migrant workers, especially Maghrebin [North African], were not evoked here."[47]

The regional papers also discussed immigration. Tensions surrounding the issue in Lyon were sufficiently high for the regional newspaper, *Le Progrès*, to run an editorial on 29 April, just days before the first round of the presidential election:

> Passerby, who frequents the center of the city, next to the recently opened construction site, just at the bottom of the overpass for the train, you will observe the regulation sign: a yellow triangle on which is pictured the silhouette of a worker with a shovel.
>
> Above of the head of the figure, an inscription in capital letters: BOUGNOUL.[48] For more than three weeks, this word has been visible. It has been read by hundreds and hundreds of people and alone the rain which started to fall erased these eight unhappy letters with which some poor fellow wanted to propagate his message of hate and stupidity. Of course, in his mind, it is the foreign workers, North Africans, or others, all combined in his malediction, who are the enemy. Portuguese, Arabs, Turks, and other faces, "not like our own," who are within our walls, wandering down our streets, admiring our daughters, working in our

---

adequate wages, housing, and working conditions were provided, foreign workers would be attracted to Germany, Switzerland, and elsewhere and France would lack an adequate labor force.

46. Freeman 1979:95 observes that, "despite the great turmoil that had existed the previous fall, immigration did not appear to be much of an issue in the [presidential] election."

47. Both citations were quoted in "Spécial: Migrants" (1974:23a).

48. This is a derogatory racist term applied mostly to North Africans, similar in connotation to the U.S. "nigger" and the British "wog." I thank Martin Schain for clarifying the use of the term.

factories and construction sites, and who, even with all that, occasionally look happy, especially when they are together, to laugh and to sing, or to talk in their dialect.

That's when the insult comes to mind but, because he is scared, he scribbles the word, hastily, as night falls, at the hour when the poor fellow is particularly disappointed by his job, which he hates, by his buddies who have abandoned him, by his wife who no longer loves him, by everything that has been done to him all day long. . . . That's when he has to do something: to cry out his misery, his disgust. He cannot live with the nausea. A piece of coal, the signpost on the construction site, BOUGNOUL, by his own hand, these eight letters, like the point of a sword.

The warm spring rain erases the inscription; . . . and the people of Lisbon sing and dance in the streets.

But editorials against xenophobia could not prevent the 10 May 1974 terrorist attack against an immigration reception center in Paris. Although no one was killed, the facility burned to the ground, preventing access to newly arrived immigrants (*Provençal*, 11 May 1974).

Politicians were aware of these anti-immigrant pressures and developed electoral platforms to "solve" the immigrant problem. These platforms were publicized in regions where immigration was an issue. Targeting campaign issues to local constituencies is common in France.[49] The electorate had a long tradition of "preference for politicians who are effective in defending local interests," and local election rallies are the primary means to address these concerns (Lord et al. 1968:153).[50] Thus, despite the absence of immigration on the national agenda, the issue was very much alive in particular constituencies and addressed by presidential candidates at that level.

For the ruling majority, the first-round campaign acted as a primary in which the Gaullist presidential candidate, Jacques Chaban-Delmas, was overshadowed by the Independent Republican Giscard d'Estaing. For the first time, Giscard d'Estaing thought it appropriate to delineate an immigration policy, which he argued could no longer be conceived exclusively as a labor market policy. He promised to give the resolution of the problem high priority by appointing a cabinet-level minister (Berne 1981).

François Mitterrand, the common candidate of the left, organized a

49. The ability of local officials to extract resources or beneficial policies from the national government in exchange for political support is well known in France. One example comes from the city of Lyon, where the exchange was labeled "pradelism," after the longtime mayor Louis Pradel. This Radical (center-right) mayor is reputed to have obtained major construction projects from President Pompidou "almost by blackmail ([by] the votes of the electors of Lyon that the mayor influenced)" (Labasse et al. 1986:52).

50. Also see Goldey and Johnson's 1973:327 description of candidates in the 1973 legislative elections who "concentrated on local matters and the benefits that they [would be] able to bring to their constituencies" and candidates "with strong local bases [who] fought on local issues."

caravan across the country, stopping to rally the faithful and convince the skeptics (Colliard 1979). Local meetings always consisted of three parts. Mitterrand began by talking about the local problems of the region where he was speaking. Only then would he criticize the opponents for their failure to resolve these problems. Finally, he ended with the campaign promises of the Common Program. These local rallies were forums that allowed politicians to tailor their national platforms to local conditions. And the itinerary for the caravan was set by electoral priorities. Before the second round of balloting, the itinerary took into account "either the results of the first round— a department . . . that was particularly unfavorable—or the express demands of local militants" (Colliard 1979:58).

The Common Program incorporated a platform on immigration, emphasizing conditions endured by immigrants. Not only was housing a problem, but a 1968 survey by the Employment Commission of the Sixth Plan found that foreign workers were paid, on average, 88 percent of French take-home wages, although regional averages ranged from 80 percent in Provence–Côte-d'Azur to 94 percent in the Lorraine ("Spécial: Migrants" 1974). To remedy these and other immigrant problems, the Common Program promoted equality. But at the same time, it promoted planned immigration within the broader context of employment policy ("Spécial: Migrants" 1974). Thus "unreserved support for the demands of immigrants who already work in France" was accompanied by "an opposition to the entry of new immigrants" (Vieuguet 1975:135).

The platform of the centrist CDP reflected the concerns of the public in regions of electoral strength such as Lyon. In the party's analysis, "the tendency of these new immigrants, deprived of any orientation, to rejoin the regions where a large number of their compatriots are already found, culminating in a growing concentration of immigrant workers in certain industrial regions or in certain suburbs of large cities, inevitably entrain[s] serious social tensions" ("Special: Migrants" 1974:5). These tensions were to be avoided by reducing immigrant flows.

And, of course, Le Pen enunciated the FN's program: "I not only agree to control severely immigration but even more to reduce progressively the volume in an important way. I hold, in effect, that the immigrant labor force prevents the necessary revalorization of manual work, the basis of a policy of social justice" (*Minute*, 1–7 May 1974). He justified this stance in part on the potential political impact of immigrants, claiming that "these millions of immigrants . . . constitute a mass of redoubtable followers in the hands of the leftists" (*Minute*, 22–28 May 1974).

The first round of the election on 5 May produced two candidates who proceeded to the second round, Valéry Giscard d'Estaing and François Mitterrand. On 12 May, as the polls showed an even race between the candidate of the left and the candidate of the right, Le Pen threw his support and that of his followers behind Giscard.[51] Le Pen had earlier warned, "Everything leads us to believe that the election will be played out within tens of thousands of votes. That is to say that the 190,000 votes I received in my name can make the difference" (*Parisien Libéré*, 9 May 1974, 3). Le Pen may have overrated the significance of his support, but *L'Humanité* captured a similar picture in its 13 May headline, "Le Pen to Giscard's Rescue."

In the second round of balloting, Giscard won by only four hundred thousand votes of the twenty-six million votes cast. And immigration retained a high priority in Giscard's program. With his presidential victory in hand, Giscard appointed the promised secretary of state for immigration. Within six weeks, a decision was taken at a council of ministers meeting to put a temporary halt to migration of permanent workers, a policy announced on 4 July 1974. It was accompanied by a halt in family immigration, although this policy was reversed the following year. The newly appointed secretary of state for immigration, Postel-Vinay, resigned shortly thereafter to protest the inadequacy of resources to carry out an ambitious project to house foreigners. But the next minister, Paul Dijoud, retained the same strategy and, in October 1974, permanently closed the door to immigration of workers.

The effects of the policy were dramatic. The level of entry of permanent workers was reduced from 132,055 in 1973 to 64,461 in 1974 and still further to 15,591 in 1975. To accommodate labor market needs without creating a permanent immigrant population, a new category of immigration was created in 1977, APT (*autorisations provisoires de travail*). APT immigrants normally held contracts of more than twelve months but less than two years. Even including APT workers, only around 20,000 permanent workers per year have been admitted since the controls were installed, a number that reflects European Union workers as well as noncitizen spouses of French citizens. Family migration, the control of which was constrained by court rulings, followed a slower descent from 72,647 in 1973 to 68,038 in 1974 and 51,824 in 1975. Family migration has ultimately leveled out at about 30,000 per year.

The date of this dramatic turn in immigration control in France might suggest that economic crisis was the crucial determinant of that policy. Such a conclusion, however, overlooks the *political* process through which such a decision might be made and contradicts many observations of the era.[52] For example, the OECD immigration experts noted in the 1974 SOPEMI report:

---

51. Giscard claimed that no deals were cut with Le Pen for this support.
52. A U.S. observer confirms that "if the futility of French policy towards immigrants had not become unmistakable during Pompidou's presidency [1969–74], it would have been possible to link the socioeconomic explanation to the . . . transformation of immigration policy (Ashford 1982:274).

These unilateral measures, that to some might appear, over time, to be linked to the energy crisis and to the international financial difficulties, were inspired by *essentially political motives.* . . . Everything happened as if the approach of a conjunctural recession, more anticipated than felt, as well, constituted an occasion and served to get accepted restrictive decisions taken based on the *social and political situation.* (Quoted in Wihtol de Wenden 1988:191)

And with the perspective that comes from distance, Catherine Wihtol de Wenden (1988:191) argued that "in France, this fundamental change in migratory policy is concomitant with a political 'inflection' linked to the election of Valéry Giscard d'Estaing to the presidency of the Republic in May 1974." Here I have traced the underlying political determinants of that "inflection."

Literature on French Immigration Control

I have argued that French politicians face the same electoral incentives as politicians in Britain and other advanced market economy countries, although those incentives are shaped by the institutional rules that govern the construction of a national government majority. Geographically concentrated immigration generated a rise in anti-immigrant pressures that the government was able to ignore, in large part because it was concentrated in opposition constituencies and because it coincided with a conservative backlash against the May events that provided the government with a broad majority in the National Assembly. The political winds were traced carefully by the Gaullist majority and, in the run-up to the 1973 National Assembly elections, the government began responding to these anti-immigrant pressures in left and centrist electoral constituencies in an effort to prevent an electoral swing that would undermine their National Assembly majority. The narrowness of the presidential election in 1974 reinforced the electoral incentives to respond to these local anti-immigrant pressures.

My analysis builds on and extends the literature on French immigration control but is distinctive in its emphasis on electoral incentives in this early period. Analysts who attempt to explain this period tend to rely on state-centered theories that contend that the state, insulated from societal pressures, pursues a state-defined interest such as cultural homogeneity or economic growth through improved productivity. Maxim Silverman (1992:71), for example, observes a "new consensus at the end of the 1960s; at the heart of this consensus was the new racialization of immigration." For analysts such as these, the shift from European immigrants (Italians, Spaniards, and Portuguese) to non-European immigrants (North Africans,

Turks, Yugoslavs, and black Africans) made the government conscious of the social costs of immigration as well as the economic benefits. My argument is consonant with their contentions that "it was not economic slowdown and manpower surplus which provided the initial justification for immigration controls in the modern period" (Silverman 1992:48). It differs from their emphasis on the "question of ethnic 'balance' and fears of the social tensions which would ensue if this balance was not maintained" (Silverman 1992:48).

It is true that the Calvez report (CES 1969), among others, makes clear the concern whether the "new" immigrants would be able to assimilate successfully into French society, and although the report explicitly denies a racist sorting of immigrants, it makes a clear distinction between European immigrants and "others." But the same concern was expressed by Georges Mauco in the 1940s, when he and other "populationists" argued for selective immigration. The analysts who focus on cultural homogeneity and assimilation provide no explanation of why these concerns elicited a reaction at one time whereas in an earlier period the same concerns were ignored.

It is also empirically accurate to point to the shift from immigrant intakes dominated by European stock to a substantial—although always less than majority—intake from non-European sources. Yet the government itself was an active recruiter of non-European immigrants, especially Moroccans, Tunisians, and Turks, and immigration streams explicitly included family members. It seems odd to rely on government actions as the source of government counteractions. Why would the government initially promote non-European immigration only to decide later that these groups were unacceptable? Moreover, the current zero-immigration policy is not particularly friendly to more ethnically homogeneous immigration from Central Europe and the Soviet successor states, now that these states have permitted emigration, a policy that is puzzling from the "racialization" perspective.[53]

A similar question arises regarding explanations that point to government goals of improved economic productivity. Juliette Minces (1973) and Georges Tapinos (1975) both describe the government's concern with modernization of the industrial base and the dampening of incentives to enhance productivity because of the availability of a cheap, immigrant labor force. These issues are reflected in the CES (1969) report as well. But the government actively promoted and permitted uncontrolled immigration for some

---

53. This is not to deny the existence of racism or its interaction with immigration. I do suggest, however, that it is more useful to separate immigration control polices from racism and to examine their interaction rather than to conflate the two variables.

twenty-five years before shifting priorities. The authors provide no basis for explaining why government priorities should have changed and why they changed in the late 1960s or early 1970s.

Explanations that rely on state interests tend to address the shift in immigration policy in an ad hominem manner. Moreover, they never elucidate the "black box" of the state, the process through which state interests are determined. The theoretical framework presented here moves beyond state-centered explanations to examine the incentive structures that drive politicians, who, in turn, determine state policy.

Alternatively, authors point to the bureaucracy itself as the source of policy (Ashford 1982).[54] It is true, in the case of France, that policies were promulgated by the bureaucracy, often without parliamentary debate. But these explanations lack a systematic account of bureaucratic interests, how they changed over time, and how power shifted among bureaucracies to produce the policy outcomes of first openness, then closure. Moreover, Marie-Claude Henneresse (1979:372), among others, has shown that the policies adopted were discussed periodically in interministerial council meetings, thereby introducing a political incentive structure exogenous to the bureaucracy.

The account developed here relies on the organization of societal interests in politically important constituencies. The rise of opposition to immigration has been traced in the preceding pages, but the same could be done for groups who supported immigration. Like the opposition, support was geographically concentrated. These geographically specific demands are visible in the efforts of the Parisian Federation of Construction (Fédération parisien du bâtiment, or FPB) and in the Parisian Chamber of Commerce (Chambre de Commerce et d'Industrie de Paris, or CCIP) to promote immigration and stand in sharp contrast to those of the national employers association (CNPF), which remained inactive on immigration issues until the mid-1970s (Henneresse 1979).[55]

The FPB's interest in immigrant workers arose from their significance to the construction industry. In 1963, 22 percent of the construction workforce was foreign, a proportion that grew to 29 percent by 1970, as compared with 8 percent of the labor force as a whole. And the figures were much higher for three of the regions discussed above: 43 percent of the construction work-

---

54. Ashford's argument is a bit more subtle, attributing the contradictory positions of the bureaucracy to the theory that "France never knew what policy to follow" (1982:267).

55. This account relies heavily on the doctoral thesis of Marie-Claude Henneresse 1979, whose research was conducted in the mid- to late 1970s. Her findings were partially validated through an examination of the FPB's records of council and bureau meetings. Unfortunately, the individuals responsible for immigration policy at the FPB were retired or deceased and their files either destroyed or uncataloged, so that a thorough examination of all source documents is now impossible.

force in Paris was foreign, 41 percent in Provence–Côte-d'Azur, and 39 percent in the Rhône-Alpes. Two-thirds of the foreigners employed in construction were in those three regions. In some of the large firms that undertook heavy construction and public works projects, as much as 85 percent of the workforce was foreign (Martin 1972:628). Moreover, these statistics probably understate the actual importance of immigrant workers to the construction sector because construction was a conduit to other sectors of the economy. Many immigrants started there, then moved into more stable employment.

It is not surprising, then, that the FPB was the sole employers' organization that developed and pursued "a long-term analysis of immigration" (Henneresse 1979:253–54). The FPB also sent several missions to various source countries to facilitate recruitment: Morocco (1963), Italy (1964), Greece (1964), Turkey (1966), Yugoslavia (1967), and Tunisia (1969). The demand for immigrant workers was sufficiently strong for the FPB to "envision prospecting [for migrants] in Iran and Brazil" (Henneresse 1979:253–54).

In addition to its direct recruitment efforts, the FPB maintained a close relationship with both parliamentarians and bureaucrats. Its leadership met regularly with the regional prefects, petitioned parliamentarians, and organized meetings with the administrative offices of the Office of Population and Migrations (Direction de la Population et des Migrations, or DPM), which oversaw the ONI. The FPB publicized its positions on immigration through advertisements in newspapers and invited journalists to public relations lunches (FPB 1965–75, Henneresse 1979). Moreover, these official contacts served as the basis for unofficial contacts between the interested parties. As a result, "thanks to the relations that they maintained with the parliamentarians, the CEOs [in the construction industry] were able to resolve to their advantage the problems posed by the employment of immigrants in their firms" (Henneresse 1979:391).

When the CNPF finally took a position on immigration at its annual conference at Lille in October 1974, it was at the bidding of the vice president of the FPB, J.-P. Dumont, who petitioned to have the issue included on the conference agenda, then directed the drafting of the policy position (Henneresse 1979:282). Even at late as October 1974, the positions taken were affected by concern over the ultimate availability of immigrants. "Employers judged that the needs of the economy still justified the entry of immigrants" (Henneresse 1979:302). The social costs of immigration were acknowledged, but the solution was to be found not in the provision of social services to immigrants but in the recruitment of unmarried foreign workers (Henneresse 1979:307). Thus the FPB, a sectorally and geographically specific organization, served as the primary pressure point in support of immigration and was recognized as playing "a point position in the domain [of immigration]" in the CNPF (Henneresse 1979:525).

That government policy was not a mere reflection of dwindling support on the part of employers is visible in the fact that employers, that is, the FPB, actively protested against government control beginning in 1972, when the Fontanet and Marcellin circulars were issued. And in response to the July 1974 halt to immigration, the FPB's president, Abel Laganne "underlined [his] astonishment in seeing such a decision taken so brutally without any advance warning." He continued, "We also and equally manifested the concern of our industry toward the possible consequences of such a decision that comes at a moment when construction activity is sustained and in the middle of vacation season" (FPB 9 July 1974:2). It was not until 1975 that the FPB and other employers relaxed their calls for continued immigration, well after the government halted migration. Thus the shift in bureaucratic positions can be closely linked, first, to geographically concentrated support for immigration and then to geographically concentrated opposition to immigration, via the political significance of specific constituencies.

The analysis I have presented to this point is closest to that of Martin Schain (1985, 1988).[56] He, too, emphasizes the political importance of the geographic concentration of immigrants, although he argues that, up through the early 1980s, immigration issues were contained at the local level and therefore were not catapulted to the national stage. But he acknowledges that immigration concerned "disproportionately, those municipalities governed by the Left and, . . . with little real access to the political system, representatives in these cities . . . had great difficulty raising the issue with which they had been preoccupied" (Schain 1985:187). Further, in describing the politicization of immigration and race in the 1980s, he emphasizes the changing electoral incentives of French politicians, associated with the rise in electoral support for the National Front, support that is geographically concentrated in departments with large immigrant populations. If I am correct, the same logic applies to the earlier period.

My analysis differs from Schain's in suggesting that, if the issue was contained at the local level until the early 1970s, it could no longer be contained by 1972, as the Gaullists prepared for the 1973 legislative elections. Moreover, Schain locates the electoral incentives in the rising volatility of the French public in the 1980s, reflected in the declining support for the PFC and rising support for the National Front. A careful analysis of electoral data, however, demonstrates that, even if the majority of French voters retained a primary party identification in this early period, this did not preclude a series of possible defections in national legislative and presidential elections.

56. Also see Ogden 1987 and Lewis-Beck 1993.

The center was composed of numerous factions, some of which, like the Independent Republicans, remained mostly loyal to the Gaullist electoral and parliamentary coalition.[57] Others tried to forge a "third path" between Gaullism and the left. Still others supported the noncommunist left. The left was also not oblivious to electoral defections. Many communist voters at the municipal level voted Gaullist in presidential elections, and many socialists, when confronted with an electoral alliance with the PCF, defected and voted for centrist parties. Thus the electoral arena represented anything but a stable and disciplined electorate, thereby providing a strategic environment that forced politicians to appeal to particular constituencies.

Schain also emphasizes the role of the elites in responding to immigration pressures, anticipating, rather than responding to, the public. Yet many accounts of the period suggest that public pressures were mounting. Moreover, what better signal for national politicians than the voices of municipal leaders who faced a set of electoral incentives of their own? As in Britain, municipal leaders in France confronted a politically unappealing policy: to provide resources to a group of nonvoters at the expense of voters, in an era of scarce resources and growing demands on those resources. This trade-off generated local demands for greater resources or the reduction of the immigrant population that absorbed those resources, with an eye on the electoral consequences in case of failure. In sum, although there are differences in emphasis, the explanation I have offered overlaps considerably with Schain's.

My analysis has less in common with other explanations of French immigration policy although I contend that these do not compete with my emphasis on political incentives. One set of authors emphasizes the continued openness to immigration in France rather than closure. Both Patrick Weil (1991) and James Hollifield (1992) suggest that the adoption of a "liberal" ideology by the republican state can account for the continued openness of the French state to immigration. As Hollifield (1994:159) puts it, "The primary reason for the continuation of immigration in France was the republican consensus and the power of rights-based politics, which prevented the state from acting to halt all forms of immigration." These authors point to the various efforts of the state to curtail immigration flows and its ultimate inability to do as, in part because court rulings voided the various decrees.

From an empirical perspective, there is some truth to the argument. The government was not completely unconstrained in its efforts to control immigration. The two highest courts in France, the Conseil d'État, the adminis-

---

57. This loyalty did not prevent occasional defections, as in 1969, when defections contributed to the defeat of a referendum and de Gaulle's subsequent resignation.

trative court, and the Conseil Constitutionel, the constitutional court, have reviewed administrative decrees and draft legislation and given opinions that overturned the decisions of the government. For example, provisions of the 1972 Marcelin and Fontanet circulars were overturned by the Conseil d'État on 13 January 1975. The court held that regularization remained possible and that the government could not require lodging as a condition for residence and work permits. Subsequent decrees were overturned on the grounds that the executive branch was empowered only to implement political decisions, forcing the government to turn to the legislative branch to authorize various control efforts (Wihtol de Wenden 1988).

But there are two reasons to suggest that this explanation is partial, at best. First, the courts' rulings affect only individuals already on French territory and do not prevent the government from excluding those without some territorial attachment. That is, the government was able to restrict the immigration of workers from other countries; it was unable to restrict family reunification with workers already established on French soil. And the government remains the decision maker regarding the intake of refugees; it is only asylum seekers already on French soil that are governed by certain due process provisions of the constitution.[58] Second, empirically, administrative and legislative controls have reduced substantially the number of immigrant workers from a peak of 174,000 in 1970 to 11,000 in 1985 and total immigration (workers, family, seasonal) from 390,000 to 130,000 in 1985 and 72,000 in 1993. The courts did not prevent the ONI from enforcing immigration regulations once the government decided to implement those regulations. The rate of regularization fell from its highest point of 82 percent in 1968 to 44 percent in 1972 and declined steadily thereafter. Moreover, employers channeled ever greater numbers of their demands for foreign workers through the ONI: between 1965 and 1968, only one of every four foreign workers was recruited under the auspices of the ONI, whereas between 1970 and 1972, one of every two foreign workers was recruited through the ONI. Ultimately, the ONI refused to adjust the status of foreign workers who failed to go through its channels (Tapinos 1975). By enforcing these regulations, the ONI was able to provide employment priority for the native population or for those immigrants already established in France.

Closing the front door to immigration resulted in a rise in undocumented immigration. For this and other reasons, France is not, and is unlikely to become, a zero-immigration country. Nonetheless, the government has demonstrated a substantial capacity to reduce the legal flow to minimal levels

---

58. Both refugees and asylum seekers are fleeing persecution; from the perspective of a country admitting "involuntary migrants," refugees are displaced from their homes but are located either in their home country or in a third country; asylum seekers, on the other hand, have arrived in the host country and are claiming the right of *nonrefoulement*, the right not to be expelled.

and has implemented both internal and border controls that reduce the undocumented population. And the courts have not prevented the state from taking some fairly onerous steps to control illegal immigration, including arbitrary identification checks and expulsion of undocumented immigrants. Weil and Hollifield have noted an important phenomenon: a series of legal protections have been extended via the courts to a resident, although foreign, population. These legal protections affect the level of immigrant intakes by guaranteeing family reunification and asylum adjudication but have not prevented the government from dramatically reducing the influx of documented and undocumented aliens. Moreover, family reunification is narrowly defined to include only the spouse and minor children. Thus the constitutional constraints on the "liberal" state are limited. An account of immigration policy would be incomplete without recognition of these constraints. By the same token, these constraints do not provide a complete picture of immigration control in France or elsewhere.

Gary Freeman (1979) presents a more complex picture of immigration policy in France, pointing to the ability of the French to avoid immigration as political issues during the 1960s and 1970s. The primary reason for the defusion of immigration and race as political issues arises from "stronger working class commitment of the French elites on the Left." This was reinforced by the fact that the Left remained in opposition throughout this period, thus avoiding potential political penalties associated with the implementation of a more generous immigration policy. Finally, in France, immigrants remained noncitizens and were therefore on the margins of the political system. Schain (1985), however, has convincingly shown that any such "working class commitment" did not extend to the local level where immigrants are concentrated. So the supposed solidarity of national leaders is not so much wrong as it is mistargeted. The second and third dimensions of Freeman's argument involve the electoral incentives of politicians and fit nicely with the analysis presented here.

The focus on the geographic concentration of immigrants and the electoral incentives that arise from the uneven distribution of costs and benefits of immigration helps to elucidate the direction and timing of immigration policy in France. It is less useful in explaining another phenomenon associated with immigration in France, the electoral popularity of Le Pen and his anti-immigrant National Front Party. France, like Britain, undertook to reduce immigrant flows in the absence of electoral support for an extremist right-wing party, yet those actions did not prevent the subsequent rise of political support for such a group. This is a puzzle that has elicited much attention (Betz 1994, Kitschelt 1995) but that remains unresolved.

Conclusions

The recruitment of immigrants by French employers and the government ultimately led to the creation of immigrant networks and the expansion of immigration to levels that created economic, social, and cultural pressures in areas where immigrants were concentrated. Because these pressures were greatest among the political opposition and because the conservative back-lash to the 1968 social upheavals provided the government with a solid National Assembly majority, the Gaullist government could afford to ignore demands for policy change. But gradually, the left opposition created a viable alternative electoral coalition and threatened the majority. The Gaullist government responded to that electoral threat, initially by seeking to reduce immigration and associated pressures by tying levels of immigration to the availability of housing. But the presence of immigrant networks decreased the effectiveness of government policy. Lacking the resources to provide an adequate infrastructure for the new arrivals and confronting a narrow presidential electoral margin, Giscard d'Estaing responded to anti-immigrant constituencies by "stopping" immigration upon his election in 1974.

There are legal, constitutionally based safeguards in France that limit the government's discretion, but it was able to reduce immigrant intakes dramatically. That move coincided with increased modernization of the productive apparatus, enhancing productivity. But there is little evidence to suggest that a shift in government preferences for productivity drove the change in immigration policy. The inflow of immigrants declined as the proportion of non-Europeans among immigrants was increasing. But the government itself created these non-European flows before deciding to constrain them, suggesting that racism alone is an insufficient explanation of the change in immigration policy. Moreover, more ethnically similar immigrants from Central Europe and the Soviet successor states have not been welcomed.

The evidence from France is consonant with the theoretical framework set out in Chapter 3 and provides parallels with the British case presented in Chapter 4. Both governments facilitated immigration through direct or indirect recruitment of immigrants, non-European as well as European. Immigration flows expanded gradually in the initial period but gathered momentum as immigrant networks were established and expanded. As immigration expanded, it became less sensitive to labor market needs, and the immigrant population tended to crowd the public goods provided by the state: transportation, housing, sewage systems, schools, and other services. In Britain, the immigrants tended to be concentrated in Conservative constituencies, and the Conservative parliamentary majority responded when economic recession and industrial restructuring aggravated the tensions created by social and cultural pressures. In France, immigrants tended to be concentrated in left, opposition constituencies. The Gaullist majority could therefore afford to ignore the calls for immigration control until the electoral margin narrowed and anti-immigrant swing constituencies became important to retaining a National Assembly majority. In both cases, the messages from anti-immigrant constituencies were organized rather than amorphous demonstrations of public opposition. Local government leaders, with electoral concerns of their own, were one group that vocally challenged government policy. Other indicators of anti-immigrant pressures came from press reports and politically organized groups, as well as from anomic displays of violence. These features are prominent in the next case as well, that of the settler state of Australia.

6 Immigration Control in Australia

with Kimberly Cole

Gough Whitlam's 1972 election campaign slogan, "It's Time," not only called for the election of a new party to government but foretold the Australian Labor Party's dramatic revision of postwar immigration control policy as well. Although the newly elected Whitlam government officially abolished the White Australia policy, the main change was a significant reduction in the level of immigration to Australia.[1] This change indicated a major shift in Australia's approach to immigration. Immediately after World War II, Australia premised its immigration policy on national security needs. But defense issues were rapidly overshadowed by political pressures for an increased labor supply, an enlarged domestic market, and economic growth. A bipartisan consensus among Australians was forged on the principle that high levels of immigration were necessary to spur the economy as well as to secure an adequate defense force. Although concerns about the costs of immigration were voiced with ever-increasing regularity in the second half of the 1960s, the policy was not modified until the election of the Whitlam government in 1972. Thereafter, immigration targets would never return to such high levels. This change in policy can be explained by the electoral incentives created by a small number of electoral constituencies, all of which experienced economic decline in the presence of a substantial and growing immigrant community and, therefore, opposed continued immigration. Because these constituencies were crucial to a Labor victory, immigration control became a part of its political agenda. Continued electoral competition assured the retention of lowered immigration intakes when the conservative coalition regained power in 1975.

---

1. The White Australia policy gradually eroded during the 1950s and 1960s, as various ethnic groups were permitted entry and as entry regulations were modified, although the broadest rule changes were implemented in 1966 under the Liberal/Country Party (LCP) government. This dimension of Australian immigration policy is discussed in further detail below.

Australian Immigration Control since 1945

Like the United States, Australia is a settler country. Immigration has been an important part of Australia's historical development since the first British convicts arrived in 1788 and the coming of free settlers shortly thereafter.[2] Assisted passage for immigrants was initiated in 1831 and continued for the next 150 years.[3] Immigration even played a crucial role in the creation of the Australian Commonwealth in 1901. The six former colonies agreed to federate only after reaching consensus on the issue of immigration (Castles 1989). The resulting Commonwealth Immigration Restriction Act of 1901 became the first major piece of legislation passed by the new Common-wealth legislature. But despite the importance of immigration, only one other major piece of immigration legislation has been enacted since this landmark law.

The Immigration Restriction Act of 1901 required all individuals entering Australia to possess a British passport or an entry permit obtained from the Ministry of Interior (after July 1945, from the Ministry for Immigration). The minister of interior defined the criteria for issuing entry permits, charac-terized by vague wording concerning the health, wealth, and special skills possessed by the potential immigrant. More important, the law specifically provided that entry permits could be predicated on literacy, as demonstrated by passing a dictation test given in a European language.

Potential immigrants could petition for entry permits in either their home country or upon arrival in Australia, but typically this evaluation was made at the point of departure. Because entry permits were not allocated uni-formly across different ports of departure, this represented an additional tool in the selection of immigrants. Moreover, the discretionary provisions in the act granted the executive virtual control over immigration policy. Each new government was able to set policy, such as immigration targets, regardless of what previous governments had done.

Through the dictation test, as well as the vagueness of entry qualifications and the wide discretionary power granted to the executive branch, Australia was able to promulgate a racist immigration policy without any explicit ref-erence in the Australian legal code. The White Australia policy, as it came to be known, virtually ensured that only British and a few European immigrants would be allowed to enter Australia. This policy effectively excluded Asians

2. For a comprehensive overview of immigration policy since 1901, see Jupp 1991. Additional sources on Australian immigration legislation are Bird 1988, Spann 1973, Plender 1972, 1987, Hawkins 1991, Patience and Head 1979, and Murphy 1993. For more on administrative regulations refer to Birrell and Birrell 1981, Jupp and Kabala 1993, and Walsh 1971.
3. Assisted passages were discontinued in 1981, except for refugees.

and also most continental Europeans. And if the dictation test were in any way insufficient for controlling entry, the 1925 Immigration Amendment Act reinforced executive power by granting the government the ability to limit the intake of any specified nationality, race, class, or occupation (Birrell and Birrell 1981). Rather than "White Australia," these policies created what could more accurately be labeled "British Australia" (Wilton and Bosworth 1984).[4]

The Migration Act of 1958 replaced the 1901 act. Although the new legislation contained several changes, the two acts were essentially the same. In conformity with the 1901 act, no immigrant would be admitted into Australia without a valid entry permit (or British passport). The executive retained wide discretionary powers to set immigration targets and to determine which applicants would be granted entry permits.[5] The act delegated to the minister for immigration the responsibility of evaluating applicants on vaguely worded criteria, "good character, good health, and proof of non-indigence" (Plender 1972:151). Again, the agents at the points of departure and entry were in charge of allocating permits on what was, practically, an ad hoc basis. The dictation test was eliminated by the 1958 act, but because the minister for immigration maintained wide discretionary powers, this de jure modification did not prevent the selection of immigrants on racial criteria.

The 1958 act has been amended several times. The first amendment, in 1959, declared non-European spouses and minor children of Australian citizens eligible for entry permits, as well as for naturalization. The legislature amended the act a second time, in 1960, to qualify spouses and children of British Commonwealth citizens legally in Australia for entry permits and naturalization (Plender 1972). Additional amendments were adopted in 1989 and 1992.

The paucity of legislation governing immigration and the broad discretion granted the executive by existing legislation suggests that the real story of immigration control lies with the executive. The party of government sets the target number for immigrant intake and determines the criteria for entry. It is virtually unconstrained by legislation or by the previous government's policies. But even though the ruling party has the ability to implement whatever

4. As an example of how seriously the White Australia policy was taken, not even Japanese wives of Australian servicemen were allowed to enter the country until a 1952 amendment granted them a five-year temporary entry permit (Plender 1972).
5. The Migration Act of 1958 extended the discretionary powers of the executive to decide the proportion of immigrants allowed as refugees, for "national need," and for family reunion. Additionally, the manner in which immigration policy was to be applied to spouses, children, and extended families of applicants for entry permits was left to the discretion of the minister for immigration.

policy it wishes, there has been a surprising continuity in immigration control policy. Although the exact target levels have fluctuated annually, there have been essentially only three immigration control policies since the end of World War II (Appleyard 1971a:3).[6] The first of these was initiated at the end of World War II by Prime Minister J. B. "Ben" Chifley of the Australian Labor Party (ALP), who proposed large immigration intakes in 1945, a program that was continued and expanded under the Menzies Liberal/ Country Party (LCP) coalition in 1949. The second was implemented by the Menzies government in 1952–53 and lowered immigration intake targets to the goal of 1 percent net population growth through immigration. The third came twenty years later, when the Whitlam Labor government dropped the 1 percent goal and dramatically reduced average immigration intake targets.

In 1945, the Chifley government announced a new immigration control policy best characterized by the slogan "populate or perish." This program grew out of Australia's experience in World War II, which suggested the country was too sparsely populated and too dependent on primary industry to secure adequately its defense against an aggressive Asian country such as Japan. On 2 August 1945, Arthur Calwell, minister for immigration, declared before the House of Representatives that "if Australians have learned one lesson from the Pacific war now moving to a successful conclusion it is that we cannot continue to hold our island continent for ourselves and our descendants unless we greatly increase our numbers. . . . We need it for reasons of defense and for the fullest expansion of our economy" (quoted in Hawkins 1991:32). Such anxiety animated postwar immigration policy.

To expand Australia's population rapidly, Chifley and his Labor government devised what was termed the "2 percent solution," so named because the program was designed to increase the total Australian population by 2 percent every year. Half of this growth would come from natural population increase, the remainder from immigration. Interestingly, immigration targets were set at twice that level, 144,400 per year, whereas the 1 percent target would have required only 70,000 immigrants (Stevens

---

6. Appleyard 1971a:3–4 identifies "two phases" in postwar immigration. The first was during the late 1940s and early 1950s, when immigrants were sought "essentially to supplement a labour force unable to satisfy pent-up demand." Although Arthur Calwell, as the first minister for immigration, defined his immigration goal as a 1% net population growth through immigration in this first period, intakes were "equal to *double* Mr Calwell's criterion." The recession of 1952–53 brought "the government's decision to cut the immigration target from 150,000 to 80,000," which Appleyard labels "the end of phase one in the immigration programme." Phase 2 was the adoption of the 1% target. To these two phases I add a third, beginning in 1972, with the entry of the ALP in government. Lloyd 1993 provides a similar description of intake levels, although he does not identify three periods per se.

1953:119).[7] To achieve this level of immigration, the government would actively recruit potential immigrants and assist with the costs of migration. A separate bureaucracy was deemed necessary to cope with the planned influx of immigrants, so the Chifley government created the Commonwealth Department of Immigration and appointed Arthur Calwell as its first minister.[8] It also created the Commonwealth Employment Service to provide information on the labor market and the economic effects of immigration.

Chifley and Calwell embarked upon a delicate balancing act. The Labor government at once sought to invigorate postwar development through immigration and to preserve the White Australia policy that had prevailed for decades. Therefore, the initial postwar program targeted British citizens, and in 1946 and 1947, Australia signed agreements with Britain to provide assisted passage to qualified British citizens who wished to immigrate to Australia (DIEA 1978).[9] But it quickly became clear that these policies were incompatible. The main source country of immigrants, Britain, experienced manpower shortages and also lacked sufficient ships to transport potential immigrants to Australia. Chifley and his Labor government were forced to look elsewhere to achieve their immigration goals.[10]

Continental Europe soon provided a solution. At the end of the war, displaced persons camps contained hundreds of thousands of Europeans who were unable or unwilling to return to their home countries. In 1947, Chifley signed an agreement with the Preparatory Commission for the International Refugee Organisation (PCIRO, later simply IRO) in which he agreed to accept an annual quota of 12,000 displaced persons; the number would be increased to 20,000 if the IRO could procure additional ships to transport the immigrants. The Australian economy quickly absorbed these new immigrants, and by 1951, a total of 170,000 settlers had come to Australia under the Displaced Persons Scheme (APIC 1977).[11]

Even though the Chifley Labor government was the architect of post–World War II immigration policy, the conservative Liberal/Country

---

7. Two other sources, DIEA 1978 and Appleyard 1971b, list the 1952 target as 150,000. Birrell and Birrell 1981 give 200,000 as the 1950 target. Kmenta 1964:41 lists the targets as follows: 1948, 70,000; 1949, 110,000; 1950, 200,000; 1951, not specified numerically; 1952 150,000. The distinction between net and gross immigration is discussed below.
8. Until 1945, immigration policy was handled by both the Department of External Affairs and the Department of the Interior.
9. Nonetheless, British immigrants remained the largest recipients of assisted passages until the early 1980s, when the policy was discontinued.
10. The department took on various names over time and is currently designated the Department of Immigration and Ethnic Affairs (DIEA).
11. Even at the higher authorized level of 20,000 per year, the displaced persons should have provided 100,000 immigrants between 1947 and 1951, rather than the actual higher number of 170,000. This provides yet another indication that the ALP and LCP governments were shooting for more than the initially stated 1 percent goal.

Party coalition continued Labor's policy of high immigrant intakes upon gaining power in 1949.[12] As the Displaced Persons Scheme wound down in the early 1950s, lower intakes of immigrants prompted the LCP government to sign several bilateral agreements with European countries to provide assisted passage to non-British immigrants (Jupp 1991:78). Agreements were negotiated with the Netherlands and Italy in 1951; with West Germany, Austria, and Greece in 1952; with Finland, Switzerland, Sweden, Denmark, and Norway in 1954; and with Spain in 1958.

Immigration intakes in the second period, beginning in 1952, were brought into line with the original 1 percent target. By the early 1950s, national security concerns had begun to wane (Appleyard 1971a).[13] The political pressures generated by the 1952 recession compelled the LCP government to curtail the 1952 intake and to reduce the 1953 program target to 80,000 from almost twice that level (Appleyard 1971b:211). This reduction, the minister of immigration declared, provided "a breather so that the substantial intake of the past can be digested the more comfortably" (quoted in Stevens 1953:116). But the breather was permanent in comparison with the previous scale of immigration. No longer would intakes be "equal to *double* Mr Calwell's criterion" (Appleyard 1971a:3). Thereafter, gross immigration targets remained close to the 1 percent initially laid out by Calwell. These targets averaged 115,000 per year in the mid-1950s, 125,000 in the late 1950s and early 1960s, 145,000 in the mid-1960s, and 170,000 in the late 1960s, with corresponding per capita figures ranging from 1.15 to 1.43 percent of the Australian population. And even though the LCP coalition remained in power for the next two decades, immigration did not become a major political issue. An unusual bipartisan consensus had been forged on immigration control policy and was not challenged until the early 1970s.

The third phase in Australian immigration control was initiated when Gough Whitlam and the Labor Party took control of government in 1972. The Whitlam government abandoned the 1 percent standard and retroactively decreased intake targets from 140,000 to 110,000. This number was reduced again to 80,000 in 1974 and still further, to 50,000, in 1975 (Patience and Head 1979).[14] The corresponding per capita figures—0.83 to 0.36 percent of the Australian population—demonstrate a clear break from previous policy (Lloyd 1993).

12. The Country Party changed its name to the National Country Party in 1975, then to the National Party in 1981. Despite these name changes, it caters to the same rural constituency.
13. Appleyard 1971a:3 observed that "the defence criterion was soon pushed into the background, partly because of the advent of the nuclear age and partly because when the danger of invasion passed the people became more concerned with immediate problems of reconstruction." Rivett 1978:68 agreed that, "in all events, the economic case for immigration became more prominent."
14. The 140,000 was roughly 1 percent of the total population of Australia in 1972.

Reduced intakes were included in a broader immigration program of which other components reflected greater continuity with the past (Price 1979). The Whitlam government officially abolished the White Australia policy, but this program had been slowly dismantled over the entire postwar period, with the most substantial modifications introduced by the LCP coalition in 1966. The White Australia policy proved unrealistic when high immigration goals were adopted in the early postwar period. Strict adherence was abandoned when Chifley introduced the Displaced Persons Scheme that brought central Europeans to Australia.[15] They were followed by immigrants from Mediterranean countries. Ultimately, regulations governing non-Europeans were relaxed. Beginning in 1957, both the Commonwealth and the states began to repeal discriminatory laws and regulations. By 1964, the LCP government had dropped all entry restrictions for part-Europeans. In 1966 the governing coalition repealed the fifteen-year rule and aligned non-European naturalization requirements with those for European immigrants.[16] Applications by non-Europeans wishing to settle in Australia were to be considered individually on their merits, and a small but growing number of non-Europeans was accepted for settlement annually (IPC 22 November 1968). Although the LCP coalition began dismantling the racist practices, it never formally abolished the policy (Price 1974). Ultimately, it was the ALP government that modified legislative and administrative wording to eliminate discrimination. Immigration policy was to be based on "understanding and tolerance" and "the avoidance of discrimination on any grounds of race or color of skin or nationality" (Reid and Samuel 1973:40–41). So the abolition of White Australia was more an acknowledgment of the status quo than the introduction of a new policy.

To be sure, the Whitlam government reinforced the changes implemented during the LCP period, in part by introducing in 1973 a standardized immigrant selection system, the Structured Selection Assessment System (SSAS). This system consisted of a two-part "interview report" completed by an immigration officer. The first part of this process evaluated the economic potential of migrants using a system that awarded various points for employment criteria. Second, the officer was required to assess the applicant's personal and social characteristics such as attitudes toward migration, initiative, self-reliance, personal appearance, and family unity. Although much was still left to the individual immigration officer's discretion, the system provided a semblance of objective protocol that heretofore had been absent from immi-

---

15. Although the displaced persons were European, they were viewed as ethnically distinct by many Australians. In Al Grassby's 1979:79 colorful language, for Australians, "Africa begins at Calais [France]."

16. The fifteen-year rule required that non-Europeans be resident in Australia for fifteen years before being allowed to bring in dependents (Rivett 1976).

gration policy. Since the introduction of the SSAS, the selection system has been refined and updated periodically. The Numerically Weighted Multi-factor Assessment System (NUMAS) was introduced in 1979. NUMAS modified migrant selection further by weighting the economic factors, such as occupational skills, as well as the preferred personal and social characteristics, such as family ties, to make the process more uniform. NUMAS was subsequently replaced by the Migration Selection System.[17]

The Whitlam government also shifted the weight of various components of the intake stream.[18] Australia placed immigrants in three major categories—family reunion, national need (persons with human or financial capital), and refugees (Hawkins 1991).[19] In the past, Australia had given priority to immigrants who had skills that the economy needed and had actively recruited immigrants otherwise unconnected to Australia. Now, higher priority would be given to those with family ties in Australia than to those without such connections. The weight awarded to sponsorship had two political advantages: it catered to the preferences of naturalized immigrants, and it reduced the costs of immigrant recruitment and relocation previously borne by the government.

The major legislative and executive immigration control initiatives are summarized in Table 6.1. Although the various selection systems were used to determine the types of immigrants granted entry permits, the decision over immigration levels was left to the discretion of the executive, in consultation with several organizations that had special interests in immigration. The Chifley government initiated this program of consultation in 1945 when the minister of immigration, Arthur Calwell, announced that the government "will need, and will seek, the assistance and the advice of the trade union movement, the Chambers of Manufactures, the Chambers of Commerce, the Primary Producers' Organisations, and any other similar organisations whose activities have a bearing on economic development" (Warhurst 1993:185). This informal consultative process was formalized through the creation of two standing committees, the Immigration Advisory Council in 1947 (IAC) and the Immigration Planning Council in 1949 (IPC), the former to advise on issues of integration, the latter on control. The LCP government retained these two councils upon gaining power in 1949 and continued to consult with these committees on immigration recruitment priorities and intake targets as well as to use the representatives to promote the government's immigration policy.

17. For the exact point system refer to Hawkins 1991.
18. These components were announced by Al Grassby, newly appointed minister of immigration, in a report to the House of Representatives titled "Australia's Decade of Decision: A Report on Migration, Citizenship, Settlement and Population."
19. There is also a "special humanitarian" category and a category of immigrants that is uncontrolled: New Zealand citizens who enter without visas as part of the Trans-Tasman Travel Arrangement.

Table 6.1. Major immigration control measures, Australia, 1901–1993

Control measure	Year	Provisions
Legislation		
Commonwealth Immigration Restriction Act	1901	Gave executive wide discretionary power to determine immigration policy and instituted dictation test; together these measures resulted in White (British) Australia policy
Migration Act	1958	Similar to 1901 act except that it abolished dictation test; first amended 1959, making non-European spouses and children of Australian citizens eligible for entry permits and naturalization; second amendment, 1960, extended eligibility to spouses and children of Commonwealth citizens legally in Australia; further amendments 1989 and 1992
Policy		
"Populate or perish" plan	1945	Called for 1% net increase in population through immigration and set immigration targets well above that level; policy based on defense needs
U.K.–Australia Assisted Passage Migration Agreement	1946	Facilitated immigration of workers
Displaced Persons Agreement	1947	Facilitated immigration of displaced persons
Government-to-government agreements	1951–71	Facilitated immigration of workers
Immigration for economic growth	1952	Immigration targets reduced to achieve about 1% net population growth
Reduction in immigration	1972	1% net increase abandoned; immigrant intake reduced, White Australia policy officially abolished; family reunification accorded priority in response to immigrant demands

(Table continues)

Table 6.1. Continued

Control measure	Year	Provisions
Selection system		
Structured Selection Assessment System (SSAS)	1973	First standardized selection system that awarded points on basis of employment criteria
Numerically Weighted Multifactor Assessment System (NUMAS)	1979	Extension of points-based selection system, with weights assigned to education, job experience, age, language skills, and ties to Australian sponsor; close family members and humanitarian entries excluded from selection criteria
Migration Selection System	1988	Refinement of points-based selection system
Consulting council		
Immigration Advisory Council (IAC)	1947	Representatives of veterans, farmers, business, trade unions, women's organizations, and local government advised on issues of immigrant integration
Immigration Planning Council (IPC)	1949	Representatives of same groups as on IAC advised on issues of immigration control
Australian Population and Immigration Council (APIC)	1975	Membership represented business, trade unions, social services, migrant/ethnic communities, and academics
Australian Council on Population and Ethnic Affairs (ACPEA)	1981	Membership represented same groups as on APIC
National Population Council (NPC)	1984	Membership represented same groups as on APIC plus aborigines and environmentalists

Until the 1970s, membership in the two councils was drawn primarily from the "growth lobby," a group of relatively powerful economic interests that profited from an expansion in the domestic market. These interests included the construction industry, land speculators and developers, farmers, manufacturers, and retailers; they were joined by unions and community leaders (Warhurst 1993). The membership of these two councils ensured that they were essentially pro-immigration. They recommended high immigration targets, providing support for large immigration intakes.

For a period of time after the Whitlam government was elected in 1972, the institutional structure maintained by the LCP coalition remained intact, although the membership of both the IAC and the IPC was adjusted, reflecting preferences for advice from those that favored lowered intakes (Warhurst 1993). But ultimately Whitlam abolished the Department of Immigration and, in 1975, created a new consultative body called the Australian Population and Immigration Council (APIC). The shift in nomenclature represented the changing perspective on immigration issues in society, from a focus on immigration to concern about population growth. The APIC was a smaller body whose composition differed significantly from those of earlier councils. Members who once played a crucial role in immigration control policy now found themselves outside the policymaking arena. For example, representatives of farmers and armed forces organizations no longer received invitations to participate. Moreover, new groups, such as academics and ethnic associations, were brought into the policymaking process. Members now included representatives from the Good Neighbour Council, the Ethnic Communities Councils, and the universities, in addition to the usual representatives from unions and employers.[20] The changed composition generated different policy advice: smaller intake levels, the abolition of racist regulations, and emphasis on family reunification.

When the Liberal and (renamed) National Country Party (Lib-NCP) coalition returned to government in 1975, it retained the services and the membership of the APIC. But in 1981, the APIC was merged into a new body called the Australian Council on Population and Ethnic Affairs (ACPEA). The game of musical councils continued when the ALP government regained power in 1983. The Hawke Labor government established the National Population Council (NPC) to "advise the Government on issues pertinent to the well being of Australia's multicultural society, including the relationship between population growth, immigration intake and the economy" (Warhurst 1993:187).

The shifting titles, membership, and focus of these various councils suggest

---

20. The Ethnic Communities Councils were themselves new, the first being established in Sydney and Melbourne in 1975, with a Federal Council following in 1979 (Jupp and Kabala 1993:xvii).

that the government sought and obtained advice consonant with its own priorities. Moreover, when the advice contradicted government priorities, the councils' recommendations were overturned. This happened for the first time in 1952, when the cabinet rejected the advice of the IPC on immigration intakes, cutting the recommended intakes by half (Birrell and Birrell 1981). Under the ALP government the IPC advised that 130,000 immigrants be received for 1973–74 and 135,000 for 1974–75, levels that the government reduced to 110,000 and 80,000 respectively (Birrell and Birrell 1981). These differences of opinion contributed to the reconfiguration of that advisory council into APIC. But its recommendations were, in turn, reduced by the Lib-NCP government during the late 1970s, when target intakes were rolled back from the recommended 110,000 per year to 90,000 (Rivett 1979).

Immigration control policy in Australia has been left to the discretion of the executive. The legislature has passed only two major pieces of immigration control legislation since Australia's federation in 1901. These two acts were sufficiently broad to give the government complete control over immigration. But despite this flexibility, there has been an amazing amount of continuity on the issue.[21] At the end of World War II, the Chifley government initially pursued a policy of extremely high immigration intakes, a program that was adopted by its conservative successor, the Menzies Liberal/Country Party coalition. These extraordinarily high intake levels were cut back to the 1 percent level in 1952–53, and a relatively steady intake was maintained until 1972, when the Whitlam government abandoned the 1 percent goal and reduced target intakes to more moderate levels. Another bipartisan consensus was formed around this reduced level of intake. No successive government has returned to the high levels of immigrant intakes represented by the 1 percent formula (Lloyd 1993). Intakes have varied over time, but there is no distinct trend in each of the three phases.

Figure 6.1 illustrates these three distinct periods of immigration control in Australia.[22] Intake targets ranged from 1.7 to 1.9 percent of the Australian population in the first period, from 0.9 to 1.4 percent in the second period, and from 0.45 to 0.85 percent in the third period.[23] There is no overlap in

---

21. The one area that has elicited a more partisan response is the type of immigrants admitted. Labor tended to emphasize family reunion whereas the Liberal coalition has tended to emphasize worker admissions.

22. Gross immigration targets were developed with specific net immigration goals in mind. If the per capita immigration targets were set at 1.2% on average during the 1953–71 period, it was because of the anticipated 18% departure rate of immigrants (see Stevens 1953 for this estimate). The level of admissions predicts the level of net migration very well, with an R^2 of 0.91; the level of programmed admissions is less good but still reasonable, with an R^2 of 0.74.

23. The statistics include long-term residents as well as settlers up through 1959, when the government began distinguishing between the two categories of alien residents. When the series is corrected for long-term residents, through modeling trends in long-term resident intakes and

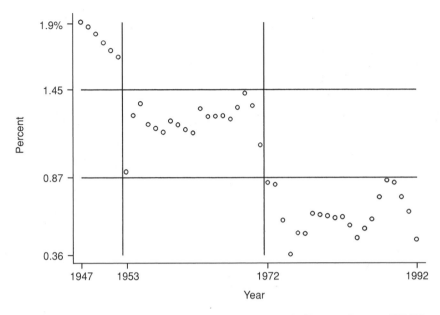

Figure 6.1. Australian immigration intake targets, 1947–1993. (*Sources:* Stevens 1953:119; DIEA, *Australian Immigration: Consolidated Statistics* and *Review of Activities*, various years; Birrell 1978; Mackellar 1979; Lloyd 1993:61.)

intake targets in these three periods, and an analysis of variance reveals that the mean target intakes for these three periods—1.8, 1.2, and 0.6 percent—are statistically different.[24]

Moreover, targets were generally met. Except for 1947, when the immigration program was still getting under way, and 1952, when the government curtailed the immigration intakes midstream, the overall variance from the target is less than 1 percent.[25] For half of the time, the deviations from target are between −6.0 and 7.0 percent. There is no systematic trend over time although, on average, actual intake was 1 percent over target in the first period, 4 percent under target in the second, and 1 percent over target in the third. These figures suggest that the Australian government was and still is very good at achieving program goals.

As a result, as illustrated in Figure 6.2, actual per capita settler intakes also

subtracting them from the series up to 1959, the series looks very similar. None of the conclusions drawn here are modified when the series is corrected for the inclusion of long-term residents.

24. The *F* statistic for the analysis of variance is 254, indicating that the likelihood that the differences are due to chance is close to zero (0.0000). The analysis of variance meets the model assumptions of similar variances.

25. I do not have the revised target for 1952 and therefore deleted it from the analysis. For 1972, I do have the revised target, so that year is included in the analysis.

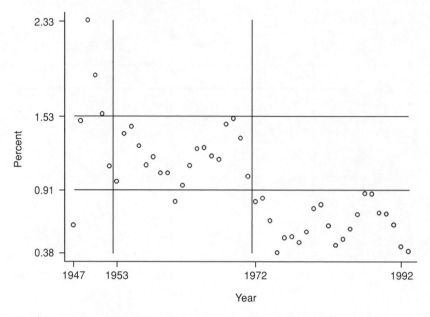

Figure 6.2. Australian gross annual settler intake, 1947–1993. (*Source:* DIEA, *Australian Immigration: Consolidated Statistics*, various years.)

reflect the periodization described above. Within each period, there is no systematic trend up or down.[26] Moreover, for the entire time frame and for the third period, the party in power was not a predictor of the level of immigration.[27] The conservative Lib-NCP government, elected in 1975, did increase the intake level gradually but reduced the level in 1982, a trend adopted by the ALP upon regaining power in 1983. And the ALP also adjusted intakes within this lowered intake range so that per capita intake targets ranged from 0.46 percent (1992) to 0.85 percent (1988). These data suggest that the description of bipartisanship on immigration control issues maintained by all observers of Australian immigration control is accurate.

The Institution of Immigration Control

The question, of course, is why parties on both sides of the political spectrum adopted specific immigration intake targets reflecting a different willingness

---

26. For all three periods, regression analysis revealed that "year" was not statistically different from zero, and the R^2s ranged from 0.004 to 0.03.
27. In regression analysis, in neither equation was "government" statistically significant.

to admit a foreign population. To answer this question, I focus on the political dynamics of immigration control surrounding the downturn in intakes in 1972. Unfortunately, for the earlier period, it is impossible to trace the impact of immigration by electoral constituency. The latter period is more amenable to analysis because census data aggregated at the constituency level are available beginning with the 1971 census.

The reduction in immigration in 1972 was a surprise to many observers of Australian immigration control policy. For years, the central object of controversy had been the White Australia policy. But although the racist aspects of Australian immigration policy were debated continually at both the international and national levels, no one seriously contested the aspect of the policy which granted a high number of entry permits to immigrants every year. Even those who did not subscribe to the national security rationale for immigration believed high immigrant intakes contributed to economic growth. Australia was a huge, sparsely populated country with abundant natural resources and a steadily growing economy. Immigrants were quickly absorbed into the expanding economy. Between 1947 and 1972, immigrants filled six out of every ten new jobs that were created. That immigrants were crucial to the growing Australian economy was a premise accepted by all major parties.

If immigration was not a political issue and the two major parties shared a long-established consensus, why did the Labor Party, in 1972, drastically reduce the level of immigration? And if the Liberal Party favored high levels of immigration, why did it not revert back to the pre-1972 levels when it was returned to power in 1975? I argue, following the theoretical framework presented in Chapter 3, that indigenous middle-class voters in swing constituencies with a large concentration of immigrants were confronted with escalating competition for government services and public goods from a rapidly growing immigrant population. This competition was aggravated by the economic downturn in 1971–72 that doubled unemployment rates. To appropriate these swing constituencies, a necessary condition for a Labor victory, the ALP had to address their concerns about increased immigration.

The political institutions that structured the electoral incentives in Australia are similar to those in Britain. Australia has a parliamentary system of government, meaning that the executive is formed by the majority party in the lower house of parliament. It also has single-member constituencies for lower house elections. It differs from Britain in its system of single, transferrable voting, in which preferences for second, third, and fourth candidates are tallied and distributed among the candidates. This system has worked to facilitate the electoral and parliamentary alliance of the Liberal Party and the (National) Country Party by allowing their constituents to award their second preferences to a political ally. Thus parliamentary coalitions are more common in Australia than in Britain.

A second major difference is that the Australian Senate has a legislative veto whereas the House of Lords in Britain is able only to delay legislation. Because immigration decisions are centered in the executive rather than the legislature, however, the upper house's legislative veto plays a minor role in immigration control policy.[28] The main set of electoral incentives comes from the lower house elections, which determine the composition of the government.

The rise of anti-immigrant pressures

Despite its reputation as a settler state, the erratic economic conditions between 1890 and 1940, combined with the 1901 immigration restrictions, substantially diminished immigration flows to Australia. In 1947, less than 10 percent of the population was foreign-born, and 90 percent of these were from the British Isles (Parkin and Hardcastle 1994). The massive influx between 1947 and 1952 created pressures to reduce immigration to more manageable levels. But for a considerable time thereafter, the economy and the broader society appeared to absorb this inflow with relative ease. The sustained impact of significant immigrant intakes, however, combined with an increase in program targets beginning in 1968 and the overshooting of those targets, generated competition between the host and immigrant communities.

By the late 1960s, immigrant networks were well established, contributing to the expanded flow and concentrating immigrants in areas of earlier settlement. As in Britain and France, these areas of settlement were highly concentrated. The immigrants were initially attracted to regions with employment opportunities in the eastern industrial cities, where manufacturing employment was growing by leaps and bounds. They settled in the city centers and industrial suburbs of Sydney and Wollongong (New South Wales), Melbourne and Geelong (Victoria), and Adelaide (South Australia), and most found employment in the metals, clothing, footwear, textiles, and building industries. In 1971, 80 percent of foreign-born citizens were concentrated in Australia's ten largest cities as compared with 60 percent of the Australian-born population (APIC 1977). Sixty percent of immigrants were located in Melbourne and Sydney alone.

At the electoral division level, the concentration of migrants is clearly

---

28. The Senate can veto immigration regulations that are introduced into the legislature, as it did in 1996, which indicates that a fuller account would include electoral incentives in the Senate. Nonetheless, historically, the Senate has played but a minor role in immigration control policy. I thank James Jupp for bringing this to my attention.

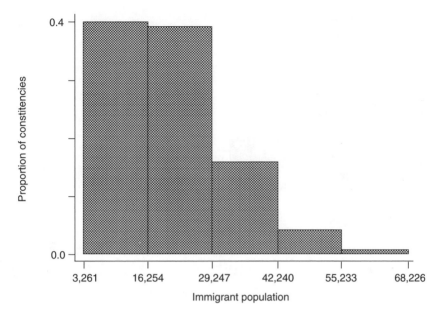

Figure 6.3. Distribution of total immigrant population among Australian electoral divisions, 1971. (*Source:* Australia, Commonwealth Bureau of Census and Statistics, 1972.)

visible. Because of the long history of immigration, every division had some immigrants. But the range was enormous, from 4 immigrants per 100 residents to 53 immigrants per 100 residents. Not only was immigration concentrated spatially, but temporally both targeted and actual immigration increased steadily during the 1960s. The target was set at 1.4 percent of the Australian population in 1969 and fell only slightly, to 1.3 percent, in 1970. In addition, immigration targets were exceeded in 1968 and 1969, so that actual levels of immigration reached 1.5 percent of the Australian population in a single year (Greenwood 1974).

These new immigrants were even more heavily concentrated than the established immigrant population and were attracted to areas of old immigrant settlement where some electoral divisions received as many as 16 immigrants per 100 residents in the five-year period between 1966 and 1971. Figure 6.3 shows the spatial distribution of migrants; Figure 6.4 provides the same illustration for new immigrants.[29]

Another measure of the distribution of immigrant pressure comes from

29. Although as a rule I normally look at the per capita level of immigration, here I focus on the absolute number of migrants per electoral division because these represent approximately equal voting populations.

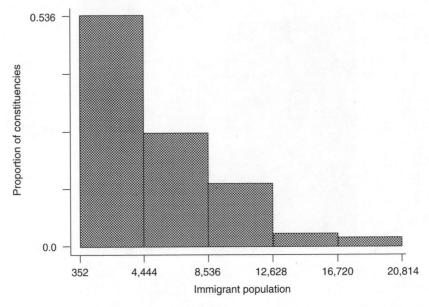

Figure 6.4. Distribution of immigrants resident less than five years among Australian electoral divisions, 1971. (*Source:* Australia, Commonwealth Bureau of Census and Statistics, 1972.)

the geographic concentration of noncitizen migrants and helps to clarify the pressures that arise from different types of migrants.[30] Australia sought to recruit migrants primarily from Britain. The major distinguishing feature between these and other immigrants was not so much their ethnic heritage as their professional training and English-language abilities. The derogatory term "Pommies" aside, British immigrants were able to replicate and exceed the earning power of native Australians (Rivett 1978, Collins 1988). The "noncitizen" category is composed of individuals born outside the Commonwealth who had not become naturalized Australian citizens. The vast majority of these people at the time of the 1971 census were southern Europeans, of "non-English-speaking background," a term so widely used that it is commonly abbreviated NESB in immigration articles. These were the unskilled workers who became factory fodder in the growing Australian manufacturing sector, whose earnings fell below the Australian average (Collins 1988). These immigrants were even more concentrated than the new arrivals, as depicted in Figure 6.5. And they placed greater pressure on

30. In the 1971 census, the actual designation is "British" and "non-British"; at that time, there was no separate designation for those born in the British Isles, those born in Australia, and those born elsewhere but naturalized.

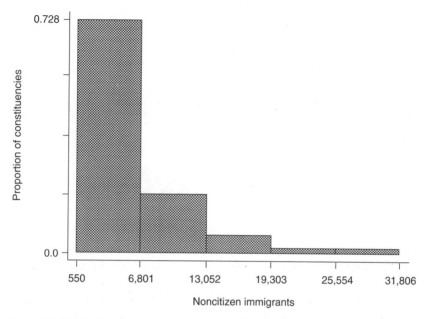

Figure 6.5. Distribution of noncitizen immigrants among Australian electoral divisions, 1971. (*Source:* Australia, Commonwealth Bureau of Census and Statistics, 1972.)

the public infrastructure than did the more affluent English-speaking migrants.

Pressures from this immigration were concentrated in the urban areas. As in the Paris region in France, immigration in Australia coincided with increased urbanization. Between 1947 and 1971, the population of Sydney grew by 65 percent, Melbourne by 87 percent (Forster 1995). For the period as a whole, well over half of this population growth came from international migration. If the children of foreign-born parents were included in the international dimension, the figure would be even higher. But urban population growth in the late 1960s, fueled by international migration, actually created a reverse flow of the Australian-born population from these major cities as the quality of urban life diminished.[31] Before the mid-1960s, only about one-quarter of the population growth in both Sydney and Melbourne was attributed to international migration (Neutze 1971). But from 1966 to 1971, as the population of Australia's state capitals continued to expand, international immigration accounted for about half the population growth of Sydney, Mel-

31. A similar story can be told of the United States, where states with large immigrant intakes between 1985 and 1995 experienced counterbalancing out-migration of the host population (Frey 1994, 1996).

Table 6.2. Populations of Australian state capitals, 1966–1971

State capital	Total population	Total increase	Percent increase			
			Total	Natural	Internal migration	International migration
Sydney	2,539,627	265,000	10.4%	47.7%	−7.6%	59.9%
Melbourne	2,228,511	273,000	12.3	52.3	−0.8	48.5
Brisbane	777,935	90,000	11.6	47.0	22.2	30.8
Adelaide	770,628	71,000	9.2	50.9	2.0	47.1
Perth	558,297	144,000	25.8	28.8	17.0	54.1
Hobart	141,238	12,000	8.5	68.1	5.0	26.9

Sources: Adapted from Australian Population and Immigration Council 1977 and Australian Bureau of Statistics, *Yearbook Australia*, 1967.

bourne, Perth, and Adelaide. Sydney and Melbourne each absorbed more than a quarter-million immigrants in the five-year period (APIC 1977). Table 6.2 summarizes the percentage increase in population between 1966 and 1971. The immigration component of population growth was concentrated in the late 1960s and exacerbated urban problems that had been festering for years, prompting an exodus of the Australian-born population. Sydney and Melbourne experienced a net out-migration of the Australian-born population between 1966 and 1971.

This rapid population growth led to the deterioration of the urban environment (Stilwell 1980, Birrell and Birrell 1981, United Nations 1982, Betts 1988). The crowding of public goods was pervasive across a broad range of services: transportation, education, sewage, and pollution, to name the most important. The housing problem was different in Australia than in Britain and France. The stock of social housing was small; market forces provided a rapidly expanding private housing stock and developers who catered to the growing demand for housing provided part of the political support for continued high levels of immigration. But on an individual level, the high demand for housing led to inflationary real estate prices, making home ownership more difficult for the Australian-born population to achieve.

In the sprawling urban environment of Australia's major cities, transportation became a major issue. According to the *Economist*, "By any standards many Australians spend a lot of time getting to and from school and work. Most of the present inhabitants of [Sydney and Melbourne]—particularly those large numbers of them who have to live 15 to 20 miles from the center—spend three hours a day commuting by deplorable public transport" ("Gough Whitlam's Australia" 1973:35). The roads that led into the city, where employment was concentrated, became congested. Public transportation was not able to alleviate the congestion because these services were overcrowded and infrequent. Because immigrants contributed heavily to population growth, immigration was the target when city residents complained that "that their cities are big enough already."

Education was a second feature of urban deterioration. Again according to the *Economist*, "The striking features of Australia's educational system include overcrowded classrooms" ("Gough Whitlam's Australia" 1973:38). The immigrants' contribution to this overcrowding was even more important than their contribution to population growth because, on average, immigrants were younger than the Australian population and had more children in school. Urban experts explained, "The age selectivity of immigration, with many southern and some north-western and eastern European migrants starting families in Australia, has exerted considerable pressure on social facilities, crèches, schools, hospitals and housing, all essential elements of the urban fabric" (Burnley 1974a:117). And this growing school population presented new challenges to educators. In Melbourne, for example, "in June 1971, of 16,895 children enrolled in 33 primary schools in the inner suburbs, 9,204 were from non-English speaking homes (54 percent)" (Burnley 1974a:170).

Sewage facilities are an important and underappreciated urban public good. Development in Australian cities proceeded so rapidly that many new residential areas had no or inadequate sewage treatment facilities for years. This uncontrolled growth also contributed to the rise in pollution, air pollution from the growing stock of automobiles and water pollution when untreated sewage was dumped into the bays around which both Sydney and Melbourne were constructed. The *Economist* reported that "Sydney's lungs and its saving grace, its harbour and beaches, grow increasingly polluted as sewage spills into the sea at an ever faster rate" ("Gough Whitlam's Australia" 1973:35).[32]

Both politicians and the public linked the declining quality of urban life to rapid population growth and to the immigrant component of that growth. Although the immigrant population was concentrated, it was not segregated and therefore was visible. According to one urban geographer (Burnley 1974b:168), "Even in the areas of densest minority group settlements, those of Greeks and Italians in central Sydney and Melbourne, . . . the immigrant groups individually did not exceed 40 percent of the total population." Thus the Australian-born population that remained in areas of immigrant settlement witnessed the growth in the immigrant population and associated it with the crowding of infrastructure.

The initial move by many Australians to the suburbs often left city centers with an adequate housing stock to meet immigrant demand so that compe-

32. See also Rivett 1978.

tition between the immigrant and indigenous populations was avoided in the early years of postwar immigration. But even in these areas of "immigrant succession," which experienced a real decline in Australian-born population, the rapid influx of immigrants in the 1960s reversed the demographic decline. And, "by 1971, new accommodation and population stresses were being felt by pre-school centres and schools in the inner city, as well as by hospitals and other welfare services and institutions, and it was evident that such pressures would increase in the immediate future" (Burnley 1974a:109).

These pressures on the infrastructure were exacerbated by an economic slowdown in 1971–72 that doubled national unemployment rates (Norton 1982). By late 1970, an uncertain position in the world economy and a continually depressed rural sector combined with an economic downturn.[33] In 1971, unemployment reached its highest point in ten years. By late 1972, unemployment reached 3 percent and all indicators showed that it was likely to continue to rise (Wilson 1978). Moreover, unemployment was not equally distributed across Australia.

Because the distribution of unemployment can be traced only through periodic censuses and statewide surveys, we do not have the range of unemployment rates by electoral division for 1972. The national unemployment rate was 1.66 percent in 1971, with a range of 0.78 to 3.15. It is likely that, as unemployment rates doubled, the upper end of the range would have exceeded 6 percent. And although manufacturing employment as a whole continued to grow until 1973, employment in the labor-intensive textile, clothing, and footwear industries, which had relied heavily on unskilled immigrant labor to expand, actually contracted as industrial restructuring of the economy proceeded (Rich 1987). Thus some pockets of unemployment were concentrated in divisions with high immigrant populations. The 1971 census figures show that three of the six highest unemployment rates were found in the Sydney, Melbourne, and Melbourne Ports electoral divisions, whose immigrant populations ranged between 32 and 40 percent and, more important, which had received 10 to 13 percent of their immigrant populations within the last five years. And Gallup polls showed unemployment to be one of the important political issues in the 1972 election (Hughes 1973).

There are scattered indications of labor market competition between the indigenous and immigrant populations. Both journalistic inquiries and

33. In the past, Australia was relatively isolated from the world economy except for the connection to its major trading partner, Britain. One example illustrates the depth of those ties. A trade mission to Latin America in the early 1960s revealed that Australian producers were still selling products via London distributors rather than developing direct trade networks (Grassby 1979:30). Britain's negotiations for European Economic Community membership (and ultimate admission in 1973) forced Australia to reexamine its position in the international economic community. For more details on Australian foreign trade, see Anderson and Crawford 1977.

Table 6.3. Coefficients of correlation among location of foreign-born population, unemployment, growth in immigration, and "anti-immigrant" constituencies in Australia 1971

	1	2	3	4	5	6	7	8	9
1. Migrants	1.00								
2. New migrants	0.91	1.00							
3. Noncitizens	0.79	0.74	1.00						
4. Unemployment	0.01	0.09	0.04	1.00					
5. Anti-immigrant 1	0.88	0.86	0.70	0.42	1.00				
6. Anti-immigrant 2	0.90	0.95	0.74	0.18	0.90	1.00			
7. Anti-immigrant 3	0.81	0.88	0.64	0.35	0.93	0.96	1.00		
8. Anti-immigrant 4	0.82	0.93	0.67	0.38	0.94	0.94	0.96	1.00	
9. Anti-immigrant 5	0.73	0.72	0.93	0.30	0.80	0.74	0.74	0.74	1.00

Source: Australia, Commonwealth Bureau of Census and Statistics, 1972. See text for definition of anti-immigrant measures.

government investigations turned up numerous reports that employers preferred immigrant workers to the Australian-born population and refused to hire from the local labor markets. Robert Birrell and Tanya Birrell (1981:88) reported that "the Melbourne newspapers splashed briefly the story that the Ford factory refused to employ native Australians on the line. Government investigation turned up similar cases, for example, BHP's attempt in 1973 to recruit through the employer nomination system 300 unskilled migrants to its Whyalla steelworks."

In addition to rising unemployment, the cost of living skyrocketed at a rate of 6.1 percent a year. In the *Economist*'s colorful language, it was "the dreaded spiral of higher wages chasing higher prices chasing higher wages" ("Gough Whitlam's Australia" 1973:21). Inflation was especially important in the housing market, where rapid increases in housing prices made home ownership virtually impossible for many native Australians. By all measures, the fiscal year 1971–72 was a poor one (Southern 1973).

Thus extremely high levels of settler arrivals in the late 1960s combined with poor economic conditions in the early 1970s (United Nations 1982). As I did for Britain and France, I have created a set of indicators to locate those electoral constituencies experiencing immigrant pressures. Using the census data from 1971, I calculated five indicators of immigrant pressures: the first based on immigrant concentration and unemployment rates, the second on immigrant concentration combined with recent immigrant intakes; the third combining the three variables, the fourth focusing on unemployment combined with recent immigrant intakes, and the final indicator combining unemployment rates with the noncitizen population. All five indicators of immigrant pressures are highly correlated (see Table 6.3). The same relationships between the variables visible in Britain and France are apparent in

Australia as well. Unemployment is not highly correlated with immigration or new immigration and only moderately correlated with the measures of anti-immigrant pressures, but the presence of a large immigrant community is highly correlated with the indicators of immigrant pressures.

Organized responses to these pressures were not long in following. Despite the political consensus favoring high immigration intakes, Australia was never entirely free from complaints about immigration. Many reports of anti-immigrant sentiment come from the earlier period, when immigration pressures culminated in 1952. The Australian Council of Trade Unions passed a measure demanding decreased immigrant intakes at its 1952 annual congress, much to the embarrassment of union and Labor Party leaders (IPC 4 March 1953).[34] And the Immigration Planning Council provided reports from the local press expressing concern over the impact of immigration. The *Sydney Morning Herald* reported on 27 January 1953 that "immigration has been a powerful inflationary factor, and that the important new economic assets represented by 700,000 migrants have not been acquired cheaply." On the same day, the *Daily Telegraph* reported that "initially [the migrants] put a big strain on inadequate supplies of houses, scarce foodstuffs, and capital equipment." The *Sydney Sun* reported on 27 January 1954 on the local difficulty of providing housing for immigrants. The *Melbourne Sun* reported on 16 August 1954 the results of a nationwide Gallup poll showing that "the housing shortage was the usual reason given for opposing increased migration."[35] That these pressures were politically important is reflected in the New South Wales ALP conference held in 1953 at which party members "formally moved that migrants be distributed across the country" to avoid "a great influx to the eastern cities which strains the economy of the country" (Wilton and Bosworth 1984:9).

The massive influx of immigrants in the second half of the 1960s, combined with the cumulative effects of two decades of substantial immigration intakes, generated new, systematic, and organized pressure against continued immigration. Again, the salience of the issue is reflected in local newspaper coverage. The *Australian* (8 June 1970, 7) devoted a three-part series to immigration issues in June 1970, listing the various issues as perceived by members of the Australian community:

> At any rate, the anti-immigrant case is broadly that Joe Dabocca's [a prototypical, fictitious Italian immigrant] need for a rented home and later for a house

34. The resolution read in part, "In view of the fact that at the present time full employment does not exist, Congress considers that the intake of migrants should be immediately stopped and confined to the wives and children, or fiancees, of migrants already in Australia" (IPC 4 March 1953:5).

35. These quotations are excerpted from the periodic IPC "Surveys of Responsible Public Opinion." One can only wonder about the comments from "irresponsible" public opinion.

of his own and the things to fill it represent an inflationary pressure. . . . Immigration means in effect that we have to spend double the amount we would otherwise need to on new houses, new suburban roads, extra school teachers, new hospitals, extra welfare spending and so on. (Hallows 1970:8)

One voice of organized opposition was the Australia Conservation Foundation (ACF), created in 1965 (Warhurst 1993). The ACF provided the organizational platform to advance the Zero Population Growth movement, which focused on the role of immigration in damaging the environment and reducing the quality of life in Australia. Another source of opposition originated in the academic community; economists began linking immigration to a wide variety of economic ills, inflation, low per capita economic growth rates, and inadequate growth in productivity (Birrell and Birrell 1981, APIC 1977). These criticisms were sufficiently strong that the government felt compelled to respond by commissioning studies on the issue in 1970 (Birrell and Birrell 1981). Although these studies were not completed until after the 1972 election, that they were commissioned at all indicates that organized political opposition to immigration was becoming politically significant.

Another indicator of the growing opposition to high immigration intakes comes from the topic selected for study in 1971 by the Australian Institute of Political Science (AIPS) for its annual summer school. The AIPS held annual summer sessions on topics of contemporary political significance but had not addressed immigration issues since 1953, the earlier conference also coinciding with the increased salience of immigration as a political issue. The session scheduled in January and February 1971 was titled "How Many Australians?" The conference proceedings discussed the many arguments advanced by the "anti-immigrant underground" or by the "new critics" of immigration, labels that capture the growing salience of immigration issues (AIPS 1971, Warhurst 1993). According to the proceedings, 1971 was a time "when immigration restriction policies have come under increasing scrutiny and criticism as have the targets of immigration policy in general" (Burnley 1971:57). A report of the proceedings divided the discussions into two main camps:

(1) ecologists and others have been advocating zero or slow population growth on the grounds that immigration is causing overcrowding in Australian capital cities, and indirectly putting stress on social services, contributing to pollution and other social and environmental evils; (2) critics of the "White Australia" policy [who] favour a liberalising of immigration policy and the admission to Australia of more non-European migrants. (Smith 1971:8)

The same report elaborated on the concerns of the former group:

The present population clearly bears two sorts of immediate costs. Firstly, there are costs of administering the immigration policy, including the costs of attracting and, in many cases, transporting new migrants. More important is the cost of providing social capital to meet the needs of the increased population. Present Australians must either forgo some current consumption, in order to provide schools, hospitals, roads, etc., for the new migrants, or they must suffer a deterioration in the quality of these services as the present facilities become over-utilised. (Smith 1971:9)

Various other indicators point to the growing opposition to immigration. One member of the business community vented his anger in an anonymous article titled "A Herd of Sacred Cows: The Economic Case against Immigration," in which he punctured both security and economic justifications for immigration.[36] Others reported that immigration received much of the blame for pollution problems and for Australia's relatively poor economic growth. A public opinion survey of the residents of Melbourne pointed out that dissatisfaction with life in Melbourne came from manmade sources: "pollution and overcrowding within the city especially with relation to transport problems" (Ware 1974:190).

If much of the organized and unorganized opposition to immigration concentrated on its economic effects, racial issues were not entirely absent from the debate. The Immigration Control Association (ICA) was established in 1966 to present the case for racial exclusiveness, joining the growing chorus of those who opposed continued high immigrant intakes (Moore 1995).

While immigrant pressures were concentrated, the effects of the economic slowdown created broader political consequences. Public opinion polls reveal that attitudes toward immigration were relatively stable in 1956 and 1963, when 43 to 45 percent of the respondents favored maintaining immigration intakes. This level of support dropped to 34 percent in 1971 and plummeted to 17 percent in 1972 (Birrell and Birrell 1981:238). Politicians were cognizant of these complaints. The Labor spokesman on urban affairs acknowledged the linkage between immigration, urban decay, and the economy more broadly and warned, "It is about time that a few more people recognised the nature and results of exponential [immigration] growth in our population" (*Sydney Morning Herald*, 13 October 1972). And these complaints provided a set of electoral incentives that shattered the immigration consensus.

Electoral incentives for immigration control, 1966–1969

There were few electoral incentives to introduce immigration control in the 1960s. Despite rising pressures from immigration, neither the conservative

---

36. *Nation*, 18 October 1969. Rivett 1978 identifies the author as Paul L. Sharp, a Sydney industrialist.

LCP coalition nor the ALP proposed reduced immigration intakes for several reasons.

First, support for immigration from the growth lobby remained strong (Birrell and Birrell 1981). The primary beneficiaries of high immigration intakes were the manufacturing sector and developers.[37] The postwar program had encouraged local manufacture of products heretofore purchased abroad. To achieve this end, tariffs were raised to provide protection for domestic producers. But because manufacturers were uncompetitive on international markets, only the growth in local demand would permit expansion—growth that could be maintained through high levels of immigration (Birrell and Birrell 1981). Moreover, expanded product demand brought a demand for labor, which immigrants could fill. Hence the manufacturing sector formed the core of the "growth lobby." A second important segment of the growth lobby consisted of developers and the construction industry. Like the manufacturing sector, this nontraded sector also depended on local demand for growth, which high immigrant streams fueled with their demands for housing and associated services.[38] At one time, developers could actually nominate immigrants for settlement in Australia, providing themselves with guaranteed customers (Australia 1975:19–20).

The core of the growth lobby was highly geographically concentrated. Although manufacturers and developers lobbied the government as "national organizations," such as the Associated Chambers of Manufacturers of Australia, they really represented employers in metropolitan areas (Warhurst 1993). Large manufacturing firms were located almost exclusively in the major metropolitan areas of the southern state capitals, Sydney, Victoria, Adelaide, and Perth. In the seventy-five urban constituencies, average manufacturing employment was 12,700, whereas in the fifty rural constituencies it was less than half that amount, 5,200.[39] In fact, in the very early period of refugee and state-assisted migration, immigrants were bound to locational job decisions made by the government (Burnley 1982: chap. 6). While some immigrants were sent to rural areas for development projects, such as the Snowy Mountains Hydro Electric scheme, most were directed to manufacturing employment in Sydney and Victoria, in addition to the sec-

37. Although the primary products sector, including agricultural and mineral products, also benefited from an expanded domestic market, these segments of the Australian economy were closely tied to international markets and could seek expansion in export markets rather than in increased local demand. These segments of the economy were less dependent on immigration streams and therefore less insistent on continued high levels of immigration to guarantee high product demand. Moreover, neither economic sector was particularly dependent on immigrant labor. Agriculture was in the process of mechanization, leading to contraction of employment, and the minerals sector was highly capital intensive.
38. "Nontraded" goods are defined in economic terms as goods and services that are not traded internationally.
39. The urban-rural distinction is taken from Mackerras 1975.

ondary industrial cites of Wollongong (NSW) and Geelong (Victoria). Thereafter, immigrant networks and employment opportunities drove the geographical concentration of migrants and the geographically specific demand for housing and associated construction jobs.

The second factor that affected the political calculation over immigration intakes was the limited pressures that immigration had placed to date on the host population. Immigration pressures were beginning to rise but were still limited by a variety of factors, among them the virtually full employment that Australia had experienced since the 1952–53 recession. In addition, the centralized bargaining system of industrial relations in Australia prevented immigrant workers from undercutting wages and working conditions. Nor was the competition over housing as intense in Australia as it was in Britain and France. The stock of public housing was small, and the free play of the market served to reduce, if not eliminate, housing shortages. And in many immigrant neighborhoods, housing was freed up when the Australian-born population moved to more desirable locations in the suburbs. Pressures were building but had not reached a critical level in a sufficient number of electoral constituencies to change the political equation.

Finally, the ALP was not well placed to challenge the LCP coalition. In 1966, the ALP had suffered a disastrous defeat at the polls, partly in response to its position against the Vietnam War that was particularly unpopular in Australia (Hughes 1973). Only a nominal number of constituencies were experiencing immigration pressures, but the LCP coalition was returned with a large margin in the 1966 federal elections: 20 seats in the 124-seat lower house. Moreover, the ALP was a divided party, without clear leadership. The state branches were almost completely autonomous and the weak federal machine was unable to control the powerfully organized state cliques. This situation began to change when Gough Whitlam won the party leadership in 1967 and set about reorganizing and reuniting the ALP as well as developing an innovative electoral platform. That process was under way but not sufficiently developed in time for the 1969 election (Butler 1968).

Electoral incentives for immigration control, 1969–1972

The picture changed with the 1969 election in which the ALP narrowed the gap between itself and the LCP coalition to seven seats so that the swing of another four seats would provide the ALP with a parliamentary majority. For the ALP, the 1969 election results came as a pleasant surprise. The large swing toward Labor reflected the shift in public opinion against the Vietnam War, Whitlam's leadership and efforts to develop a forward-looking program, the inroads made by Whitlam in party reorganization, and the length of the LCP coalition's governing tenure. This narrow margin combined with the increasing salience of immigration pressures modified the electoral incentives to respond to anti-immigrant constituencies.

The ALP's narrow defeat in the 1969 election renewed hope that the Labor Party could return to power.[40] Under the leadership of Gough Whitlam, the party made every effort to ensure that it would win the 1972 elections. The 1972 Labor election campaign was historic in organizational terms because the ALP initiated, for the first time, a highly centralized and tightly controlled campaign. Mick Young, the full-time campaign manager, was responsible for this aggressive campaign. He wrote that "victory in 1972 depends upon many things . . . but a properly held campaign would give a huge boost to our chances" (Blewett 1973:10). A proper modern campaign for the ALP meant a significantly larger national election budget for everything from a national advertising campaign to conducting public opinion polls. Additionally, Young created the National Campaign Committee (NCC) to advise the party and Whitlam and to keep the campaign centralized. The national campaign slogan, "It's Time," represented not only the idea that control of government needed to change but also the way the ALP ran campaigns. The ALP's highly centralized, professional, and costly election campaign changed electoral politics in Australia irrevocably.

The ALP left nothing to chance. To complement its national "It's Time" campaign, the NCC planned an electoral strategy focused on marginal federal divisions, Australia's term for constituencies. For the first time, the federal party decided which divisions to target and the campaign strategy in each without interference from the state party organizations. The NCC closely managed the state campaigns. It controlled state party leaders' itineraries, determined the national issues to which the states adhered, especially in Victoria, and supervised all state advertising. State campaign funds were administered by the NCC. In short, Labor adopted a coherent, national electoral strategy.

This national campaign strategy did not ignore local issues. "Election campaigns by the major political parties are two-level affairs having not only a central campaign emphasizing broad policies and concentrating on the personal qualities of the party leader, but also a local electorate campaign where broad policies are to be related directly to the people in that area" (Murphy 1970:54).

The Labor Party needed only four seats to win the election and return to government after a twenty-three-year absence. The three least populous states were a lesser electoral concern because they provided substantial Labor support. The ALP held four of the five seats in Tasmania. In South

---

40. The ALP was defeated by seven seats. The Liberal Party won forty-six seats and the Country Party twenty, so that the LCP coalition had a majority of sixty-six compared to the ALP's fifty-nine seats.

Australia and West Australia, Labor held 70 percent of the seats (Blewett 1973). Nonetheless, Adelaide and Perth had experienced heavy immigrant intakes in the 1960s, and all three of the marginal Labor seats in South Australia experienced both relatively high unemployment and high immigration intakes, as did the two marginal Country Party seats in West Australia.

The three most populous states presented an even more serious problem. Labor was the minority party in all three—New South Wales, Queensland, and Victoria. Compounding this disadvantage was the fact that Labor had never governed at a national level without an electoral majority in New South Wales, and party leaders believed that any ALP victory would not be considered legitimate without substantial support in Victoria.

As the second largest state in the Commonwealth, Victoria was thus essential to a Labor victory in 1972. Indeed, Victoria had always been a trouble spot for the ALP, and the party had held less than one-third of the Victorian federal seats since 1969 (Blewett 1973). The Victorian Labor Party was characterized by bitter infighting and often had disagreements with the federal party. In 1972, however, the federal Labor Party successfully dismantled what was tantamount to an apostate party clique. Further, the New South Wales branch was restructured and brought on board with the federal campaign.[41] The Labor Party was united as it had not been for decades and could concentrate on targeting its campaign to specific divisions. Therefore, in 1972, the ALP's main focus was on the metropolitan electoral divisions in Melbourne (Victoria), Sydney (New South Wales), and Brisbane (Queensland). Special emphasis was placed on the Victorian divisions.[42] These divisions were specifically targeted by Whitlam at the beginning of the electoral campaign (*Sydney Morning Herald*, 27 November 1972, 3). Table 6.4 provides a list of Labor's marginal federal electoral divisions in all six states.[43]

To gain those constituencies for Labor, as well as hold onto marginal Labor seats, the ALP needed to convince the swing voters that "It's Time" to vote Labor. Politics in Australia is a struggle between the Liberal Party and the ALP over such swing voters.[44] "Electoral outcomes are typically

41. For more detail on the restructuring of the two state party branches see Walker 1971.
42. Although historically a substantial part of ALP support came from rural voters, it has gradually shifted is electoral bases to urban areas. The Country Party (in 1975, the National Country Party) now holds a firm grip on rural voters, and the ALP platform contained little to attract rural voters. Since the rural vote was not essential to victory (because urban seats make up more than two-thirds of the federal total), the Labor Party focused its attention on metropolitan areas where the swing voters were located (Jupp 1991, Aitkin 1977).
43. I have adopted Mackerras's definition of marginals as those divisions where a swing of 5.9% or less would change the electoral outcome. For a more detailed description of how marginals were calculated, see Mackerras 1972. A less conservative definition of marginal comes from Hughes 1977, who defines a 0 to 4.9% swing as "ultra marginal" and a 5 to 9.9% swing as marginal. If one used Hughes's definition, the list of marginal constituencies would be longer.
44. For a detailed discussion of the stability of electoral politics in Australia see Aitkin 1977.

Table 6.4. Marginal electoral divisions, 1972 election

Division	Percent swing to change outcome	Classification	Anti-immigrant sentiment[a]	Swing to ALP
Bass (Tasmania)	5.2%	Marginal Labor	48	
Denison (Tasmania)	2.6	Marginal Liberal	96	X
Canning (Western Australia)	**4.9**	**Marginal C.P.**	**1,020**	
Forrest (Western Australia)	1.2	Marginal Labor	112	
Moore (Western Australia)	**5.6**	**Marginal C.P.**	**274**	
Swan (Western Australia)	**4.3**	**Marginal Labor**	**624**	
Grey (South Australia)	**2.1**	**Marginal Labor**	**278**	
Kingston (South Australia)	**4.2**	**Marginal Labor**	**382**	
Sturt (South Australia)	0.8	Marginal Labor	208	
Bowman (Queensland)	2.7	Marginal Labor	59	
Brisbane (Queensland)	4.1	Marginal Labor	146	
Griffith (Queensland)	1.6	Marginal Liberal	152	
Herbert (Queensland)	1.8	Marginal Liberal	52	
Lilley (Queensland)	1.8	Marginal Liberal	43	X
Moreton (Queensland)	3.4	Marginal Liberal	52	
Petrie (Queensland)	4.0	Marginal Liberal	49	
Batman (Victoria)	**3.1**	**Marginal Labor**	**404**	
Bendigo (Victoria)	4.6	Marginal Labor	9	
Casey (Victoria)	5.1	Marginal Liberal	177	X
Corio (Victoria)	**4.7**	**Marginal Labor**	**297**	
Holt (Victoria)	**3.6**	**Marginal Liberal**	**448**	**X**
La Trobe (Victoria)	**5.2**	**Marginal Liberal**	**259**	**X**
Maribyrnong (Victoria)	1.5	Marginal Labor	180	
McMillan (Victoria)	5.4	Marginal Liberal	37	
Barton (N.S.W.)	3.2	Marginal Labor	61	
Cook (N.S.W.)	2.9	Marginal Liberal	60	X
Eden-Monaro (N.S.W.)	3.7	Marginal Labor	35	
Evans (N.S.W.)	**1.3**	**Marginal Liberal**	**461**	**X**
Gwydir (N.S.W.)	3.5	Marginal C.P.	9	
Hume (N.S.W.)	1.0	Marginal C.P.	9	X
Macarthur (N.S.W.)	3.4	Marginal Liberal	131	X
Mitchell (N.S.W.)	2.6	Marginal Liberal	86	
Phillip (N.S.W.)	**0.5**	**Marginal Liberal**	**604**	**X**
Riverina (N.S.W.)	2.6	Marginal Labor	15	
Robertson (N.S.W.)	2.3	Marginal Labor	54	
St. George (N.S.W.)	0.2	Marginal Labor	139	
Australian median			111	
Australian mean			226	

Note: Rows in **boldface** designate electoral divisions where anti-immigrant scores were above the national mean of 226.

[a] See text for definition of anti-immigrant scores; the score presented here corresponds to "anti-immigrant 3."

Sources: Adapted from Mackerras 1972; Australia, Commonwealth Bureau of Census and Statistics 1972.

decided by changes in the voting decisions of a small proportion of the electorate" (McAllister 1994:198). This struggle takes place against a backdrop of deep-rooted party loyalties dating back to 1910 that continue to shape electoral politics in Australia today. The last major shift in party support occurred in the 1920s with the emergence of the (National) Country Party, which attracted the rural vote. Australians hold strong party loyalties that often seemed impervious even to the most aggressive issue-based campaigns (Aitkin 1977). Labor's task in 1972 was by no means an easy one.

The Liberal Party's constituency base is composed mostly of middle-class urban and suburban dwellers who are professionals, industrialists, manufacturers, and businesspeople. But they also enjoy a substantial provincial and rural electorate base. This base is complemented by the rural base of their coalition partner, the (National) Country Party. The ALP, on the other hand, has traditionally relied on trade unions and the working class for support. Gough Whitlam brought teachers, intellectuals, and college students into the Labor fold by making education a major domestic political issue for the first time, but the main electoral base continues to come from the working classes and trade union organizations.

The parties' discrete electoral bases ensure that all federal elections in Australia are won at the margins. Although the Liberal Party has tight control over the inner suburbs of both Sydney and Melbourne, the outer suburbs are always contested. The latter middle-class urban seats, defined as those divisions in which 35 percent of the workforce is employed in professional, administrative, or clerical sectors, are essential to electoral success (Jupp 1982).

To win these marginal Liberal seats, the ALP promised to resolve urban problems, in part by reduced immigration intakes.[45] A significant part of the ALP platform was accordingly devoted to urban issues. The program was revolutionary for Australia because for the first time it promised federal intervention in urban affairs, an arena of public policy that had previously been the preserve of state and local governments. In fact, Whitlam was reported to feel "more deeply about the cities than probably any other issue" ("Gough Whitlam's Australia" 1973:35). The campaign platform sought to express these concerns:

> Increasingly, a citizen's real standard of living, the health of himself and his family, his children's opportunities for education and self-improvement, his access to employment opportunities, his ability to enjoy the nation's resources

---

45. McAllister and Mughan 1987 make a distinction between "conversion" of voters, where those with different party loyalties are induced to vote differently, and "mobilization" of voters, ensuring that those loyal to the party turn out to vote. See below for efforts to "mobilize" Labor voters.

for recreation or culture, his ability to participate in the decisions and actions of the community are determined not by his income, not by the hours he works, but by where he lives. This is why Labor believes that the national government must involve itself directly in cities. (*Sydney Morning Herald*, 14 November 1972)

The ALP promised a variety of policies to improve the urban environment. The ALP campaign platform (*Sydney Morning Herald*, 14 November 1972) noted that "Australians pay some of the world's highest rates [i.e., property taxes] for some of the world's worst municipal services," and it promised funds to improve those services. The platform addressed sewerage, transportation, and education. Control over the skyrocketing real estate market was promised as well as access to cheap mortgages. To address the variety of urban issues outlined in the platform, the ALP also promised a new Ministry of Urban Affairs. Overall, Labor's "declared intention of investing in more social projects [was concentrated] in . . . urban development . . . [which accounted] for a large part of the social expenditure budgeted in the next three years" ("Gough Whitlam's Australia" 1973:6, 35). According to one election observer, by 1972, "Mr Whitlam's urban policies . . . were seen as the centerpiece of Labor's grand strategy" (Hughes 1973:25).

At the same time, the ALP promised an immigration policy premised on the ability to provide employment, housing, education, and social services, specifically tying immigration intakes to the adequacy of the urban infrastructure. The change in immigration policy was part and parcel of Whitlam's efforts to develop an innovative and attractive electoral platform (Grattan 1993). It was debated and adopted at the ALP's 1971 conference, which determined that "Labor's immigration policy would no longer be directed to the goal of increasing population" (Grattan 1993:129, Price 1974). Thus the ALP's 1972 electoral platform added a reference to the adequacy of public goods (clause [b]) while eliminating a call for a "vigorous and expanding immigration program." The contrast between the ALP's 1969 and 1972 electoral platforms is presented in Table 6.5. Whitlam brought attention to this change in his policy speech opening the 1972 campaign, when he announced, "We will change the emphasis in immigration from government recruiting to family reunion and to retaining the migrants already here" (ALP 1972:7).

The connection made between immigration and urban amenities in the party's platform became apparent in the election campaign as well. The Labour spokesman on urban affairs, Tom Uren, clarified this connection: "I feel I must point out to you why we decided to cut back on migration. A great part of that decision is the realisation that . . . we must relieve the pressure placed on our large cities by migration. Rectifying the past neglect will

Table 6.5. Australian Labor Party's electoral platforms on immigration control, 1969 and 1972

1969	1972
Convinced that increased population is vital to the future development of Australia, the Australian Labor Party will support and uphold *a vigorous and expanding immigration program* administered with sympathy, understanding and tolerance. The basis of such a policy will be: a. Australia's national and economic security; b. the welfare and integration of all its citizens; c. the preservation of our democratic system and balanced development of our nation; d. the avoidance of the difficult social and economic problems which may follow from an influx of peoples having different standards of living, traditions and cultures.	The Australian Labor Party supports an immigration policy administered with sympathy, understanding and tolerance. The basis of such a policy shall include: a. Australia's national and economic security; b. *the capacity to provide employment, housing, education and social services;* c. the welfare and integration of all her citizens; d. the preservation of our democratic system and the balanced development of our nation; e. the avoidance of the difficult social and economic problems which may flow from an influx of peoples having different standards of living, traditions and cultures; f. the avoidance of discrimination on any grounds of race or colour of skin or nationality.

Source: Hawkins 1991:99.

take a great deal of money, time, and, above all, a great slowdown in the growth rate of Sydney and Melbourne" (*Sydney Morning Herald*, 13 October 1972).

These policies were used in targeting those electoral divisions that had experienced high immigration pressures. Of all the forty electoral divisions with high immigration pressures, eleven were marginal.[46] Additionally, half of these (six) were located in either Victoria or New South Wales. The ALP needed only to pick up four marginal seats from the Liberal/NCP coalition and retain the marginal Labor ones. Of the eleven marginal divisions with high immigration pressures, five were marginal Labor, four were marginal Liberal (Holt, La Trobe, Evans, and Phillip), and two were marginal Country Party (Moore and Canning). Providing policies that would alleviate immigration pressures in these districts could secure the ALP precisely the swing divisions that it needed for national electoral victory.

The policy package of urban renewal accompanied by immigration control was also compatible with mobilizing Labor's core constituency. Of the forty

46. The forty divisions are all of those with a score of anti-immigration sentiment above the average score of 226.

divisions experiencing immigration pressures, eleven were safe Labor seats and nine were fairly safe Labor seats. Immigration was thus an issue that could attract swing voters as well as keep those voters who had, in the past, voted Labor. The ALP's immigration policy was compatible with other elements of its platform, including a program to restructure the economy. But it retained a political dynamic of its own, centered on the appeal to swing constituencies in areas of high immigration pressure.

The outcome of this electoral strategy was a historic Labor victory and a return to power after twenty-three years in opposition. The ALP won sixty-seven seats, the Liberal Party thirty-eight, and the Country Party twenty; overall this gave the ALP a nine-seat majority, against the combined fifty-eight seats of the LCP coalition. As the *Economist* noted, "Mr. Whitlam would say that dissatisfaction in the big cities played a big part in the ALP's victory last December. He would very probably be right" ("Gough Whitlam's Australia" 1973:35).

Revisiting Table 6.3 places the role of marginal immigrant constituencies in perspective. The table presents all of Labor's marginal electoral constituencies. The 1972 Labor victory is indivisible from its electoral gains in Victoria, where it picked up three seats and lost one, and New South Wales, where it picked up six seats. Outside of these two states, few seats changed hands, and these were a wash overall, with Labor losses being compensated by gains. Whitlam and his advisers were aware that the electoral balance of power rested in these two states and targeted the marginal divisions in those states. Moreover, Whitlam's predictions were correct; the campaign generated a swing in Holt and Casey in Victoria, as well as in Evans, Phillip, and Mitchell in New South Wales. Parramatta was the sole seat targeted by Labor and lost.

As in Britain and France, immigration was never the central national campaign issue. But the ALP was not interested in making it one. Rather, it simply wanted to reassure those key marginal electoral divisions that they would not experience a flood of immigrants into their communities. Mick Young knew that reductions in immigration levels would get the attention of a few key constituencies and swing voters, namely the middle-class urban voters in the outer suburbs of Sydney and Melbourne, such as Mitchell and Casey. In key swing constituencies, immigration control was part of the political dialogue. In Evans, for example, an Independent ran on a single-issue platform of reduced immigration (*Sydney Morning Herald*, 29 November 1972). The ALP would employ a similar strategy in the 1983 Hawke election campaign. "Given the political mileage wrought out of the record unemployment levels, Stewart West, the Hawke Government's first Immigration Minister, immediately announced a scaling down of immigration" (Collins 1988:27). Thus, although it was not a central national campaign issue, immigration played a key role in Labor's 1972 electoral victory, a key role at the margin.[47]

Labor kept its promises. On the heels of the December 1972 electoral victory, the ALP announced immediate reductions from 140,000 to 110,000 in 1972–73, thereby retroactively cutting immigration targets for the current fiscal year. Further reductions were made in 1974–75 to bring the target to 80,000. By the end of 1975–76 fiscal year, actual immigration intakes were down to 52,700, resulting in a net migration total of only 20,800, the lowest net intake since 1947 (Patience and Head 1979). Even more notably, this reduction was not a temporary response to poor economic conditions in 1971 and 1972. Economic growth returned in 1973 and with it increased demand for immigrant labor. But requests from even the most powerful Australian corporations were turned down. Broken Hill Proprietary, Australia's largest corporation and the sole steel manufacturer in the country, was told that "it would not be allowed to recruit immigrants to work in its South Australian shipbuilding yard, the reason given being that the company could attract labour locally if only it would pay enough" ("Gough Whitlam's Australia" 1973:22, Birrell and Birrell 1981:88). This statement suggests that the reduction in immigration intakes was not a temporary response to poor economic conditions but rather a response to the electoral significance of constituencies where immigration pressures were concentrated.

In Australia, as in Britain and France, the costs of immigration associated with the geographic distribution of immigrant communities facilitated the organization of opposition to immigration. This opposition offset the continued support for immigration leading to the maintenance of lower intake targets.

Electoral incentives for immigration control, 1972–1975

The period between the December 1972 ALP victory and the 1975 return of the conservative coalition to government was a bitterly contested time in Australian political history. The LCP coalition, out of power for the first time since 1949, employed every possible means to discredit the ALP government, including blocking the government budget in the upper house for the first time in Australia's history. As a result, the ALP called for dissolution of both houses of parliament in the spring of 1974 less than eighteen months after its election victory. In the subsequent elections, the ALP retained its majority, but its parliamentary margin narrowed to five seats in the lower house and the LCP retained control in the upper house. The coalition employed

47. There were obviously many reasons for Labor's 1972 victory, including the long tenure of the LCP coalition and the prime minister's lack of popularity. This does not undermine the point that immigration played a key role in a few critical constituencies.

the same tactics in 1975, again followed by a joint dissolution and elections. This time, however, the governor general (nominally appointed by Her Majesty's government in Britain) appointed Malcolm Fraser, the Liberal Party leader, as head of the interim government. This intervention threw the country into a constitutional crisis, and the 1975 federal election is best remembered for these issues.

Nonetheless, the Lib-NCP coalition, upon returning to power in 1975 with a wide parliamentary majority, abandoned the 1 percent solution and retained the principle of lower intakes established by the ALP. It did so because growing unemployment expanded the number of anti-immigrant constituencies and forced the Lib-NCP coalition to control immigration intakes despite continued pressure from the growth lobby. The contraction of immigration intakes contrasts dramatically with the LCP's enthusiastic support of high immigration intakes during the 1950s and 1960s.

During the 1950s and 1960s, the Liberal Party continued to maintain that immigration was needed for economic growth even when government reports, initiated by the LCP itself, began to indicate that high levels of immigration were hurting the economy. In 1965, the LCP prime minister, Robert Menzies, rejected the Report of the Committee of Economic Enquiry which called for a freeze on immigration levels, noting that "it will be clear that the Government cannot accept any artificial ceiling on migration for a term of years. We will therefore continue our present policy of securing as large an inflow of migrants as Australia can usefully absorb" (quoted in Birrell and Birrell 1981:66). That commitment was maintained during the 1972 electoral campaign. In fact, in January 1972, A. J. Forbes, LCP minister for immigration, delivered a major attack on the ALP's new immigration policy, labeling it as "equivalent to national economic euthanasia" (Birrell and Birrell 1981:86, Hawkins 1991). But that election was lost.

Placed in opposition for the first time in twenty-three years, the Liberal Party had time to reflect. When it had day-to-day responsibility for government, the party had tended to lose any sense of strategic vision (Aitchison 1974, March 1976, Oakes 1976). Neither the party organization nor its electoral strategies had been renovated. The Liberal Party used its time in opposition to good effect, examining its strategies in light of the policy agenda adopted by the ALP as well as on the techniques it had employed to win the 1972 election (Oakes 1976: chap. 14). Liberal politicians undertook a major overhaul of the party platform, policies, and organization.[48] Ultimately, the

48. The Liberal Party draws a distinction between the party "platform," which delineates general party values and philosophy and is the responsibility of the organization wing of the party, and party "policies," which are specific policies proposed to the electorate and developed by the parliamentary party (March 1976).

Liberal Party adopted not only the more centralized electoral machine of the ALP but much of the electoral program that had appealed to voters in 1972.

The revision of the party platform was complete by the 1974 elections, when the refusal of the LCP coalition in the Senate to pass the budget forced the Whitlam government to call for a double dissolution of the House and Senate and new elections, scheduled for May. But the Liberal Party had not yet developed a compelling policy program to attract voters and was defeated at the polls, although Labor's parliamentary margin was narrowed to five seats.[49] The 1974 defeat brought a new party leader, Malcolm Fraser, and a renewed effort within the Liberal Party to proceed with the reevaluation of policies.[50] Policy working parties were set in place, bringing together shadow ministers, staff, and outside experts in a real effort to develop new and responsive policies (Rubenstein 1993).[51] To ensure coordination among the various policy arenas, Fraser also established in 1975 the Policy Coordination Committee (March 1976). Thus, by the time that parliament was dissolved again in November 1975, the Liberal Party was ready to contest those very seats it had lost in 1972. The party was well aware that "the areas most responsible for the swings to Labor in 1969 and 1972 and which proved crucial when they stuck to Labor in 1974 were the outer metropolitan areas" (Mackerras 1976:43). These were the very seats that Labor had swayed with its more restrictive immigration policy.

Under the ALP government, economic conditions had begun to change as well. The oil shocks of 1973 modified world economic conditions at the very moment when Australia was opening its markets to freer trade. The 25 percent across-the-board tariff cut implemented by the ALP caused a contraction of the manufacturing sector, hitting Australian-born workers in provincial areas harder than immigrant workers.[52] Inflation was rising; unemployment, after dropping in 1973, began to rise as well. Therefore, despite the slowdown in immigration under the ALP government, indicators of immigrant pressure continued to grow. As unemployment rates rose, indicators of anti-immigrant constituencies rose in unison.

The manufacturing sector was especially hard hit, experiencing both absolute and relative employment losses (Rich 1987). These sectors of the economy had been major employers of immigrant labor. Therefore, demand for immigrant labor declined as opposition rose with rising unemployment

49. In the Senate, the LCP coalition retained its edge.
50. William "Billy" Snedden, the Liberal party leader defeated at the polls in 1974, was removed from his position in March 1975.
51. Rubenstein 1993:148 argues that the "liberal opposition underwent a significant reorientation under the new leadership of Malcolm Fraser. These new policies were incorporated in the August 1975 policy document."
52. Jupp, personal correspondence.

rates. These indicators of anti-immigrant sentiment are consistent with a survey commissioned by the Liberal Party in 1974 that found that "often some long-standing neighbourhood or regional inconvenience, some local thorn in the side, could swing an electorate from one party to another" and that immigration was one of the potential "local thorns" (Aitchison 1974:249). As a result, although the Liberal/NCP tone on immigration remained positive, they too acknowledged that the 1 percent solution was outmoded and retained Labor's commitment to lowered immigration levels.

This change was evident in the policy debates in the Liberal Party during its period in opposition. In 1974, the new party platform acknowledged "the need for flexibility in the determination of the desirable migrant intake and a continuing review of all aspects of immigration planning including the availability of employment opportunities" (Liberal Party 1974:27). But the 1974 electoral platform, developed by the parliamentary party, still promoted "the active encouragement of the maximum number of migrants to Australia" (*The Way Ahead* 1974:103). Efforts to change the electoral platform and the chances for electoral success were under way even before the May 1974 election. Phillip Lynch (1974: chap. 9), the LCP minister for Immigration from 1970 to 1971, argued, "Our future immigration policies must emphasize levels of migration that are consistent with changing national needs, . . . in the context of an overall manpower policy." These sentiments were echoed by Malcolm Fraser (1974: chap. 8), even before he became party leader, when he claimed, "I have found that, in my view, present circumstances require changes in our past policies and attitudes [on immigration]." Fraser emphasized programs that catered to the migrant population, reflecting the perceived growth in political power of the "ethnic vote," but also acknowledged that "the character of immigration programme has changed." Ultimately, the Liberal Party adopted a policy on immigration that "pay[s] due regard to Australia's national needs," not to the rote formula of 1 percent population growth through immigration (Combe, Hartung, and Hawker 1982:24). The 1 percent mantra was no longer a viable electoral policy.

The change in immigration policy may also have been affected by one of the many lessons learned during the 1972 and 1974 electoral defeats. One of the few seats lost by the ALP in 1974 was the Riverina constituency, held previously by Al Grassby, the ALP minister of immigration. Riverina was the only rural electoral division in New South Wales with a large Italian immigrant population. And although ALP policies had been rather unfriendly to rural constituencies, no one anticipated that the highly popular Grassby would be defeated (Mackerras 1975:263). But in the last ten days of the election campaign, the Immigration Control Association waged a campaign against Grassby's immigrant-friendly policies.[53] Although political commentators of the day noted that "Grassby had reason to complain; the campaign waged against [him] by the Immigration Control Association was one of the most unsavory and contemptible seen in Australia in recent years," Grassby lost the election by a slim margin (Oakes and Solomon 1974:491).

In the 1975 election, immigration was hardly a burning issue despite the deteriorating economic conditions. The LCP coalition had again blocked the budget in the Senate, but this time around, the governor-general requested the resignation of Whitlam and appointed the Liberal Party leader, Malcolm Fraser, as interim prime minister. New elections were called for both the House of Representatives and the Senate. The national campaign issues centered on the constitutional crisis and management of the economy. Nonetheless, for particular constituencies, immigration remained a salient issue and the Liberal Party's electoral campaign promised that immigration intakes in the future would be modulated to Australian economic conditions. These promises, along with the Liberal Party's ability to convince voters that it could better manage the economy, produced a wide Liberal–National Country Party victory, with constituencies in the outer metropolitan areas producing the biggest average swing against Labor—9.2 percent (Mackerras 1976).

Upon regaining office in 1975, the Lib-NCP coalition reinstituted the Department of Immigration, now renamed the Department of Immigration and Ethnic Affairs (DIEA), but "continued the policy ... of keeping intake relatively low" (Rivett 1978:71). Michael Mackellar (1979:103), minister for immigration, announced that "Australia's present policy entails a broad population growth goal of 0.5% annually." Targets rose from 50,000 set by the last ALP government to 70,000 for the next two fiscal years. And in 1978, the government authorized a three-year immigration program of 70,000 net annual immigration intakes for 1978–79 to 1980–81. But because net intake targets were not directly comparable to the gross intake targets of the past, a heated debate was generated about the appropriate level of gross intakes necessary to achieve net goals. Mackellar was an enthusiastic supporter of immigration and recommended high intakes. He cited an APIC report suggesting that gross flows of 90,000 to 120,000 would yield a net intake of 50,000 per year. But ultimately, the cabinet rejected those recommendations and rolled back the proposed target for 1978–79 of 110,000 to 90,000, where it remained.

Immigration continued to remain an electoral issue. Birrell and Birrell

---

53. The fact that the ALP reduced immigrant intakes did not preclude the provision of services that catered to the immigrant community. See below on immigrant policy preferences.

(1981:224–25) discuss a 1979 internal electoral tactics report "which cited refugees as one of the potentially troublesome issues needing to be 'neutralized' for the 1980 election." So immigration targets remained at 90,000 in 1981 and 92,500 in 1982 before dropping to 85,000 in 1983. These figures corresponded to gross intake levels of 0.5 percent, 0.6 percent, and 0.55 percent of the Australian population respectively.

The Lib-NCP coalition did raise immigration targets above the lowest level set by the ALP government in 1975, 50,000. But a comparison of the average program targets under the ALP between 1972 and 1975 and the Lib-NCP coalition between 1975 and 1983 reveals that, on average, Labor actually projected higher immigration targets of 87,500 when compared to the Lib-NCP targets of 84,700. Moreover, it was the Lib-NCP coalition that, in 1981, finally did away with the assisted passage program that underwrote immigration flows to Australia. This evidence reinforces the notion that a new consensus on immigration had been reached.

Literature on Australian Immigration Control

I have argued that the rapid increases in immigration intakes in the second half of the 1960s contributed to pressures on the social infrastructure in areas where immigrants concentrated. In response, the "new critics" of immigration began to organize a political opposition to continued high immigrant intakes. When these pressures combined with economic recession, the stage was set. The ALP promised reduced immigration intakes to those swing constituencies hardest hit by these pressures. That decreased immigration was compatible with other dimensions of the ALP platform, economic restructuring and urban renewal, only made the overall platform more appealing electorally. The Liberal/NCP coalition miscalculated the significance of immigration issues in swing constituencies and lost the election but adopted the ALP's low immigration targets to help ensure electoral victory in 1975.

Overall, there is a lacuna in the Australian immigration literature addressing the Whitlam government's reduction of immigration levels in 1972. The lion's share of attention has gone to the demise of the White Australia policy.[54] In those discussions, authors often devote no more than a paragraph to Whitlam's abandonment of the 1 percent annual targets around which both the Liberal and Labor governments had formed a consensus. When the literature does address the reduction, it is usually descriptive in nature, listing the actual numbers. Although the abolition of the racist policy is important, it is only part of the story. The Whitlam government's decision to make a

---

54. See, among others, Betts 1988.

political issue out of a traditionally bipartisan one presents an interesting puzzle that has elicited some attention.

A few scholars have noted the shift in immigration intakes and have advanced explanations for the ALP's decision to reduce dramatically the immigrant intake levels. The first provides a parallel to explanations advanced for British and French immigration policies, focusing on racism and the linkage between the demise of White Australia and reduced levels of immigration. A second set of authors focuses on structural changes in the economy. A third examines the continued openness of Australia to immigration intakes.

Freda Hawkins (1991) and Charles Price (1974, 1979) posit that the reduction in immigration intakes should be understood in conjunction with the official abolition of the White Australia policy. According to Hawkins, Whitlam had always been interested in foreign policy and when the ALP returned to power in 1972, he made foreign affairs a top priority. He was committed to increasing Australia's standing in the international community and advancing a more independent foreign policy. The White Australia policy was a major obstacle to achieving this goal. Some objections arose from international power players. Countries such as Italy were increasingly critical of Australia for discriminating against their citizens. Britain was offended by Australia's denial of entry permits to black British applicants. Canada and the United States had already abandoned their racially based immigration policies several years previously. Other objections came from neighboring countries. Australia was pushing for a regional economic organization in which Pacific countries would form a loose economic association, similar to the Organisation for Economic Cooperation and Development. But these countries were troubled about becoming significant trading partners with Australia given its racist immigration policies against their citizens, thus straining international relations. Australia was viewed as "a white imperialist puppet, flaunting an immigration policy designed to consolidate white supremacy in the south-western Pacific" (Price 1979:205).

If Australia was to take on a more prominent role in the international arena as well as become a leader in the Pacific region, the White Australia policy had to go. But Australia was in a difficult position. Price (1974) argues that countries such as the United States and Canada could easily abandon their discriminatory policies because their immigration intake levels were much smaller, only around 0.2 percent of their total population. Any increase in non-European immigrants would not alter their overall ethnic composition. Australia was a different story. Because of high immigration intakes, eradication of the racial discrimination in immigration policy would alter noticeably the ethnic composition of the country.

Such a policy was a major political liability, threatening electoral defeat.

A solution to this dilemma came in the form of reduced immigrant intakes. According to Hawkins, this reduction was essential to reassure the party's hard-liners that there would not be a large inflow of non-European migrants. Both Price and Hawkins argue that Whitlam reduced immigration intakes to ensure that the ethnic composition of the country would not be altered dramatically. Combining intake reductions and the abolition of racial discrimination into one immigration policy enabled Whitlam and the ALP to neutralize an otherwise electorally fatal policy.

There are problems with the scenario painted by Price and Hawkins. First, it assumes that high immigration intakes necessitated or were compatible with racial sorting of immigrants. But in practice, these two dimensions of immigration policy were incompatible. The supply of desirable British settlers was insufficient from the start, leading first the ALP, then the LCP coalition, to waive restrictionist criteria. The LCP coalition, over the following twenty years, gradually reduced de facto and de jure racial dimensions of immigration policy. Second, because of this incompatibility and the LCP's de facto reduction of restrictions, the ALP's rejection of White Australia really represented little new. Rejection of White Australia was not an insurmountable political liability; it was merely an acknowledgment of the status quo. And third, ultimately, non-European immigrant streams have come to represent over half the Australian immigrants in any one year (Bureau of Immigration 1995). They are in the process of changing the racial composition of Australia, and they vote.[55] Thus the policy was not implemented to achieve what Price and Hawkins give as the purported goal, to restrict the influx of non-European immigrants.

The timing of the policy also raises questions about the validity of Hawkins's and Price's analyses. The ALP had been concerned with the abolition of the White Australia policy long before the 1972 election. In 1965, the ALP struck all discriminatory wording from its platform. Had it been concerned with the electoral ramifications regarding the ethnic composition of Australia, the ALP could have introduced lower immigration targets at that point. But the ALP debate over immigration levels awaited its 1971 convention. There, delegates took note of the wider political debate, "questioning whether high numbers of immigrants were not putting too much pressure on scarce resources of health, education, sewerage, and other social services." The party concluded at that time that "Because of recession and other problems, immigration policy could no longer be directed to the goal of increased population" (Grattan 1993:129).[56]

55. That is, once they become naturalized citizens, voting is mandatory. The requirements for naturalization have varied over time and among applicants. Currently, two years' residence is a minimum requirement (Davidson 1997).
56. Other scholars such as Charles Price 1974 and Jock Collins 1988 make similar arguments.

Hawkins also attributes Labor's abandonment of the racist White Australia policy, in part, to Whitlam's leadership. But Whitlam became the head of the party in 1967. Hawkins overlooks the fact that Whitlam failed to propose immigration restrictions in time for the 1969 election. The ALP did not add immigration restrictions until the 1972 election campaign, when immigration pressures combined with unemployment to place immigration control on local political agendas.

Moreover, the policies of the Liberal Party raise more questions regarding timing. The Liberal Party, as well as state governments, began to erase discriminatory language from legislation as far back as 1956. Additionally, the easing of entry conditions for non-Europeans in 1964 and the alteration of the fifteen-year rule in 1966 resulted in a total of forty thousand Asians and Pacific and Indian Ocean islanders acquiring Australian citizenship between 1956 and 1971 (Price 1974:198).[57] Again, if White Australia and reduced intakes are intimately linked, the LCP's policy of increased intakes accompanied by increased ethnic diversity is incomprehensible. As a contemporaneous analyst observed, "The two policies of non-discrimination and of keeping intakes relatively low . . . complement each other but, after all, were adopted for quite distinct reasons" (Rivett 1978:71).

The puzzle is even more significant in comparative perspective. Race and racism have been used to explain policies in France and Britain that appear diametrically opposed to policies in Australia that are also reportedly due to race and racism. Moreover, France and Britain, among other countries, have combined "racist" policies with low levels of immigration, while Australia has adopted nondiscriminatory admissions standards at higher levels of immigration. It is also important to remember that racism toward the aboriginal population in Australia has been greater and remains greater than that toward the immigrant population. Again, the caution is not to overlook racism but to separate its effects from those associated with "alien" populations.

Other Australian immigration scholars have proposed an economic explanation for the reductions in 1972. These scholars argue that immigration must be understood in the context of structural changes in the Australian economy. "The decade of the seventies turned up a slightly different set of pressures favouring immigration, and, more importantly, a new set of limitations on immigration. These limitations were the result of fundamental economic problems and immigration in this period cannot be understood apart from the issue of the pressures to restructure the Australian economy" (Birrell and Birrell 1981:85).

---

57. In 1974, individuals from the Middle East, from Lebanon, Syria, and Turkey, were included in this group, as "Mediterranean Asians."

According to Birrell and Birrell (1981), immigration before the 1970s was closely linked to the manufacturing industry. The expansion of the industry was dependent on growing markets, which were in turn dependent on population growth, which high levels of immigration provided. Because the ALP did not have strong ties to the manufacturing industry, when the Whitlam Labor government came to power in 1972, it was able to sever the connection between immigration and manufacturing in order to achieve economic rationalization. Labor's economic program focused on growth through the more efficient use of Australia's resources of capital and labor. It included a 25 percent across-the-board reduction in tariffs, producing a contraction of the high-cost manufacturing sector and the associated demand for immigrant labor. Under economic rationalization, high levels of immigration were not necessary; therefore, annual intakes were cut drastically. The reduction also made it easier for the Immigration Department to fill the targets with skilled immigrants, thus reducing the proportion of unskilled immigrants, which was large before 1972.

Birrell and Birrell acknowledge that Labor's plan to restructure the economy was not the sole reason for reduced immigration intakes. A second, related, factor was the ALP's campaign strategy to make social and environmental costs of immigration a political issue. I give priority to the electoral incentives created by immigrant pressures in urban areas for three reasons. The first, again, involves timing. If Whitlam and the ALP were interested in reducing immigration as part of a plan to restructure the economy, the policy should have been adopted in time for the 1969 campaign, when economic restructuring was initially introduced by the ALP. But the evidence presented here links the timing more closely to the rising opposition to immigration and its political organization in the early 1970s. There is nothing in the Birrells' explanation to indicate why the policy was adopted in the 1972 election but not in 1969.

A second reason is the geographic focus of the ALP's election campaign. The Labor Party directed its campaign at swing constituencies in Victoria and New South Wales. Although the party did not ignore constituencies in other states, it concentrated its time, energy, and resources in very specific constituencies where it promised reduced immigration intakes. If economic restructuring were the primary consideration for immigration reduction, such campaign targets and promises would be extraneous. Yet we have seen that these electoral strategies were crucial to the 1972 Labor victory.

Third, the Birrells cannot explain adequately why the Liberal Party failed to return to high levels of immigration when it regained power in 1975. They argue that the conservative Liberal/NCP coalition, with the exception of those in the Immigration Department, adopted Labor's economic program, as indicated in their White Paper on Manufacturing Industry, issued in 1975 and, therefore, they did not wish to return to a policy of growth through immigration. Moreover, the Birrells contend that high unemployment rates, which climbed to around 10 percent in the late 1970s, made it virtually impossible to return to the old policy. But their explanation ignores continued political pressure to maintain high immigrant intakes from previous politically important clients, developers and manufacturers. Even if the Liberals adopted the ALP's program on economic restructuring, the Birrells do not adequately address the political incentives and disincentives for such a policy.

While economic restructuring promoted by the ALP is compatible with reduced immigration intakes, I conclude that it was not the driving political force behind the reduction in immigration. Clearly, the 1972 ALP platform contained many policy elements, including economic restructuring, that were congruent with reduced immigration intakes and that responded to specific bases of political support. The Liberal/NCP's subsequent adoption of the policy, with a distinct political clientele, suggests that marginal electoral constituencies were critical in explaining policy changes.

Before concluding this review of the Australian literature on immigration, it is important to note that, although Australia has experienced periods of zero immigration in the past, in the postwar period it has continued to maintain a partially open door, with programmed immigration intakes averaging 0.62 percent of the Australian population since 1972. Katherine Betts takes up this issue, although she examines a period only partially explored in this chapter, that between 1976 and 1987. She asks why immigration targets increased during this period, achieving levels "as high as they had ever been at any time since the immediate postwar years" (Betts 1988:3). Whether one looks at programmed or actual levels of immigration, Betts's presentation of immigration levels is exaggerated. The best basis of comparison is on a per capita basis; Figure 6.1 reveals that, in the period after 1972, the highest per capita level of programmed immigration never exceeded the lowest per capita level of immigration in the period between 1953 and 1971. The same is true for actual immigration levels with the exception of 1961, as exhibited in Figure 6.2. Nonetheless, one may ask why immigration has been maintained at all, given the experience in many European countries, where the door has been closed much more tightly.

To answer this question, Betts argues that support for immigration from the growth lobby has remained strong while opposition to immigration has been silenced by the intellectual class. This new intellectual class has used the immigration issue as a marker of its status, labeling all opposition to immigration as racist, thereby undercutting more legitimate arguments against continued immigration based on environmental and national cohesion concerns. Without taking a position on the issues of intellectuals and status markers, I would agree that the continuation of immigration in Australia can be attributed to the support for immigration among important political actors, in contrast to European countries where such support has all but evaporated. What Betts's argument misses is the real opposition to immigration and its effect on immigration levels, reducing those from, first, about 2 percent of the Australian population, to about 1 percent, and then to about 0.5 percent.

The continued strength of support for immigration can be contrasted to the European case. If sources and levels of opposition are similar, why doesn't the same apply to sources of support? One explanation is linked to the immigrant community itself. Birrell and Birrell (1981:221) remark that "ethnic organizations operating in the political arena generally support an expansionary immigration program." Kenneth Rivett (1978:78) makes an even more explicit reference to the political power of the immigrant community: "It has been said . . . that some twenty seats in the Commonwealth Parliament are held by majorities appreciably smaller than the numbers of migrants in the electorates concerned. Their power is being used, not only to bring improvement (though how slowly!) in the treatment of migrants now here, but also to keep alive the hope of a wider measure of family reunion than is permitted at present."

First, it should be remarked that, politicians began to recognize immigrants' political power only in the 1970s. Until then, reports on immigrants' political participation indicated a significant degree of apathy on their part (Davies 1966). Immigrants were not always eager to naturalize and to participate in the political process. Moreover, representatives of immigrant communities were not incorporated in the advisory boards of the IPC or the IAC until 1970, and when they were invited to participate beginning in the 1970s, they were always more heavily represented on councils associated with integration of immigrants than on those associated with planning for immigration (Jupp 1993). So the early support for immigration was not located in the immigrant community.

The notion that ethnic communities were politically powerful thereafter is contested by James Jupp (1993). Nonetheless, if the political power of immigrants, at least as perceived by politicians, expanded in the 1970s, immigrants' preferences on intake levels were not dramatically different than those of the host population. Immigrants were and remain eager for equal treatment and access to services. And they are interested in ensuring that the immigration program favors family reunion over the "national need"–based immigration that places greater emphasis on language skills and human and physical capital. But immigrants are not markedly more interested in high immigration levels. Jupp, a close observer of Australian immigration (1993: 217), argues that,

Table 6.6. Public opinion on immigration intake, 1993 (percent)

Question: The statements below indicate some of the changes that have been happening in Australia over the years. For each one, please say whether you think the change has gone too far, not gone far enough, or is it about right?

The number of migrants allowed into Australia at the present time has gone ...	Australian-born	Foreign-born	All respondents
Much too far	43.4%	25.8%	39.4%
Too far	29.9	30.8	30.1
About right	21.6	34.6	24.5
Not far enough	3.1	6.3	3.8
Not nearly far enough	1.9	2.4	2.1
All responses	99.9%	99.9%	99.9%
Number of responses	2,228	647	2,875

Source: Jones et al. 1993.

in general, [the ethnic councils] have more influence over (and are more interested in) settlement and cultural issues than in immigration policy. Indeed the current policy statement of [one ethnic council] does not mention immigration at all as one of its concerns. . . . [And the federal ethnic council] has consistently believed that "Family Reunion and the Refugee and Special Humanitarian programs should be the cornerstone of an equitable and just Immigration policy" while refusing to be "drawn into a debate over optimum annual intake figures."

The positions of the ethnic councils accurately reflect the attitudes of the immigrant population. Table 6.6 shows that, in the early 1990s, neither the Australian-born population nor the foreign-born population favored increased immigration. And although the immigrant population more strongly favored current intake levels than the Australian-born population, a majority of the immigrant population favored reduced intakes.

If the immigrants themselves are not the source of support for continued levels of immigration, the growth lobby continues to support it. The strength of the growth lobby, especially in the early period of high immigration intakes, is based in part on the insulated domestic market, which required a growth in domestic demand to expand (Birrell and Birrell 1981, Betts 1988, Warhurst 1993). But even as the Australian economy has become more open to market forces, those sectors of the economy that rely on domestic demand, those that produce nontraded goods, continue to benefit from immigration streams, as do industries that rely on immigrants for labor. Moreover, the growth lobby is finding new support among those who benefit from the influx of foreign capital associated with immigration based on "national needs" (Warhurst 1993).

The various dimensions of Australian immigration policy, like those of Britain and France, have generated a substantial literature. Country-level attributes undoubtedly play a role in policy outcomes, as the excellent text by Jupp and Marie Kabala (1993) suggests. There is a common underlying political dynamic to immigration policy formation, however. It is only in a comparative context that these common features of the policy process become apparent.

Conclusions

Australia represents yet another case where local immigration pressures are associated with rapid increases in immigration, placing pressures on the local infrastructure. When these pressures are combined with economic recession, communities began to organize against immigration. These pressures ultimately bubbled up to the national political agenda because of the political significance of those constituencies to national electoral outcomes.

An interesting comparison can be drawn between Australia, on the one hand, and Britain and France, on the other. In the latter two countries, immigration control was initiated by the conservative party or coalition, despite potential opposition from an important political base, employers seeking an increased supply of labor. In Australia, it is the Labor Party that initiates the reduction in immigration. Thus immigration control does not appear to be a partisan issue that systematically divides parties of the right from parties of the left. I leave further parallels with Britain and France to be drawn in the following, concluding chapter.

7　Conclusions

The geographic concentration of immigrants in the host state is central to understanding the political dynamics of immigration policy. The spatial distribution of immigrants concentrates both the costs and the benefits of immigration and contributes to the organization of political pressures for and against immigration. But the organization of interests does not necessarily assure the adoption of policies they prefer. Geographic concentration often means that the number of legislators who want to add immigration control to the national agenda is small. Therefore, we must look to the national political arena and the need for politicians to construct a national electoral alliance to obtain or maintain the reins of national government. If "immigration" constituencies are crucial to national electoral outcomes, immigration control is likely to be added to the national political agenda. And because national electoral alliances are constructed within the constraints of national political institutions, the analysis must be sensitive to these institutions.

In Britain and Australia, political incentives are straightforward. Single-member constituencies, combined with a parliamentary system, place the focus on national parliamentary elections, the parliamentary margin, and swing constituencies. The semipresidential system in France, combined with the two-round ballot system, provides a more complicated set of incentives. Attention must be paid to the presidential election as well as the National Assembly elections because the president has the power to dissolve the National Assembly. Moreover, because of the likelihood of parliamentary coalitions in the two-round electoral system, politicians must consider not only the size of the opposition but the balance of power among the parties of the governing coalition as well.

The evidence presented in Chapters 4, 5, and 6 is consonant with this picture. Rapid growth in immigration placed pressure on localities in which immigrants were concentrated to provide the infrastructure necessary to support the expanding population. When combined with economic recession, the competition for state services intensified and anti-immigrant pressures mounted, even though pro-immigration pressures often remained strong. In some instances, unemployment, associated with industrial restructuring or recession, aggravated the tensions between the immigrant and host communities. Indicators of cultural competition are more difficult to measure; nonetheless, there is reason to believe that cultural competition contributed to the rise of anti-immigrant sentiment as well.

National politicians took note of these local demands through various means. Local government officials were one source of information about the degree of anti-immigrant pressures. They faced a set of electoral incentives themselves because providing scarce resources to a nonvoting population threatened their political support.[1] Political parties, unions, community organizations, and other organized interests provided alternate sources of information to politicians about the stakes of ignoring these local demands. This organization of interests resolves one of the puzzles associated with immigration policy. Public opinion toward immigration tends to be both relatively negative and constant. Yet immigration control policy swings from relative closure to relative openness, and back again to relative closure. Analysts who emphasize continued openness to immigration tend to focus on the inability of public opinion to organize, while analysts who emphasize policies of closure point to politicians' sensitivity to public opinion. The geographic concentration of immigrants resolves this paradox by reference to the spatial concentration of costs that facilitates political organization under specific circumstances and, hence, a political response.

In Britain, analysts commonly attribute immigration control legislation to the power of swing constituencies when the national parliamentary margin is narrow. This is a traditional interpretation of Labour's changing position on immigration control between 1961, when it opposed the Conservative introduction of the Commonwealth Immigrants Act (CIA), and 1964, when it reduced the quota of New Commonwealth immigration vouchers upon acceding to office. These same analysts have more difficulty with the timing of the Conservative shift from openness to NCW immigration and the 1961 introduction of the CIA. This change is variously attributed to the 1958 race riots, or to Commonwealth relations, or to Britain's shift toward Europe. The evidence presented here, however, suggests that the timing is more proximately located in the rapid rise of immigration in the late 1950s combined with the recession of 1961. And these anti-immigrant pressures were broader

---

1. Internal migration can also create the same competition for jobs and social infrastructure between the local population and the newly arriving indigenous population. But internal migrants can vote and hence provide political support to politicians who cater to their demands.

in Conservative than in Labour constituencies in this early period, presenting a threat to the Tory national parliamentary majority. Hence the theoretical framework systematically explains both the timing and the direction of the immigration control legislation, by reference to the same, rather than different, explanatory variables.

There is a curious tension between the localized impact of immigration and the national decision-making arena. An alternative strategy for national politicians would be to channel immigration to the opposition constituencies and to devolve the associated problems to local governments. Unfortunately, this is easier said than done. In the British case, if the Conservative government had hoped that delegation of immigration issues to local governments would avoid political controversy (Bulpit 1986), they were sadly mistaken. Unlike the French Gaullist party, which had either the policy tools or, more likely, the good fortune to direct the immigrant population into the opponents' constituencies, the Conservative Party found the concentrated immigrant population in its own constituencies. Moreover, the devolution of immigration issues is a policy that can backfire if the electoral margin narrows and these constituencies become important to maintaining a national government majority.

In France, local governments confronted pressures similar to those experienced in Britain as immigration networks took hold and immigration expanded. Immigration networks contributed to the rising tension because they diminished the nexus between labor market needs and immigration by reducing the costs of migration borne by the individual immigrants. The initial impetus to channel immigration may have come from the 1967 legislative elections when the Gaullist coalition in the National Assembly was razor thin. But the conservative backlash to the May events in 1968 provided a cushion that allowed the Gaullist party to ignore the mounting pressures. The opposition, in particular, the communist mayors in and around Paris, was vocal. The mayors represented communities that were experiencing the pressures associated with rapid population growth and were forced to provide services to a population that could not vote. These were politically dangerous policies for local officials because the immigrant population could not provide political support in exchange for the allocated resources. The presidential election of 1969, following de Gaulle's resignation, did not provide electoral incentives to add immigration control to the national political agenda. But the 1971 municipal elections demonstrated that the Gaullist electoral honeymoon was over, triggering the implementation of controls in 1972, in an effort to persuade voters that the problem had been resolved, in the run-up to the 1973 legislative elections. The narrowness of the 1974 presidential election clinched the electoral pressures to address immigration control at the national level and, shortly after Giscard d'Estaing's victory, a stop to immigration was initiated.

Much the same story was told about Australia. In a country of immigration since British colonization in the eighteenth century, the political bargain establishing the Commonwealth of Australia in 1901 was based on immigration control; thereafter immigration flows into Australia in the first half of the twentieth century were small. Security concerns elicited by World War II and the changing balance of power in the Pacific were important catalysts in prying open Australia's door after hostilities ended. But support from employers and developers who benefited from the influx of immigrants sustained the 2 percent solution.

The extraordinarily high levels of immigration directly after World War II were cut in half in response to political opposition to immigration during the 1952–53 recession. But the cumulative effects of immigration thereafter combined with rising intakes in the 1960s to create pressure on the infrastructure in cities where the immigrants moved, Sydney and Melbourne. When compounded by the 1971–72 economic downturn and sectoral decline in labor-intensive manufacturing, creating pockets of unemployment, immigration control became important in a small number of constituencies. The Australian Labor Party capitalized on this trend in the 1972 election and promised urban renewal and reduced immigration intakes to the few swing anti-immigrant constituencies necessary to win a parliamentary majority for the first time in over twenty years. The policy of reduced immigration was closely connected with the ALP's emphasis on urban renewal and consistent with its economic plans to restructure the economy. In addition, it reassured citizens who were worried about the official demise of the White Australia policy. Thus immigration control fit nicely into a broader political program. But the political significance of these swing constituencies, even in the context of a different political program, remained visible in the conservative coalition's retention of reduced immigration levels when it returned to power in 1975.

Several parallels among the cases need to be underscored. First is the rapid increase in immigration before the implementation of controls and the associated pressure on the infrastructure created by this population growth. The significance of competition over social services is emphasized by similar findings in the United States (Smith and Edmonston 1997). That, ultimately, these immigrants contributed to national wealth and paid taxes to support the expanded infrastructure is less important to immigration control policy outcomes than the short-term competition for scarce resources between the immigrants and the indigenous population. With elections never more than five years distant (or three years in the case of Australia), politicians of necessity have a short-term perspective.

A second parallel is the role of local elected officials in signaling to national elected officials the salience of immigration control in local constituencies. In Britain, when MPs from constituencies affected by immigration voiced their concerns to party leaders, in many cases they could point to local council election results as the consequence of responding to or ignoring local interests in immigration control. In France, local demonstrations were actually organized by the French Communist Party in conjunction with local elected PCF officials. Where the political salience of the issue is crucial to national politicians, these signals are critical. There are always a small number of voices raised against immigration. Cyril Osborne began his campaign in Britain as early as 1952, and Le Pen was initially elected to the French legislature in 1956. The question is whether these voices reflect a broader political base that has national electoral consequences. And the experience of local elected officials provides an important clue.

A third parallel among the three cases is the presence of distinct local labor market conditions in a theoretically unified national economy. Regions with undiversified economies are often affected more severely by mild national recessions and, in case of industrial restructuring, can become significant pockets of unemployment even within a broader national context of economic growth. Internal mobility of capital and labor can ease these disparities but only in the medium to long term.

In Britain, the West Midlands' dependence on the auto industry made that region particularly sensitive to national recession, especially when combined with the overall decline of the British auto industry. In France, Marseille faced the restructuring of its dominant port industries while the Lorraine experienced the decline of its coal and steel industries. The Paris region faced a peculiar set of circumstances, a concerted government effort to decentralize the French industrial base. In Australia, the contraction of labor-intensive textile and apparel firms in Sydney and Melbourne produced an unemployed, unskilled labor force that was poorly suited for the higher-skill jobs being generated in the economy. These local labor market conditions intensified the pressures created by the rapid influx of immigrants that would otherwise have been mitigated.

Yet another parallel among the three cases is the impact of immigrant networks in sustaining immigrant flows even under changing labor market conditions. Immigrant networks are important social and economic networks that dramatically reduce the costs of immigration. They promise food and shelter to newly arrived immigrants until they can become self-sustaining, thereby reducing the connection between labor market demands and immigration and further straining the capacity of the local community to cope with the growing population.[2] The impact of chain migration was clearly

---

2. In some instances, immigrant entrepreneurs create jobs for members of their own ethnic community, for other immigrants, or for the indigenous population (Light et al. 1997). Where these circumstances exist, immigrants do not necessarily create labor market competition, but crowding of the social infrastructure and competition for social services continue to exist.

visible in Marseille and the surrounding region as it continued to sustain immigrant inflows under conditions of industrial restructuring with an undiversified economic base. Evidence from Australia, cited in Chapter 3, also indicated the coincidence of large new immigrant flows into areas with large old immigrant populations, despite high local levels of unemployment.

In contrast to these similarities, it is more difficult to establish a particular threshold that triggers the political organization of pro- and anti-immigration groups. We lack data that are sufficiently disaggregated to define specific combinations of labor market and social conditions that would give rise to petitions in support of or in opposition to immigration. Because the geographic concentration of immigrant communities may produce politically important consequences, we should begin to collect disaggregated data that would improve our ability to study the impact and interaction of these factors.

U.S. Immigration Control in Comparative Perspective

Without presenting the plethora of evidence necessary to make a convincing case that U.S. immigration control policy follows a pattern similar to that found in Britain, France, and Australia, it is interesting to note many similar features in the contemporary period.

Following the parallels drawn above, the United States, and the several states where immigrants are concentrated, experienced a rise in immigration intakes in the late 1970s that accelerated in the mid-1980s. The visibility of these immigrants increased with the 1986 passage of the Immigration Reform and Control Act that allowed some 1.5 million undocumented aliens already present in the United States to legalize their status. And IRCA also brought in another wave of almost 1 million immigrants through its provisions of amnesty for seasonal agricultural workers (the Special Agricultural Worker program). This influx was compounded by the passage of the 1990 Immigration Act, which raised the annual immigration quota from 290,000 plus immediate relatives of U.S. citizens to 700,000 overall.[3]

Pressures on state services and infrastructure followed. James Smith and Barry Edmonston (1997) document the short-term costs associated

---

3. The quota of 700,000 applies to the 1992–94 fiscal years; thereafter the quota dropped to 675,000. As with much immigration policy, these quotas are not, strictly speaking, comparable. The 290,000 quota excludes immediate family members of U.S. citizens who are admitted without a numerical quota. The new quota includes immediate family members of U.S. citizens, but the quota is "pierceable." Because immediate family members are exempt from numerical limitations, the quota allocated to other family members is adjusted year to year to account for high levels of immediate family member admissions the previous year. Family member admissions cannot drop below 226,000 as a result of this adjustment, however, hence the possibility that the quota will be exceeded (Briggs 1992:232).

with this influx. State and local net expenditures on immigrants in New Jersey in 1989–90 were estimated at $323 per native-headed household (in 1996 dollars). A similar study in California for the 1994–95 fiscal year estimated the net costs at $1,178 per native-headed household. These figures contrast with the net fiscal benefit at the federal level of $1 to $4 per native household, on a nationwide basis. Smith and Edmonston also document the long-term fiscal benefit of immigration, although this benefit varies with immigrants' characteristics. The net fiscal benefit (at present value) of an immigrant with less than a high school education is a negative $13,000, whereas the net fiscal benefit of an immigrant with more than a high school education is a positive $198,000. But they point out that, even though the federal fiscal impact of immigration is positive in the long term, the impact on those communities where immigrants are concentrated remains negative.

The geographic specificity of economic conditions is also reflected in the U.S. case. In California, at least, the rapid expansion of the immigrant population accompanied a deep recession. Between 1990 and 1995, unemployment rates in California ranged between 8 and 11 percent, up to twice the national rate of unemployment during most of this period. The recession produced net negative internal migration between 1990 and 1995, as native Californians moved to adjacent states (Frey 1996). Recession also reduced government services as declining tax revenues forced the state to slash its annual budget. The costs were widely felt by politically powerful classes. Among others, state employees received no cost-of-living increases and in some cases experienced temporary pay cuts. Tuition in the publicly supported system of higher education skyrocketed.

The parallel to the country analyses continues with the role of local politicians in signaling the significance of immigration as a political issue. For example, during this time frame, both of the senators from California, Barbara Boxer and Dianne Feinstein, introduced immigration control initiatives in the U.S. Senate. Proposition 187, a California initiative to withdraw state services from undocumented aliens, qualified for the 1994 ballot. And Republican governor Pete Wilson rode to reelection in part by supporting this initiative, which California voters passed at the same time.

Finally, the last parallel to be drawn with the country analyses is the role of migrant networks in sustaining immigrant flows despite poor economic conditions. Even as the recession was creating incentives for the native population to leave California for more prosperous states, international migration continued to expand the state's population (Frey 1996).

These messages were not lost on national politicians and, in particular, on presidential candidates. Bill Clinton, since his election in 1992, has funneled substantial resources to the Border Patrol in an effort to reduce the flow of undocumented migrants and established the Commission on Immigration Reform, which quickly recommended reduced annual immigration quotas. That this legislation was not passed can be attributed to at least three factors. One is the continued and strong support for immigration by employers and in particular by those in California's service and agricultural sectors. Second, although opposition to immigration remains substantial, as the California economy began to revive, that opposition diminished as competition over state resources diminished. And finally, efforts to reduce undocumented migration have provided some perceived relief. Although it is difficult to evaluate the effectiveness of those efforts, the increased costs of crossing the U.S.-Mexican border with the help of guides, or *coyotes*, suggest an increased measure of border control.

This brief sketch of the parallels between the detailed case analyses and contemporary U.S. immigration policy is no substitute for a comprehensive analysis. Yet it suggests many similarities while pointing out an area that needs additional research—the sources and strength of support for immigration. As noted in Chapter 1, the country analyses took support for immigration more or less for granted while delving very deeply into the opposition to immigration. The role of the immigrant community has been discounted with evidence substantiating similar preferences to the host population. Nonetheless, we need to flesh out our understanding of the role of employers and others who lobby for expanded immigration.

Racialization or Demonization of Immigrants?

In distinction to much of the contemporary literature on immigration in advanced market economy countries, I focus on the spatial distribution of costs and benefits of migration rather than on the racial distinctiveness of contemporary immigrant streams. Nonetheless, immigration in the postwar period has been characterized accurately as one of growing racial distinctiveness. As we saw in the British case, the dominant stream of immigrants came from New Commonwealth countries. "Black" or "coloured" was the label applied to both Afro-Caribbeans and Asians from the Indian subcontinent, a label confusing to U.S. citizens, for whom those words refer solely to people with ethnic origins in sub-Saharan Africa, but one that clearly captures the racial distinctiveness of the immigrant stream. In France, it was the North African Arab Muslim population that came to epitomize the distinctiveness of the immigrant community. In the third case, the White Australia policy was directed in the postwar period in part against Asians and Southeast Asians. Thus immigration has been racialized. From this perspective, immigrants are targets of the population and of politicians because they look different from the indigenous population, rather than because of their immigrant or guest worker status.

Yet one has only to scratch the surface to find that immigrants have always been demonized in periods of high immigration pressures, regardless of the color of their skin. Whatever trait is most distinctive is selected to differentiate the newcomer from the established members of society. Language, religion, political attitudes, and race are all markers that serve to distinguish and disparage the newcomer.[4] Nonetheless, with the notable exception of slavery and the African American experience, these distinctions have generally not prevented immigrants from ultimately achieving a degree of acceptance in their new society.

Because of its long history of immigration, the United States provides an excellent example of the variety of traits used to distinguish the immigrant population from the indigenous (host) population. In the first instance, language was an issue. Benjamin Franklin complained of the German immigration (quoted in Seller 1984:142): "Why should the *Palatine Boors* be suffered to swarm into our Settlements and, by herding together, establish their language and Manners, to the Exclusion of ours? Why should *Pennsylvania*, founded by the *English*, become a Colony of *Aliens*, who will shortly be so numerous as to Germanize us instead of our Anglifying them." In the 1830s to 1850s, the rallying cry was against Catholics—the Irish and, again, the Germans. The inventor Samuel Morse was only one of many to warn that "immigrants were agents of the Pope, who had sent them to prepare for a Catholic takeover of the United States" (Seller 1984:145). At the turn of the century, Southern Europeans were described alternately as radicals ready to overthrow the democratically constituted political order and as mental defectives. Of all the immigrant streams, only the Chinese were denounced in particularly racist terms. These once reviled immigrants are now full members of U.S. society.

The Australian immigrant population was overwhelmingly British until after World War II. The literacy test was used with administrative discretion to exclude undesirable immigrants from around the world. Yet when the demand for immigrants expanded after World War II, exceptions were made for displaced persons from Central Europe. Continued support for immigration required additional exceptions, for Southern Europeans from Greece and Italy and then from Yugoslavia. The common European origins of these immigrants did not prevent discrimination against them sufficient to elicit complaints from their home-country governments. Yet they are now full participants in the Australian polity and economy.

In Britain, immigration control was first established against Jews fleeing

---

4. I take "ethnicity" as a term that denotes a wide variety of differences, distinctive racial, national, religious, linguistic, or cultural heritage. Race is one, narrower, dimension of ethnic differences.

from the pogroms of Eastern Europe and Russia. Earlier, the Irish were the despised immigrant population. In France, before the turn of the century, the objects of derision were the Belgians employed as strikebreakers in the coal mines of the Nord–Pas-de-Calais region, immortalized in Emile Zola's novel *Germinal*. A leading French social scientist, Gérard Noiriel, documents that "practically every new wave of migrants—from Italy at the end of the 19th century, Poland between the wars, North Africa since the 1960s—has met with the same prejudices and pessimistic evaluations of its 'assimilability'" ("Review" 1996:156). Nonetheless, as in the United States, the earlier waves are now perceived as assimilable.

Probably the purest example of anti-immigrant sentiment, devoid of any distinguishing immigrant ethnicity, comes from Switzerland. There, Italians formed the vast majority of the immigrant population when referenda on immigration controls were introduced in the 1970s, in a country where several cantons are ethnically Italian and where Italian is one of the official languages. Ethnic Germans and ethnic Japanese, returning to their countries of origin after several generations' absence, also face considerable discrimination and exclusion.

These examples suggest that all newcomers, at least in periods of high immigrant pressures, are demonized and that race is only one possible characteristic that can serve as a basis for distinguishing between the established population and the new arrivals. It remains to be seen whether race will make incorporation more difficult than it was for earlier groups.

The distinction I have drawn between anti-immigrant sentiment and racism hardly means that racism is no longer an issue. Moreover, there may be racists who raise the anti-immigrant flag. Cyril Osborne and Enoch Powell in Britain and Le Pen in France have certainly been labeled as such. Nonetheless, the distinction is important because all immigrants are outsiders, nonmembers of the host society, and, as nonmembers, they may generate politically important pressures for immigration control. It is therefore inaccurate to label all who oppose immigration as racist. And it is only by distinguishing between these two concepts that we can understand the different dynamics and how they interact.

Net Costs or Benefits of Immigration v. Distribution of Costs and Benefits

I have argued that support for and opposition to immigration depends in the short term on the costs and benefits that accrue to various elements of the host population. The question of whether immigration produces a net cost or a net benefit to the nation as a whole has generated a large literature of its own. Moreover, it is a politically charged literature: those who argue for net costs are seen as anti-immigrant and those who argue for net benefits are seen as pro-immigrant.

The economic case for open borders is relatively straightforward (Hamilton and Whalley 1984).[5] Economic theory suggests that labor migration is similar to international trade.[6] Provided that markets are competitive and there are constant returns to scale, trade allows a nation to specialize in those goods and services it produces most efficiently and to trade for other goods produced with similar efficiency in other countries.[7] Nations are then able to consume more than they could under conditions of autarky; trade makes the world wealthier.

Similarly, borders artificially limit the most efficient deployment of productive factors. In a capital-scarce nation, a worker has relatively little capital to work with and is relatively unproductive. Such a worker who migrates to a capital-abundant country works with more capital and produces more output. If labor is able to migrate from nations where capital is scarce to nations where capital is abundant, economic gains arise from the more efficient allocation of productive resources (Hamilton and Whalley 1984).[8] If trade makes the world wealthier, so does international migration. Few estimates exist of the economic gains from migration, but those that do suggest that even modest increases in migratory flows increase world wealth. The potential gains from migration are believed to equal or exceed the gains from a package of trade and capital liberalization measures.[9]

Even though global output may increase with liberalized migration and the more efficient allocation of productive factors, there is no guarantee that the gains will be evenly or equitably distributed among nations. The international distribution of gains from migration has been evaluated from three complementary perspectives (Grubel and Scott 1966a, 1966b; Berry and Soligo 1969; Usher 1977; Simon 1989; Borjas 1990). The first involves the

5. See Carens 1987 on the moral case for open borders.
6. For a different view, see Simon 1989: chap. 2.
7. There are, of course, many occasions when the conditions of competitive markets and constant returns to scale do not hold; in those cases, gains from trade are not necessarily provided for all parties to the trade. See Krugman 1986 and 1990 for an examination of trade under alternative assumptions.
8. Economists often exclude from the equation the disruptive effect of drawing local, previously autonomous, economies into the international economic system. Both Massey 1988 and Sassen 1988 point out that the development of a market economy tied to the international economy actually creates a migrant flow where none existed before. Nonetheless, once a local economy is integrated into the global economy, incentives exist for abundant factors of production to move to regions where they are scarce.
9. Hamilton and Whalley 1984 estimate that a level of migration that reduces regional and global wage rate disparities by 10% increases world wealth by 5% (adjusted for population, workforce, exchange rates, and productivity differences). This figure is calculated by combining Hamilton and Whalley's table 5 on partial liberalization with their table 6, which adjusts for population, workforce, exchange rates, and productivity.

migrant's physical and human capital. The second is the "social compact" dimension, the migrant's contributions to and use of social capital and services. The third dimension consists of external effects, both positive and negative, resulting from migration. This third dimension incorporates noneconomic costs and benefits of immigration, the social aspects that are often difficult to quantify. Unfortunately, the devil lies in the details. The characteristics of migrants, the social milieu they enter, and the external effects vary across countries and over time. Sweeping generalizations cannot capture the shifting nature of the migratory flows and thus the international distribution of benefits. I thus refer readers to this literature to gauge whether advanced market economy countries have accrued net benefits from international migration.[10]

To reiterate, my argument—that some individuals or groups experience different net balances than others—does not take a position on the net balances for the nation as a whole. It is neither an anti-immigrant nor a pro-immigrant argument. Rather it points out that, whatever the immigration policy of the state, groups *within* that state do not experience the same net balance, at least in the short term. For politicians, the politically important costs and benefits are all short-term, and that term ends with the next election. This is the political battleground of immigration policy.

Policy Prescriptions

The fact that immigration policy distributes benefits and costs unequally brings us back to the political forum. I address the politics of immigration policy from the perspective of societal equity: equity among members of the host society; equity between the members of the host society and the immigrants; equity between the host society and the home society. Let us begin in reverse order.

Increased global migration, from poor countries to wealthy countries, promises increased economic efficiency. But prevailing international laws and norms place the decision-making power over the attributes of migrants and the level of migration in the hands of host states. Controls over entry are governed by one set of rules, those of national sovereignty, which permit states to prevent entry. Controls over exit fall under a different set of rules, those of human rights, which promote freedom of movement. Therefore, individuals are theoretically free to leave a country, but can do so only after

---

10. Also see my analysis (1994a) where I argue that, because of prevailing international laws and norms, on average, advanced market economy countries have reaped net economic gains from immigration, to the possible detriment of developing nations.

another country has granted them permission to enter. This divergence in governing principles conveniently places control over immigrant flows in the hands of the receiving states and seemingly permits host countries to appropriate the bulk of the economic gains from migration.

Thus, although nation-states have a mutual economic interest in increased migration, they may have conflicting interests over the level and characteristics of migrants. In the first three decades after World War II, wealthy countries accepted flows that were relatively large and dominated by unskilled labor. More recently, wealthy countries have sought to reduce the flow or to attract highly skilled immigrants (King 1993b).[11] If global efficiency points in the direction of continued openness to immigration, global equity suggests that the size of the flow and the attributes of the migrants be determined jointly by the host and home countries. This joint decision will ensure that the net gains from immigration are equitably distributed rather than captured by the wealthy nations. Immigration could then serve to reduce income disparities between rich and poor nations as well as to increase world wealth.

A second dimension of equity is that between the immigrants and the members of the host society. Immigrants, at least "voluntary" immigrants to advanced market economy countries, gain from migration; if costs exceeded benefits, they would stay home. But their gains do not necessarily translate into equality with members of the home society.[12] Immigrants are often exploited by employers, employees, the government, or taxpayers, as well as by the growing group of licit and illicit labor brokers. But that exploitation comes at a cost of inequality in democratic societies that pride themselves on equality of opportunity, if not equality of outcomes.

Two analysts of French immigration policy, Weil (1991) and Hollifield (1992), remind us that advanced market economy countries often have substantial legal safeguards that define a base against which treatment of immigrants is measured. But the potential for exploitation grows if the immigrants themselves are excluded from participation in the political arena, if they are excluded from organizing themselves to ensure equal treatment. Equity between members of the host society and the immigrants requires the latter's participation in the political process. And this, in turn, requires the ability of immigrants and their offspring to become citizens, through naturalization and the principle of jus soli. To improve prospects for equitable treatment of immigrants, host societies should not only offer political participation

---

11. Although undocumented migration exists and is becoming increasingly costly to control, developed states today have substantial abilities to control their borders (Miller 1994).

12. As noted in Chapter 3, immigrants usually have a lower reservation wage than the indigenous population. Even inequitable treatment does not necessarily reduce the benefits of immigration to zero.

through naturalization and jus soli but should facilitate participation through citizenship training programs as well.

Global equity and efficiency demand continued immigration from poor nations to wealthy market economy countries; societal equity suggests that the social rights and responsibilities extended to citizens be extended to immigrants as well. If my arguments are correct, however, these two aspects of equity lead to the inequitable distribution of costs and benefits among members of the host society, at least in the short term. Thus it behooves those who seek the first two dimensions of equity to strike a more equitable domestic political bargain, to deter the ultimate rise of anti-immigrant political pressures. The theoretical framework presented here suggests some solutions. There are at least two pertinent issues: the economic and the social consequences of immigration.

The economics of immigration

If the costs and benefits of immigration are likely to be spatially concentrated, equity among the members of the host society entails both a reduction of those costs and a transfer from those groups who benefit from immigration to those who experience the costs. If competition between the host and home populations increases the costs of immigration, efforts to reduce the costs entail the reduction of that competition. Where competition is related to the business cycle, immigration intakes should be tailored to the business cycle. A standard annual quota set by legislation prevents the flexibility in immigration intakes that would reduce competition for employment and social services. But in efforts to formulate a flexible immigration scheme, national economic indicators are insufficiently sensitive to local economic conditions. A growing economy and low unemployment do not in themselves imply that these conditions apply equally across either spatial or sectoral groups in the United States. Therefore, immigration streams should be tailored to economic conditions in those areas where immigrants are likely to locate.

Competition between the host and immigration populations, where it exists, arises in part from the substitutability of immigrant labor for domestic labor rather than from patterns of complementarity.[13] Indigenous workers who compete with immigrant labor experience lower wages and fewer work opportunities (Simon 1989). This is true for unskilled labor as well as skilled labor, as nurses and computer programmers in the United States are likely

---

13. The significance of this competition is debated. Smith and Edmonston 1997 indicate that, for the United States, internal labor mobility diffuses immigrants' impact on wages widely over the U.S. population, thereby diminishing the impact on any one group. It is likely that the degree of labor market competition varies both temporally and cross-nationally.

to understand. To decrease this competition, training should be provided to those who compete with immigrants to ensure complementarity rather than competition. Therefore, a more equitable domestic outcome would entail training these native workers for higher-skilled, higher-value-added jobs. As complements to the immigrant workforce, rather than as competitors, this group of workers would ultimately benefit. Without training and alternative job opportunities, increased immigration would only cause increased competition and increased anti-immigrant pressures.[14]

An important dimension of local immigrant pressures is the crowding of public services and infrastructure. Equal treatment of immigrants means that they will ultimately pay for those services according to the rules of the society: when tax structures are progressive, poor immigrants, just like the poor indigenous population, pay less than wealthier immigrants and the wealthier indigenous population. In the short term, however, the indigenous population faces costs. Even when funds are available, schools, roads, and sewage systems cannot be built overnight. Thus intake levels should be tailored to the ability of local communities to provide an adequate infrastructure for immigrants who settle there.

Efforts to reduce the costs of immigration accruing to the specific segments of the population do not ensure that these costs are reduced to zero. Therefore, equity suggests that the remaining short-term costs should be borne by those who reap the benefits of immigration. In economic terms, if immigration creates short-term externalities, these externalities can be mitigated by policies that incorporate them into the employment cost structure (Taylor and Martin 1996). Just as housing developers are required to build or to contribute to the local social infrastructure, employers of immigrants can be required to build or to contribute to the local social infrastructure. Alternatively, a tax on the employment of immigrants could provide the funds to expand the infrastructure appropriately.[15]

Just as immigration brings concentrated benefits, it brings diffuse benefits as well. If immigration benefits the economy as a whole, those living outside the areas of immigrant concentration experience the diffuse gains from migration arising from cheaper, immigrant-produced goods while avoiding the associated short-term costs. A portion of the short-term costs of providing social infrastructure for the immigrants, then, should be borne in part by the nation as a whole rather than by those citizens in areas where immigrants are concentrated.

14. Active labor market (or active manpower) policies are also emphasized as an efficacious method of reducing unemployment more generally. See Layard, Nickell, and Jackman 1991.
15. Singapore and Malaysia are two countries that charge a relatively large head tax on the employment of immigrant workers, for the purported purpose of social infrastructure (Martin 1997).

The politics of multicultural societies

The cultural competition engendered by immigration has been more difficult to measure. Foreigners are often perceived as a threat to the host society because they bring with them their own language, culture, race, and religion. If the global bargain raises the level of immigration, this increase will affect the social organization of a multicultural society. Three basic models have been followed historically.

The assimilationist model, as exemplified by the United States, helped to integrate millions of immigrants during the nineteenth and twentieth centuries. The immigrants forged new identities as U.S. citizens by learning the language, adopting the customs, and participating in the body politic of their adopted country. The process was lengthy, however, and involved partial or total loss of their previous cultural and ethnic identities. Moreover, the assimilationist path was in many ways closed to some immigrant groups, notably the African American community.[16]

The consociational model addresses the political and social organization of heterogeneous societies such as Belgium and the Netherlands (Lijphart 1968, 1977). Quite the opposite of encouraging assimilation, the consociational model allows distinct communities to retain their separate ethnic, religious, and linguistic identities. These communities coexist through particular institutional arrangements characterized by hierarchical pillars and elite bargaining. But if this model has lessened the tension between communities, it has not erased those tensions. In Belgium, for example, conflict over the distribution of state resources led to the decentralization of decision making in a growing number of issue areas and contributed to the decline of social solidarity.

A third alternative, cultural pluralism or multiculturalism, has been adopted by Australia. In theory, it propounds the principles of cultural identity, social justice, and economic efficiency (Castles 1992, Zubrzycki 1987). Cultural identity is defined as a civil right for all members of the society, including the original white settler population. A welfare net protects all members of the society, regardless of race or ethnicity. In theory, all residents have equal opportunity to participate in and contribute to the economic wealth of the nation; in practice, there are shortcomings. The Australian model depends on strict control of entry, ignores the special needs of ethnic minorities previously addressed through welfare policies, and tends to marginalize minority ethnic groups (Castles 1992). Despite efforts to erase the problem, ethnic discrimination has not disappeared from Australian life.

---

16. Heisler 1992 argues that assimilation was possible historically but that the changed social and political environment precludes this alternative in modern-day societies, except on an individual level.

None of these models is perfect. Nonetheless, they suggest at least two principles worth underscoring.[17] First, in a heterogeneous society, conflict can be diminished by enlarging the arena of personal privacy over which the state relinquishes control. Second, immigrants should have rapid access to citizenship and other formal rights. Providing newcomers with such a stake in the society diminishes the potential for disruption and promotes social solidarity. It facilitates their incorporation into the host society and reduces cultural competition. Thus efforts to promote equity among the indigenous population complement efforts to diminish inequality between the indigenous and immigrant populations.

Global migration represents both an opportunity and a threat. As a result, the long-term patterns of immigration control tend to be cyclical: periods of openness followed by periods of closure generated by the ultimate political victory of those who incur the costs associated with immigration. These cycles generate costs of their own, as patterns of communication, trade, and production are periodically broken. If global and domestic equity are appropriate goals, political entrepreneurs have the ability to craft a set of policies to maintain a level of relative openness to immigrants that avoids the stop-and-go nature of immigration policy to date. These policies would reduce the short-term costs of immigration in communities that receive large immigrant intakes by tailoring the flow of immigration to the business cycle and to the ability to provide social infrastructure. They would also transfer some of the benefits of immigration to pay for the associated costs. The construction of such policies would also diminish the destructive anti-immigrant rhetoric visible in advanced market economy countries today.

17. Castles 1992 argues for five principles: planning and strict control of entry; nondiscrimination among migrants but selectivity; rapid access to citizenship and other formal rights; support services for the settlement process; and cultural pluralism within carefully defined limits.

References

Aitchison, Ray, ed. 1974. *Looking at the Liberals.* Melbourne: Cheshire.

Aitkin, Don. 1977. *Stability and Change in Australian Politics.* New York: St. Martin's Press.

Amar, Marianne, and Pierre Milza. 1990. *L'immigration en France au XXe siècle.* Paris: Armand Colin.

Anderson, Nancy, and John Crawford. 1974. "Foreign Trade." In Gordon Greenwood and Norman Harper, eds., *Australia in World Affairs, 1966–1970*, pp. 105–30. Vancouver: University of British Columbia Press.

Année politique (économique, sociale et diplomatique) en France. Various years. Paris: Presses Universitaires de France.

Appleyard, R. T. 1971a. "Immigration and the Australian Economy." In Australian Institute of Political Science, ed., *How Many Australians? Immigration and Growth*, pp. 1–36. Melbourne: Angus & Robertson.

———. 1971b. "Immigration: Policy and Progress." In Australian Institute of Poltiical Science, ed., *How Many Australians? Immigration and Growth*, pp. 205–26. Melbourne: Angus & Robertson.

Ashford, Douglas E. 1982. *Policy and Politics in France: Living with Uncertainty.* Philadelphia: Temple University Press.

Australia. Commonwealth Bureau of Census and Statistics. 1972. *Census of Population and Housing, 30 June 1971: Characteristics of the Population and Dwellings, Commonwealth Electoral Divisions.* Canberra: Commonwealth Bureau of Census and Statistics.

———. Conference of Australian and State Ministers for Immigration. 1975. *Report.* Perth: State Ministry of Immigration.

Australian Bureau of Statistics. Various years. *Yearbook Australia.* Canberra: Australian Bureau of Statistics.

———. 1976. *Census of Population and Housing, 1976: Federal Electoral Division Summary File* [machine-readable data file]. Canberra: Australian Bureau of Statistics.

Australian Institute of Political Science (AIPS). 1971. *How Many Australians? Immigration and Growth.* Melbourne: Angus & Robertson.

Australian Labor Party (ALP). 1972. *Policy Speech.* Canberra.

Australian Parliamentary Handbook. 1975. Canberra: Australian Government Publishing Service.

Australian Population and Immigration Council (APIC). 1977. *Immigration Policies and Australia's Population: A Green Paper.* Canberra: Australian Government Publishing Service.

Baldwin-Edwards, M., and Martin A. Schain. 1994. *The Politics of Immigration in Western Europe.* London: Frank Cass.

Beck, Nathaniel, and Jonathan N. Katz. 1995. "What to Do (and Not to Do) with Time-Series Cross-Section Data in Comparative Politics." *American Political Science Review* 89 (3): 634–47.

Bell, David S. 1973. "The French General Election of March 1973 in Marseilles." *Political Studies* 21 (3): 343–47.

Berne, Jacques. 1981. *La campagne présidentielle de Valéry Giscard d'Estaing en 1974.* Paris: Presses Universitaires de France.

Berry, R. Albert, and Ronald Soligo. 1969. "Some Welfare Aspects of International Migration." *Journal of Political Economy* 77 (5): 778–94.

Betts, Katharine. 1988. *Ideology and Immigration: Australia, 1976 to 1987.* Melbourne: Melbourne University Press.

Betz, Hans-Georg. 1994. *Radical Right-Wing Populism in Western Europe.* New York: St. Martin's Press.

Bhagwati, Jagdish N. 1984. "Incentives and Disincentives: International Migration." *Weltwirtshaftliches Archiv* 120 (4): 678–701.

Bird, Greta. 1988. *The Process of Law in Australia.* Sydney: Butterworths.

Birrell, Robert. 1978. "The 1978 Immigration Decisions and Their Impaction the Australian Labour Force." *Australian Quarterly* 50 (4): 30–43.

Birrell, Robert, and Tanya Birrell. 1981. *An Issue of People: Population and Australian Society.* Melbourne: Longman Cheshire.

Blewett, Neal. 1973. "Labor 1968–72: Planning for Victory." In Henry Mayer, ed., *Labor to Power: Australia's 1972 Election*, pp. 6–16. Sydney: Angus & Robertson.

Böhning, W. R. 1972. *The Migration of Workers in the United Kingdom and the European Community.* London: Oxford University Press for Institute of Race Relations.

Booth, Heather. 1992. *The Migration Process in Britain and West Germany.* Aldershot: Avebury.

Borjas, George J. 1990. *Friends or Strangers: The Impact of Immigrants on the U.S. Economy.* New York: Basic Books.

——. 1994. "The Economics of Immigration." *Journal of Economic Literature* 32 (December): 1667–1717.

Boyer, Jean-Claude, Jean-François Deneux, and Pierre Merlin. 1986. "Paris–Île-de-France." In Yves Lacoste, ed., *Géopolitiques des régions françaises.* Paris: Fayard.

Braud, Philippe. 1973. *Le comportement électorale en France.* Paris: Presses Universitaires de France.

Briggs, Vernon M. 1992. *Mass Immigration and the National Interest.* Armonk, N.Y.: M. E. Sharpe.

British Social Attitudes Survey. 1983. Social and Community Planning Research Group, University of Essex Economic and Social Research Council Data Archive. Colchester, Essex.

Brochmann, Grete. 1993. "Control in Immigration Policies: A Closed Europe in the Making." In Russell King, ed., *The New Geography of European Migrations.* London: Belhaven.

Brubaker, William Rogers, ed. 1989. *Immigration and the Politics of Citizenship in Europe and North America*. Lanham, Md.: University Press of America.

Bulpit, Jim. 1986. "Continuity, Autonomy and Peripheralisation: The Anatomy of the Centre's Race Statecraft in England." In Zig Layton-Henry and Paul B. Rich, eds., *Race, Government and Politics in Britain*. London: Macmillan.

Bureau of Immigration, Multicultural and Population Research. 1995. *Australian Immigration Consolidated Statistics*, no. 18, 1993–94. Canberra: Australian Government Publishing Service.

Burnley, I. H. 1971. "Immigrants in Australian Cities." *Australian Quarterly* 43 (4): 57–69.

———. 1974a. "International Migration and Metropolitan Growth in Australia." In I. H. Burnley, ed., *Urbanization in Australia: The Post-War Experience*. Cambridge: Cambridge University Press.

———. 1974b. "Social Ecology of Immigrant Settlement in Australian Cities." In I. H. Burnley, ed., *Urbanization in Australia: The Post-War Experience*. Cambridge: Cambridge University Press.

———. 1982. *Population, Society, and Environment in Australia: A Spatial and Temporal View*. Melbourne: Shillington House.

Butler, D. E., and Anthony King. 1965. *The British General Election of 1964*. London: Macmillan.

Butler, D. E., and Richard Rose. 1960. *The British General Election of 1959*. London: Macmillan.

Butler, David. 1968. "Aspects of Australian Elections." *Australian Journal of Politics and History* 14 (1): 12–23.

———. 1973. "Thoughts on the Election." In Henry Mayer, ed., *Labor to Power: Australia's 1972 Election*, pp. 1–5. Sydney: Angus & Robertson.

Butler, David, and Dennis Kavanaugh. 1980. *The British General Election of 1979*. London: Macmillan.

Butler, David, and Donald Stokes. 1972. *Study of Political Change in Britain, 1963–1970*. Michigan: Inter-University Consortium for Political Research.

Carens, Joseph H. 1987. "Aliens and Citizens: The Case for Open Borders." *Review of Politics* 49 (Spring): 251–73.

Carmel, Samnut. 1976. "L'immigration clandestine en France depuis les circulaires Fontanet, Marcellin et Gorse." In Philippe Bernard, ed., *Les travailleurs étrangers en Europe occidentale*. Paris: Mouton.

Castells, Manuel. 1975. "Immigrant Workers and Class Struggles in Advanced Capitalism." *Politics and Society* 5 (1): 33–66.

Castles, Francis G. 1989. "Social Protection by Other Means: Australia's Strategy of Coping with External Vulnerability." In Francis G. Castles, ed., *The Comparative History of Public Policy*. Cambridge: Polity.

Castles, Stephen. 1992. "The Australian Model of Immigration and Multiculturalism: Is It Applicable to Europe?" *International Migration Review* 26 (2): 549–67.

Castles, Stephen, and Godula Kosack. 1973. *Immigrant Workers and Class Structure in Western Europe*. Oxford: Oxford University Press.

Castles, Stephen, and Mark J. Miller. 1993. *The Age of Migration: International Population Movements in the Modern World*. London: Macmillan.

Cazeaux, Maurice. 1997. "Ils voulaient casser la banlieue rouge." *Le Parisien*, Île-de-France regional ed., 4–5 October 1997, p. 4.

Charlot, Jean, and Monica Charlot. 1970. "Les campagnes de Georges Pompidou et Alain Poher." *Revue française de science politique* 20 (2): 224–48.

Charon, Jean-Marie. 1991. *La presse en France de 1945 à nos jours*. Paris: Seuil.

Clout, Hugh D. 1972. *The Geography of Post-war France*. Oxford: Pergamon.

Colliard, Sylvie. 1979. *La campagne présidentielle de François Mitterrand en 1974*. Paris: Presses Universitaires de France.

Collins, Jock. 1988. *Migrant Hands in a Distant Land: Australia's Post-war Immigration*. Sydney: Pluto.

Collinson, Sarah. 1993. *Beyond Borders: West European Migration Policy towards the 21st Century*. London: Royal Institute of International Affairs.

Combe, David, Greg Hartung, and Geoffrey Hawker. 1982. *Platforms for Government: The National Platforms and Policies of Australia's Political Parties Analysed and Compared*. Yarralumla, A.C.T.: Yarralumla Soft.

Commonwealth Bureau of Census and Statistics. 1968. *Official Yearbook of the Commonwealth of Australia No. 53, 1967*. Canberra: Commonwealth Government Printer.

Conseil Économique et Social (CES). 1964. *Problèmes posés par l'immigration des travailleurs africains en France*, no. 15. Paris: Journal Officiel de la République Française.

——. 1969. *Le problème des travailleurs étrangers*, no. 7. Paris: Journal Officiel de la République Française.

Conservative Party (National Association of Conservative and Unionist Associations). Various years. *Annual Report*. London: Conservative Central Office.

Cooper, Kristin, and Danilo Martucelli. 1994. "L'expérience britannique." In Michel Wieviorka, ed., *Racism et xénophobie en Europe*. Paris: Découverte.

Cornelius, Wayne A. 1998. "The Structural Embeddedness of Demand for Immigrant Labor in California and Japan." Paper presented at the Workshop of the Comparative Immigration and Integration Program, University of California, San Diego, 20 February.

Cornelius, Wayne A., Philip L. Martin, and James F. Hollifield, eds. 1994. *Controlling Immigration: A Global Perspective*. Stanford: Stanford University Press.

Craig, F. W. S. 1990. *British General Election Manifestos, 1959–1987*. Aldershot: Dartmouth for Parliamentary Research Services.

Cross, Gary S. 1983. *Immigrant Workers in Industrial France: The Making of a New Laboring Class*. Philadelphia: Temple University Press.

Cross, Malcolm. 1993. "Migration, Employment and Social Change in the New Europe." In Russell King, ed., *The New Geography of European Migrations*. London: Belhaven.

Davidson, Alastair. 1997. *From Subject to Citizen: Australian Citizenship in the Twentieth Century*. Cambridge: Cambridge University Press.

Davies, Alan. 1966. "Migrants in Politics." In Alan Stoller, ed., *New Faces: Immigration and Family Life in Australia*. Melbourne: F. W. Cheshire.

Davison, R. B. 1966. *Black British: Immigrants to England*. Oxford: Oxford University Press for Institute of Race Relations.

Deakin, Nicholas. 1968. "The Politics of the Commonwealth Immigrants Bill." *Political Quarterly* 39 (1): 25–45.

——. 1969. "The 1966 General Election." In Sheila Patterson, ed., *Immigration and Race Relations in Britain, 1960–67*. London: Oxford University Press for Institute on Race Relations.

Department of Immigration and Ethnic Affairs (DIEA). Various years. *Australian Immigration: Consolidated Statistics*. Canberra: Australian Government Publishing Service.

———. Various years. *Review of Activities*. Canberra: Australian Government Publishing Service.

———. 1978. *1788–1978: Australia and Immigration*. Canberra: Australian Government Publishing Service.

Dummett, Ann, and Andrew Nicol. 1990. *Subjects, Citizens, Aliens and Others*. London: Weidenfeld & Nicolson.

Étrangers. 1970. Paris: Journal Officiel de la République Française.

Fassman, H., and R. Munz, eds. 1994. *European Migration in the Late Twentieth Century*. Aldershot: Edward Elgar.

Fédération Parisien du Bâtiment (FPB). Various dates. *Comptes rendus des reunions du bureau et du conseil*. Paris.

Ferrier, Jean-Paul, et al. 1986. "Provence–Alpes–Côte d'Azur." In Yves Lacoste, ed., *Géopolitiques des régions françaises*. Paris: Fayard.

Fielding, Anthony. 1993. "Migrations, Institutions, and Politics: The Evolution of European Migration Policies." In Russell King, ed., *Mass Migration in Europe: The Legacy and the Future*. London: Belhaven.

FitzGerald, Marian. 1984. *Political Parties and Black People: Participation, Representation and Exploitation*. London: Runnymede Trust.

———. 1987. *Black People and Party Politics in Britain*. London: Runnymede Trust.

FitzGerald, Marian, and Zig Layton-Henry. 1986. "Opposition Parties and Race Policies, 1979–83." In Zig Layton-Henry and Paul B. Rich, eds., *Race, Government, and Politics in Britain*. London: Macmillan.

Foot, Paul. 1965. *Immigration and Race in British Politics*. Baltimore: Penguin.

Forster, Clive. 1995. *Australian Cities: Continuity and Change*. Melbourne: Oxford University Press.

Fransman, Laurie. 1982. *British Nationality Law and the 1981 Act*. London: Fourmat.

Fraser, Malcolm. 1974. "A National View." In Ray Aitchison, ed., *Looking at the Liberals*. Melbourne: Cheshire.

Frears, J. R. 1977. *Political Parties and Elections in the French Fifth Republic*. London: Hurst.

Frears, John. 1991. *Parties and Voters in France*. London: Hurst.

Freeman, Gary P. 1979. *Immigrant Labor and Racial Conflict in Industrial Societies: The French and British Experience, 1945–1975*. Princeton: Princeton University Press.

———. 1986. "Migration and the Political Economy of the Welfare State." *Annals of the American Academy of Political and Social Science* 485:51–63.

———. 1989. "Immigrant Labour and Racial Conflict: The Role of the State." In Philip E. Ogden and Paul E. White, eds., *Migrants in Modern France*. London: Unwin Hyman.

———. 1994. "Britain, the Deviant Case." In Wayne A. Cornelius, Philip L. Martin, and James F. Hollifield, eds., *Controlling Immigration: A Global Perspective*. Stanford: Stanford University Press.

———. 1995. "Modes of Immigration Politics in Liberal Democratic States." *International Migration Review* 29 (4): 881–913.

Frey, William H. 1994. "The New White Flight." *American Demographics* 16 (4):40–58.

———. 1996. "Immigration, Domestic Migration, and Demographic Balkanization in America: New Evidence for the 1990s." *Population and Development Review* 22 (4): 741–63.

Frybes, Marcin. 1992. "France: Un équilibre pragmatique fragile." *Notes et études documentaires* 4952:83–110.

Gani, Léon. 1972. *Syndicats et travailleurs immigrés*. Paris: Editions Sociales.

Girard, Alain. 1971. "Attitudes des français à l'égard de l'immigration étrangère." *Population* 26 (5): 827–75.

———. 1977. "Opinion publique, immigration et immigrés." *Éthnologie française* 7 (3): 219–28.

Glebe, Gunther, and John O'Loughlin, eds. 1987. *Foreign Minorities in Continental European Cities*. Stuttgart: Franz Steiner.

Goguel, François. 1983. *Chroniques électorales: La cinquième république du général de Gaulle*. Paris: Presses de la Fondation Nationale des Sciences Politiques.

Gokalp, Catherine, and Marie-Laurence Lamy. 1977. "L'immigration maghrébine dans une commune industrielle de l'agglomeration parisienne: Gennevilliers." In *Les immigrés du Maghreb*, pp. 237–406. Paris: Presses Universitaires de France.

Goldey, D. B., and R. I. W. Johnson. 1973. "The French General Election of March 1973." *Political Studies* 21 (3): 321–42.

Goldin, Claudia. 1993. "The Political Economy of Immigration Restriction in the United States, 1890 to 1921." National Bureau of Economic Research Working Paper no. 4345.

"Gough Whitlam's Australia." 1973. *Economist* 247 (2) (23 June 1973).

Grant, Lawrence, and Ian Martin. 1982. *Immigration Law and Practice*. London: Cobden Trust.

Grassby, Al. 1979. *The Morning After*. Canberra: Judicator.

Grattan, Michelle. 1993. "Immigration and the Australian Labor Party." In James Jupp and Marie Kabala, eds., *The Politics of Australian Immigration*, pp. 127–60. Canberra: Australian Government Publishing Services.

Great Britain. General Register Office. 1969. *Census 1966: United Kingdom, General and Parliamentary Constituency Tables*. London: H.M.S.O.

———. 1984. *Census 1981: United Kingdom, General and Parliamentary Constituency Tables*. London: H.M.S.O.

Greenwood, Gordon. 1974. "The Political Debate in Australia." In Gordon Greenwood and Norman Harper, eds., *Australia in World Affairs, 1966–1970*, pp. 31–102. Vancouver: University of British Columbia Press.

Griffith, J. A. G., and Michael Ryle. 1989. *Parliament: Functions, Practices and Procedures*. London: Sweet & Maxwell.

Grosser, Alfred. 1975. "The Role of the Press, Radio, and Television in French Political Life." In Howard R. Penniman, ed., *France at the Polls: The Presidential Election of 1974*. Washington, D. C.: American Enterprise Institute for Public Policy Research.

Grubel, Herbert G., and Anthony D. Scott. 1966a. "The International Flow of Human Capital." *American Economic Review: Papers and Proceedings* 56 (May): 268–74.

———. 1966b. "The Immigration of Scientists and Engineers to the United States, 1949–61." *Journal of Political Economy* 74 (4): 368–78.

Hallows, John. 1970. "Three-Part Report on Australian Immigration." *Australian*, 8 June, p. 7; 9 June, p. 9; 10 June, p. 13.

Hamilton, Bob, and John Whalley. 1984. "Efficiency and Distributional Implications of Global Restrictions on Labour Mobility." *Journal of Development Economics* 14:61–75.

Hamilton, Kimberly A., and Kate Holder. 1991. "International Migration and Foreign Policy: A Survey of the Literature." *Washington Quarterly* 14 (2): 195–211.

Hammar, Tomas. 1985. *European Immigration Policy*. Cambridge: Cambridge University Press.

———. 1990. *Democracy and the Nation State: Aliens, Denizens, and Citizens in a World of International Migration.* Aldershot: Avebury.

Hansard Parliamentary Debates, House of Commons (Great Britain). Various years. London: Her Majesty's Stationery Office.

Hardcastle, Leonie, Andrew Parkin, Alan Simmons, and Nobuaki Suyama. 1994. "The Making of Immigration and Refugee Policy: Politicians, Bureaucrats and Citizens." In Howard Adelman, Allan Borowski, Meyer Burstein, and Lois Foster, eds., *Immigration and Refugee Policy: Australia and Canada Compared.* Toronto: University of Toronto Press.

Harrop, Martin, et al. 1980. "The Bases of National Front Support." *Political Studies* 28 (2): 271–83.

Haus, Leah. 1995a. "Transnational Migration and International Political Economy." *International Studies Notes* 20 (1): 32–37.

———. 1995b. "Openings in the Wall: Transnational Migrants, Labor Unions, and U.S. Immigration Policy." *International Organization* 49 (2): 285–314.

Hawkins, Freda. 1991. *Critical Years in Immigration: Canada and Australia Compared.* Montreal: McGill–Queen's University Press.

Hayward, Jack, and Vincent Wright. 1971. "The 37,708 Microcosms of an Indivisible Republic: The French Local Elections of March 1971." *Parliamentary Affairs* 24 (4): 284–311.

———. 1974. "'Les deux France' and the French Presidential Elections of May 1974." *Parliamentary Affairs* 27 (3): 208–36.

Heisler, Barbara Schmitter. 1992. "The Future of Immigrant Incorporation: Which Models? Which Concepts?" *International Migration Review* 26 (2): 623–45.

Heisler, Martin. 1992. "Migration, International Relations and the New Europe: Theoretical Perspectives from Institutional Political Sociology." *International Migration Review* 26 (2): 596–622.

Henneresse, Marie-Claude. 1979. "Le patronat et la politique française d'immigration, 1945–1975." Diss., Institut d'Études Politiques, Paris.

Hepple, B. A. 1968. *Race, Jobs, and the Law in Britain.* London: Penguin.

Higham, John. 1963. *Strangers in the Land.* New York: Atheneum.

Hillman, Arye L. 1994. "The Political Economy of Migration Policy." In Horst Siebert, ed., *Migration: A Challenge for Europe.* Tübingen: J. C. B. Mohr.

Hoare, A. G. 1983. *The Location of Industry in Britain.* Cambridge: Cambridge University Press.

Hollifield, James F. 1992. *Immigrants, Markets, and States: The Political Economy of Postwar Europe.* Cambridge: Harvard University Press.

———. 1994. "Immigration and Republicanism in France: The Hidden Consensus." In Wayne A. Cornelius, Philip L. Martin, and James F. Hollifield, eds., *Controlling Immigration: A Global Perspective.* Stanford: Stanford University Press.

Holt, H. E. 1956. *What Immigration Means to Australia.* Canberra: Government Printer.

Hughes, Colin A. 1973. "The 1972 Australian Federal Election." *Australian Journal of Politics and History* 19 (1): 11–27.

———. 1977. "The Electorate Speaks—and After." In Howard R. Penniman, ed., *Australia at the Polls: The National Elections of 1975.* Washington, D.C.: American Enterprise Institute for Public Policy Research.

Humanité, L'. Various dates.

Husbands, Christopher. 1988. "The Dynamics of Racial Exclusion and Expulsion:

Racist Politics in Western Europe." *European Journal of Political Research* 16:701–20.

Immigration Planning Council (IPC). Various years. "Agenda, Notes and Minutes." Canberra: Typescript.

——. 1968. *Australia's Immigration Programmes for the Period 1968 to 1973.* Canberra: Australian Government Printing Service.

Institute of Race Relations. 1969. *Colour and Immigration in the United Kingdom.* London.

Institut National de Statistiques et des Études Économiques (INSEE). Various years. *Recensement général de la population. Résultats des sondages au 1/20 et au 1/4. Structure de la population totale.* Paris: Imprimerie Nationale.

——. Various years. *Statistiques et indicateurs des régions françaises.* Paris: Imprimerie Nationale.

Ireland, Patrick R. 1994. *The Policy Challenge of Ethnic Diversity: Immigrant Politics in France and Switzerland.* Cambridge: Harvard University Press.

Jackman, Robert W. 1985. "Cross-National Statistical Research and the Study of Comparative Politics." *American Journal of Political Science* 29 (1): 161–82.

James, Scott. 1992. "A Party System Perspective on the Interstate Commerce Act of 1887: The Democracy, Electoral College Competition, and the Politics of Coalition Maintenance." *Studies in American Political Development* 6 (2): 163–200.

——. 1995. "Building a Democratic Majority: The Progressive Party Vote and the Federal Trade Commission." *Studies in American Political Development* 9 (2): 331–85.

——. 1997. "Parties, Presidents, and the State: The Construction of American Regulatory Institutions, 1887–1935." Unpublished manuscript, University of California, Los Angeles.

Johns, Brian. 1972. "PM Hits at ALP Immigration Policy." *Sydney Morning Herald,* 1 December 1972, p. 1.

Jones, K., and A. D. Smith. 1970. *The Economic Impact of Commonwealth Immigration.* London: Cambridge University Press.

Jones, Peter C. 1989. "Aspects of the Migrant Housing Experience: A Study of Workers' Hostels in Lyon." In Philip E. Ogden and Paul E. White, eds., *Migrants in Modern France.* London: Unwin Hyman.

Jones, Roger, et al. 1993. "Australian Election Study, 1993" [computer file]. Canberra: Social Science Data Archives, Australian National University.

Jupp, James. 1982. *Party Politics: Australia, 1966–1981.* Sydney: George Allen & Unwin.

——. 1991. *Australian Retrospectives: Immigration.* Melbourne: Sydney University Press.

——. 1993. "The Ethnic Lobby and Immigration Policy." In James Jupp and Marie Kabala, eds., *The Politics of Australian Immigration.* Canberra: Australian Government Publishing Services.

Jupp, James, and Marie Kabala, eds. 1993. *The Politics of Australian Immigration.* Canberra: Australian Government Publishing Services.

Kabala, Marie. 1993. "Immigration as Public Policy." In James Jupp and Marie Kabala, eds., *The Politics of Australian Immigration.* Canberra: Australian Government Publishing Services.

Katznelson, Ira. 1973. *Black Men, White Cities.* London: Oxford University Press.

Keely, Charles B. 1979. *U.S. Immigration: A Policy Analysis.* New York: Population Council.

Kennedy-Brenner, Carliene. 1979. *Foreign Workers and Immigration Policy: The Case of France*. Paris: OECD.

Kindleberger, Charles P. 1967. *Europe's Postwar Growth: The Role of the Labor Supply*. Cambridge: Harvard University Press.

King, Russell. 1993a. "European International Migration, 1945–90: A Statistical and Geographical Overview." In Russell King, ed., *Mass Migration in Europe: The Legacy and the Future*. London: Belhaven.

———. 1993b. *Mass Migration in Europe: The Legacy and the Future*. London: Belhaven.

———. 1993c. *The New Geography of European Migrations*. London: Belhaven.

———. 1996. "Of Free Movement and the Fortress: Recent Books on European Migration." *West European Politics* 19 (1): 176–81.

Kitschelt, Herbert. 1995. *The Radical Right in Western Europe: A Comparative Analysis*. Ann Arbor: University of Michigan Press.

Kmenta, Jan. 1964. "Australian Postwar Immigration: An Econometric Study." Ph.D. diss. Stanford University.

Kopras, Andrew. 1993. "Comparisons of 1991 Census Characteristics: Commonwealth Electoral Divisions." Canberra: Parliamentary Research Service Background Paper no. 20.

Krugman, Paul R., ed. 1986. *Strategic Trade Policy and the New International Economics*. Cambridge: MIT Press.

———. 1990. *Rethinking International Trade*. Cambridge: MIT Press.

Kubat, Daniel, ed. 1979. *The Politics of Migration Policies: The First World in the 1970s*. New York: Center for Migration Studies.

———. 1993. *The Politics of Migration Policies, Settlement, and Integration: The First World into the 1990s*. 2d ed. New York: Center for Migration Studies.

Labasse, Jean, Olivier Brachet, and Paul Bacot. 1986. "Rhône-Alpes." In Yves Lacoste, ed., *Géopolitiques des régions françaises*. Paris: Fayard.

Lacoste, Yves, ed. 1986. *Géopolitiques des régions françaises*. Paris: Fayard.

Lancelot, Alain. 1988. *Les élections sous la Cinquième République*. 2d ed. Paris: Presses Universitaire de France.

Layard, Richard, Stephen Nickell, and Richard Jackman. 1991. *Unemployment: Macroeconomic Performance and the Labour Market*. Oxford: Oxford University Press.

Layton-Henry, Zig. 1980. "Immigration." In Zig Layton-Henry, ed., *Conservative Party Politics*. London: Macmillan.

———. 1985. "Great Britain." In Tomas Hammar, ed., *European Immigration Policy*. Cambridge: Cambridge University Press.

———. 1987. "The State and New Commonwealth Immigration, 1951–56." *New Community* 14 (1–2): 64–75.

———. 1989. "Great Britain." In M. C. LeMay, ed., *The Gatekeepers: Comparative Immigration Policy*. New York: Praeger.

———. 1992. *The Politics of Immigration*. Oxford: Blackwell.

———. 1994. "Great Britain: The Would-be Zero Immigration Country." In Wayne A. Cornelius, Philip L. Martin, and James F. Hollifield, eds. *Controlling Immigration: A Global Perspective*. Stanford: Stanford University Press.

Le Gall, Gérard, and Marc Riglet. 1973. "Les circonscriptions marginales aux élections législatives de 1967 et 1968." *Revue française de science politique* 23 (1): 86–109.

Leitner, Helga. 1995. "International migration and the politics of admission and exclusion in postwar Europe." *Political Geography* 14 (3): 259–78.

Le May, M. C., ed. 1989. *The Gatekeepers: Comparative Immigration Policy*. New York: Praeger.

Le Moigne, Guy. 1986. *L'immigration en France*. Paris: Presses Universitaires de France.

Lequin, Yves, ed. 1992. *Histoire des étrangers et de l'immigration en France*. Paris: Larousse.

Lewis-Beck, Michael S. 1993. "French Electoral Theory: The National Front Test." *Electoral Studies* 12 (2): 112–27.

Liberal Party (Australia). 1974. *Federal platform*. Canberra.

Light, Ivan, Richard Bernard, and Rebecca Kim. 1997. "Immigrant Incorporation in the Garment Industry of Los Angeles." Paper presented at the Center for German and European Studies Working Group on Comparative Immigration and Integration Policy, Berkeley, 11 April 1997.

Lijphart, Arend. 1968. *The Politics of Accommodation: Pluralism and Democracy in the Netherlands*. Berkeley: University of California Press.

——. 1977. *Democracy in Plural Societies: A Comparative Exploration*. New Haven: Yale University Press.

Lloyd, Peter. 1993. "The Political Economy of Immigration." In James Jupp and Marie Kabala, eds., *The Politics of Australian Immigration*. Canberra: Australian Government Publishing Service.

Lord, J. H. G., A. J. Petrie, and L. A. Whitehead. 1968. "Political Change in Rural France: The 1967 Election in a Communist Stronghold." *Political Studies* 16 (2): 153–76.

Lynch, Phillip. 1974. "The Economy." In Ray Aitchison, ed., *Looking at the Liberals*. Melbourne: Cheshire.

Macdonald, Ian A. 1969. *Race Relations and Immigration Law*. London: Butterworths.

——. 1972. *The New Immigration Law*. London: Butterworths.

——. 1983. *Immigration Law and Practice in the United Kingdom*. London: Butterworths.

Macdonald, Ian A., and Nicholas Blake. 1982. *The New Nationality Law*. London: Butterworths.

——. 1991. *Immigration Law and Practice in the United Kingdom*. 3d ed. London: Butterworths.

Mackellar, Michael. 1979. "The 1978 Immigration Decisions—a reply." *Australian Quarterly* 51 (2): 93–103.

Mackerras, Malcolm. 1972. *Australian General Elections*. Sydney: Angus & Robertson.

——. 1973. "The Swing: Variability and Uniformity." In Henry Mayer, ed., *Labor to Power: Australia's 1972 Election*. Sydney: Angus & Robertson.

——. 1975. *Elections 1975*. Sydney: Angus & Robertson.

——. 1976. "Uniform Swing: Analysis of the 1975 Election." *Politics* 11 (1): 41–46.

March, Ian. 1976. "Policy Making in the Liberal Party: The Opposition Experience." *Australian Quarterly* 48 (2): 5–17.

Marcus, Jonathan. 1995. *The National Front and French Politics: The Resistible Rise of Jean-Marie Le Pen*. London: Macmillan.

Martin, Jean. 1978a. "Forms of Recognition: Migrants and Unions, 1945–1970." In

Ann Curthoys and Andrew Markus, eds., *Who Are Our Enemies? Racism and the Australian Working Class*, pp. 189–207. Canberra: Hale & Iremonger.

Martin, Jean. 1978b. *The Migrant Presence: Australian Responses, 1947–1977*. Sydney: George Allen & Unwin.

Martin, Jean-Maurice. 1972. "Les travailleurs en France. Un exemple concret: Le bâtiment et les travaux publics." *Population et avenir* 509 (January–February): 628–34.

Martin, Philip. 1997. "International Migration: Challenges and Opportunities." Paper presented at the Conference on Immigration and Welfare, Program on Economics, Justice and Society, University of California, Davis, 2–3 May.

Martin, Philip, and Elizabeth Midgley. 1994. "Immigration to the United States: Journey to an Uncertain Destination." *Population Bulletin* 19:2.

Massey, Douglas S. 1988. "Economic Development and International Migration in Comparative Perspective." *Population and Development Review* 14 (3): 383–414.

———. 1989. *Economic Development and International Migration in Comparative Perspective*. Washington, D.C.: Government Printing Office, Commission for the Study of International Migration and Cooperative Economic Development.

Massey, Douglas S., Rafael Alarcón, Jorge Durand, and Humberto González. 1987. *Return to Aztlán: The Social Process of International Migration from Western Mexico*. Berkeley: University of California Press.

Mayer, Henry. 1973. *Labor to Power: Australia's 1972 Election*. Sydney: Angus & Robertson.

McAllister, Ian. 1994. "Political Behavior." In Andrew Parkin, John Summers, and Dennis Woodward, eds., *Government, Politics, Power, and Policy in Australia*, pp. 198–225. Melbourne: Longman.

McAllister, Ian, and Anthony Mughan. 1987. "Party Commitment, Vote Switching, and Liberal Decline in Australia." *Politics* 22 (1): 75–83.

Meissner, Doris. 1992. "Managing Migrations." *Foreign Policy* 86 (Spring): 66–83.

Messina, Anthony M. 1989. *Race and Party Competition in Britain*. London: Clarendon.

Meyers, Eytan. 1995. "The Political Economy of International Immigration Policy— A Comparative and Quantitative Study." Ph.D. diss., University of Chicago.

Migration News. Various dates.

Miles, Robert, and Dietrich Thranhardt. 1995. *Migration and European Integration: The Dynamics of Inclusion and Exclusion*. London: Pinter.

Mill, John Stuart. 1970. "Two Methods of Comparison." In Amitai Etzioni and Frederich L. Dubow, eds., *Comparative Perspectives: Theories and Methods*. Boston: Little, Brown.

Miller, Mark. 1994. "Preface to Strategies for Immigration Control: An International Comparison." *Annals of the American Academy of Political and Social Sciences* 534:8–16.

Minces, Juliette. 1973. *Les travailleurs étrangers en France*. Paris: Seuil.

Minute. Various dates.

Le Monde. Various dates.

Money, Jeannette. 1994a. "Fences and Neighbors: Immigration Issues in the 1990s." Working Paper no. 6. Center for International Relations, University of California, Los Angeles.

———. 1994b. "The Political, Economic, and Cultural Determinants of Immigration Policy in OECD Countries." Manuscript, University of California, Davis.

Moore, Andrew. 1995. *The Right Road? A History of Right-Wing Politics in Australia*. Oxford: Oxford University Press.

Moulier, Yann, and Georges Tapinos. 1979. "France." In Daniel Kubat, ed., *The Politics of Migration Policies*. New York: Center for Migration Studies.

Murphy, Brian. 1993. *The Other Australia: Experiences of Migration*. Melbourne: Cambridge University Press.

Murphy, D. J. 1970. "Notes of a Campaign Director." *Politics* 5 (1): 54–61.

Neutze, Max. 1971. "The Growth of Cities." In Australian Institute of Political Science, ed., *How Many Australians? Immigration and Growth*, pp. 61–96. Melbourne: Angus & Robertson.

Noiriel, Gérard. 1988. *Le creuset français: Histoire de l'immigration, XIXᵉ–XXᵉ siècle*. Paris: Seuil.

Norton, Philip. 1994. *The British Polity*. New York: Longman.

Norton, W. E. 1982. *The Deterioration in Economic Performance: A Study of the 1970's with Particular Reference to Australia*. Sydney: Reserve Bank of Australia.

Oakes, Laurie. 1976. *Crash Through or Crash: The Unmaking of a Prime Minister*. Richmond, Victoria: Drummond.

Oakes, Laurie, and David Solomon. 1974. *A Grab for Power*. Melbourne: Cheshire.

Ogden, Philip. 1987. "Immigration, Cities, and the Geography of the National Front in France." In Gunther Glebe and John O'Loughlin, eds., *Foreign Minorities in Continental European Cities*. Stuttgart: Franz Steiner.

——. 1993. "The Legacy of Migration: Some Evidence from France." In Russell King, ed., *Mass Migration in Europe: The Legacy and the Future*. London: Belhaven.

Olson, Mancur. 1965. *The Logic of Collective Action*. Cambridge: Harvard University Press.

Olzak, Susan. 1992. *The Dynamics of Ethnic Competition*. Stanford: Stanford University Press.

OMISTATS/ONISTATS. Various years. *Annuaire des migrations*. Paris: Imprimerie Nationale.

ONI (Office National d'Immigration). Various years. *Statistiques de l'immigration*. Paris: Imprimerie Nationale.

Le Parisien Libéré. Various dates.

Parkin, Andrew, and Leonie Hardcastle. 1994. "Immigration Policy." In Andrew Parkin, John Summers, and Dennis Woodward, eds., *Government Politics, Power, and Policy in Australia*. Melbourne: Longman.

Parkin, Andrew, John Summers, and Dennis Woodward. 1994. *Government, Politics, Power, and Policy in Australia*. Melbourne: Longman.

Parodi, Maurice. 1981. *L'économie et la société française depuis 1945*. Paris: Armand Colin.

Patience, Allan, and Brian Head, eds. 1979. *From Whitlam to Fraser: Reform and Reaction in Australian Politics*. Melbourne: Oxford University Press.

Patterson, Sheila. 1963. *Dark Strangers*. London: Tavistock.

——. 1969. *Immigration and Race Relations in Britain, 1960–67*. London: Oxford University Press for Institute on Race Relations.

Paul, Kathleen. 1997. *Whitewashing Britain: Race and Citizenship in the Postwar Era*. Ithaca: Cornell University Press.

Peach, Ceri. 1987. "Immigration and Segregation in Western Europe since 1945." In Gunther Glebe and John O'Loughlin, eds., *Foreign Minorities in Continental European Cities*. Stuttgart: Franz Steiner.

Peltzman, Sam. 1976. "Toward a General Theory of Regulation." *Journal of Law and Economics* 19:211–40.

Penniman, Howard R., ed. 1975. *France at the Polls: The Presidential Election of 1974.* Washington, D.C.: American Enterprise Institute for Public Policy Research.

Petras, Elizabeth McLean. 1981. "The Global Labor Market in the Modern World Economy." In Mary Kritz et al., eds., *Global Trends in Migration.* New York: Center for Migration Studies.

Pilkington, Edward. 1988. *Beyond the Mother Country: West Indians and the Notting Hill White Riots.* London: I. B. Tauris.

Piore, Michael. 1979. *Birds of Passage.* New York: Cambridge University Press.

Plender, Richard. 1972. *International Migration Law.* Netherlands: A. W. Sijthoff International.

———. 1987. *International Migration Law.* Dordrecht: Martinus Nijhoff.

Price, Charles. 1974. "Immigration, 1949–1970." In Gordon Greenwood and Norman Harper, eds., *Australia in World Affairs, 1966–1970,* pp. 171–205. Vancouver: University of British Columbia Press.

———. 1979. "Immigration and Ethnic Affairs." In Allan Patience and Brian Head, eds., *From Whitlam to Fraser: Reform and Reaction in Australian Politics,* pp. 201–13. Melbourne: Oxford University Press.

Le Provençal. Various dates.

Pryles, Michael. 1981. *Australian Citizenship Law.* Sydney: Law Book Co.

Przeworski, Adam, and Henry Teune. 1970. *The Logic of Comparative Social Inquiry.* New York: Wiley-Interscience.

"Régularisation de la situation des travailleurs étrangers immigrés" (lettre circulaire no. 127 du 29 juillet 1968). 1968. *Liaisons sociales* (législation sociale) no. 3425 (28 October), p. 5.

Reid, Alan, and Peter Samuel. 1973. *A Complete Guide to the Policy of the Australian Labor Party.* Sydney: Bulletin.

"Review of *The French Melting Pot: Immigration, Citizenship, and National Identity* by Gérard Noiriel." 1996. *Foreign Affairs* 75 (6): 156–57.

Rich, David C. 1987. *The Industrial Geography of Australia.* London: Croom Helm.

Rivett, Kenneth. 1976. "Race, Immigration, and the Borrie Report." *Australian Quarterly* 48 (3): 12–22.

———. 1978. "Immigration and the Green Paper." *Australian Quarterly* 50 (1): 67–79.

Robinson, Vaughan. 1984. "Asians in Britain: A Study in Encapsulation and Marginality." In Colin Clarke, David Ley, and Ceri Peach, eds., *Geography and Ethnic Pluralism.* London: Allen & Unwin.

Roemer, John E. 1997. "The (Non-Parochial) Welfare Economics of Immigration." Working Paper 97–05. Department of Economics, University of California, Davis.

Roeder, Philip. 1994. "Politicians' Incentives and the Ethnic Agenda in Soviet Successor States." Paper presented at the IGCC conference on the International Spread and Management of Ethnic Conflict, University of California, San Diego, September 1994.

Rose, E. J. B. 1969. *Colour and Citizenship: A Report on British Race Relations.* London: Oxford University Press for Institute of Race Relations.

Rubenstein, Colin. 1993. "Immigration and the Liberal Party of Australia." In James Jupp and Marie Kabala, eds., *The Politics of Australian Immigration.* Canberra: Australian Government Publishing Service.

Safran, William. 1989. "Minorities, Ethnics and Aliens: Pluralist Politics in the Fifth Republic." In Paul Godt, ed., *Policy-Making in France: From de Gaulle to Mitterrand,* pp. 197–90. London: Pinter.

Sassen, Saskia. 1988. *The Mobility of Labor and Capital.* Cambridge: Cambridge University Press.

Schain, Martin A. 1985. "Immigrants and Politics in France." In John S. Ambler, ed., *The French Socialist Experiment.* Philadelphia: Institute for the Study of Human Issues.

———. 1988. "Immigration and Changes in the French Party System." *European Journal of Political Research* 16:597–621.

Seller, Maxine S. 1984. "Historical Perspectives on American Immigration Policy: Case Studies and Current Implications." In Richard R. Hofstetter, ed., *U.S. Immigration Policy.* Durham, N.C.: Duke University Press.

"Le VIᵉ plan et les travailleurs étrangers." 1971. *Hommes et Migrations* 118.

Shuck, Peter H. 1984. "The Transformation of Immigration Law." *Columbia Law Review* 84 (1): 1–90.

Shughart, William F., Robert D. Tollison, and Mwangi S. Kimenyi. 1986. "The Political Economy of Immigration Restrictions." *Yale Journal on Regulation* 4 (1): 79–98.

Silverman, Maxim. 1992. *Deconstructing the Nation: Immigration, Racism, and Citizenship in Modern France.* London: Routledge.

Simon, Julian L. 1989. *The Economic Consequences of Immigration.* Oxford: Basil Blackwell.

Singer-Kérel, Jeanne. 1976. "Conjoncture économique et politique française d'immigration, 1954–1974." In Philippe J. Bernard, ed., *Les travailleurs étrangers en Europe occidentale,* pp. 23–57. Paris: Mouton.

Singham, A. W. 1965. "Immigration and the Election." In D. E. Butler and Anthony King., *The British General Election of 1964.* London: Macmillan.

Smelser, Neil J. 1976. *Comparative Methods in the Social Sciences.* Englewood Cliffs, N.J.: Prentice-Hall.

Smith, B. 1971. "Immigration Policy: A Survey of the Issues." *Australian Quarterly* 43 (2): 8–15.

Smith, James P., and Barry Edmonston, eds. 1997. *The New Americans: Economic, Demographic, and Fiscal Effects of Immigration.* Washington, D.C.: National Academy Press for National Research Council.

Système d'observation permanente des migrations internationales (SOPEMI). Various years. *Trends in International Migration.* Paris: Organisation for Economic Cooperation and Development.

Southern, Michael. 1973. *Australia in the Seventies: A Survey by the Financial Times.* Blackburn: Penguin.

Soysal, Yasemin Nuhoglu. 1994. *Limits of Citizenship: Migrants and Postnational Membership in Europe.* Chicago: University of Chicago Press.

Spann, R. N. 1973. *Public Administration in Australia.* Sydney: V. C. N. Blight, C.B.E., Government Printer.

"Spécial: Élections 1973." 1973. *Faim-développement,* no. 12 (January).

"Spécial: Migrants." 1974. *Faim-développement,* no. 23 (February).

Spencer, Ian R. G. 1997. *British Immigration Policy since 1939: The Making of Multi-Racial Britain.* London: Routledge.

Stalker, Peter. 1994. *The Work of Strangers: A Survey of International Labour Migration.* Geneva: International Labour Office.

Steel, David. 1969. *No Entry: The Background and Implications of the Commonwealth Immigrants Act, 1968.* London: C. Hurst.

Stevens, Sir Bertram. 1953. "Immigration Policy for the Future: Australia's 1946–52

Immigration Programme." In Harold E. Holt et al., eds., *Australia and the Migrant*, pp. 112–65. Sydney: Angus & Robertson.

Stilwel, Frank J. B. 1980. *Economic Crisis: Cities and Regions*. Rushcutters Bay, N.S.W.: Pergamon.

Stimson, James A. 1985. "Regression in Space and Time: A Statistical Essay." *American Journal of Political Science* 29:914–47.

Studlar, Donley T. 1977. "Social Context and Attitudes toward Coloured Immigrants." *British Journal of Sociology* 28 (2): 168–84.

——. 1978. "Policy Voting in Britain: The Colored Immigration Issue in the 1964, 1966, and 1970 General Elections." *American Political Science Review* 20:46–72.

——. 1980. "British Public Opinion, Colour Issues, and Enoch Powell: A Longitudinal Analysis." *British Journal of Political Science* 4:371–81.

Tapinos, Georges. 1975. *Immigration étrangère en France*. Paris: Presses Universitaires de France.

Taylor, J. Edward, and Philip L. Martin. 1996. "The Immigrant Subsidy in Agriculture: Farm Employment, Poverty, and Welfare in Rural Towns." Paper presented at the Center for German and European Studies Working Group on Comparative Immigration and Integration Policy, University of California, Berkeley, 11 April 1997.

Textes et documents relatifs a l'élection présidentielle des 5 et 19 mai 1974. 1975. Paris: Documentation française (Notes et Études Documentaires no. 4201-3).

Thompson, Ian B. 1973. *The Paris Basin*. London: Oxford University Press.

——. 1975. *The Lower Rhône and Marseille*. London: Oxford University Press.

Thranhardt, Dietrich. 1992. "Europe—A New Immigration Continent: Policies and Politics since 1945 in Comparative Perspective." In Dietrich Thranhardt, ed., *Europe—A New Immigration Continent: Politics and Politics in Comparative Perspective*. Hamburg: Lit.

Tobin, Gregory. 1989. "Australian Immigration Policy and Politics." In Michael C. Le May, ed., *The Gatekeepers: Comparative Immigration Policy*, pp. 23–58. New York: Praeger.

Tsebelis, George, and Jeannette Money. 1997. *Bicameralism*. New York: Cambridge University Press.

Tuppen, John N. 1980. *France*. Boulder: Westview.

United Nations. Economic and Social Commission for Asia and the Pacific. 1982. *Population of Australia*. Vol. 2. New York: United Nations.

United States. Commission on Immigration Reform. 1994. *U.S. Immigration Policy: Restoring Credibility*. Washington, D.C.: Government Printing Office.

Usher, Dan. 1977. "Public Property and the Effects of Migration upon Other Residents of the Migrants' Countries of Origin and Destination." *Journal of Political Economy* 85 (5): 91–126.

Vieuguet, André. 1975. *Français et immigrés: Le combat du P.C.F.* Paris: Éditions Sociales.

Waever, Ole. 1993. "Societal Security: The Concept." In Ole Waever, Barry Buzan, Morten Kelstrup, and Pierre Lemaitre, *Identity, Migration, and the New Security Agenda in Europe*. London: Pinter.

Walker, Judith. 1971. "Restructuring the A.L.P.—N.S.W. and Victoria." *Australian Quarterly* 43 (4): 28–43.

Walsh, Maximilian. 1971. "The Politics of It All." In Australian Institute of Political Science, ed., *How Many Australians? Immigration and Growth*, pp. 168–204. Melbourne: Angus & Robertson.

Ware, H. 1974. "The Social and Demographic Impact of International Immigrants on

Melbourne: A Study of Various Differentials." In I. H. Burnley, ed., *Urbanization in Australia: The Post-War Experience*. Cambridge: Cambridge University Press.

Warhurst, John. 1993. "The Growth Lobby and Its Opponents: Business, Unions, Environmentalists, and Other Interest Groups." In James Jupp and Marie Kabala, eds., *The Politics of Australian Immigration*. Canberra: Australian Government Publishing Service.

The Way Ahead with a Liberal Country Party Government. 1974. Canberra: Liberal Party of Australia.

Weil, Patrick. 1991. *La France et ses étrangers: L'aventure d'une politique de l'immigration de 1938 à nos jours*. Paris: Gallimard.

Weiner, Myron. 1992–93. "Security, Stability, and International Migration," *International Security* 17 (3): 91–126.

——. 1993. *International Migration and Security*. Boulder: Westview.

"What the Election Is About . . . The Economy." *Sydney Morning Herald*, 28 November 1972, p. 6.

White, Paul. 1987. "The Migrant Experience in Paris." In Gunther Glebe and John O'Loughlin, eds., *Foreign Minorities in Continental European Cities*. Stuttgart: Franz Steiner.

——. 1993a. "The Social Geography of Immigrants in European Cities: The Geography of Arrival." In Russell King, ed., *The New Geography of European Migrations*. London: Belhaven.

——. 1993b. "Immigrants and the Social Geography of European Cities." In Russell King, ed., *Mass Migration in Europe: The Legacy and the Future*. London: Belhaven.

"Whitlam: Labor's Policy for Australia: Call to Revive Spirit of National Co-operation." *Sydney Morning Herald*, 14 November 1972, pp. 15–18.

"Whitlam Sees ALP Gaining 17 Seats." *Sydney Morning Herald*, 27 November 1972, p. 3.

Wieviorka, Michel. 1992. *La France raciste*. Paris: Seuil.

Wihtol de Wenden, Catherine. 1988. *Les immigrés et la politique*. Paris: Presses de la Fondation Nationale des Sciences Politiques.

Wilson, James Q., ed. 1980. *The Politics of Regulation*. New York: Basic Books.

Wilson, Paul R. 1978. "Immigrants, Politics, and Australian Society." In Graeme Duncan, ed., *Critical Essays in Australian Politics*, pp. 164–83. Melbourne: Edward Arnold.

Wilton, Janis, and Richard Bosworth. 1984. *Old Worlds and New Australia: The Post-War Migrant Experience*. Ringwood, Victoria: Penguin.

Wong, Carolyn. 1995. "The Political Economy of U.S. Immigration Legislation: Congressional Votes in the Postwar Period." Paper presented at the annual meetings of the American Political Science Association, Chicago (August).

Ysmal, Colette. 1990. *Le comportement électoral des français*. New ed. Paris: Découverte.

Zolberg, Aristide R. 1981. "International Migrations in Political Perspective." In Mary Kritz et al., eds., *Global Trends in Migration*. New York: Center for Migration Studies.

——. 1983. "Contemporary Transnational Migrations in Historical Perspective: Patterns and Dilemmas." In Mary M. Kritz, ed., *U.S. Immigration and Refugee Policy: Global and Domestic Issues*. Lexington, Mass.: Lexington Books.

——. 1989. "The Next Waves: Migration Theory for a Changing World." *International Migration Review* 23:403–30.

——. 1990. "Reforming the Back Door: The Immigration Reform and Control Act of 1986 in Historical Perspective." In Virginia Yans-McLaughlin, ed., *Immigration Reconsidered: History, Sociology, and Politics*. New York: Oxford University Press.

——. 1992. "Labour Migration and International Economic Regimes." In Mary M. Kritz et al., eds., *International Migration Systems*. Oxford: Clarendon.

Zubrzycki, J. 1987. "Public Policy in Multicultural Australia." *International Migration* 25 (1): 63–72.

Index

241